The Holy People of God

"This book offers a diverse collection of essays, bonded by their concern with the identity and mission of God's holy people. But don't expect bland, theoretical discussions. These essays speak into tough contexts like the climate crisis, systemic racism, and gender identity. Global in its scope, perceptive, and at times provocative, *The Holy People of God* will lead you to a deeper grasp of a church called to embody holiness in an unholy world."

—DEAN FLEMMING, professor emeritus of New Testament, MidAmerica Nazarene University

"As Kent Brower's first PhD student, it is my singular honor to write an endorsement for this Festschrift. The contributors, beyond the immediate task of celebrating the life of Kent Brower, have produced a masterpiece and must-read book on holiness that touches every sphere of human life. It also shows the multi-faceted nature and relevance of holiness for contemporary society. These essays reflect Brower's legacy and lifelong interest in holiness and underscore the reason that the issues to which he has devoted so much of his work will hardly die or fade away."

—J. AYODEJI ADEWUYA, professor of New Testament, Pentecostal Theological Seminary

"In a period of holiness-amnesia occurring within the Western church, this set of essays engages not only the biblical imperative to holiness but also what holiness means regarding some of the most pressing contemporary issues facing Christians today. Through this collection of essays, the reader is afforded exposure to the best of Wesleyan living theology."

—GRAHAM MCFARLANE, senior lecturer in systematic theology, London School of Theology

"Kent Brower, himself a fine scholar and teacher, has guided many students and scholars along the road of truth and practical holiness. This fine tribute to Professor Brower is itself a valuable piece of scholarship that engages both biblical truth and contemporary issues. The depth and quality of Kent Brower's life is beautifully reflected in this superb volume."

—HOWARD A. SNYDER, author of *The Community of the King*

"Kent Brower faithfully serves the Church of the Nazarene through his leadership, teaching, and scholarship. With his gentle, compassionate heart and keen intellect, Kent has invested in the development of Nazarene Theological College's PhD program and in students from around the world. I am grateful for Kent's friendship and collegiality, and along with the chorus of many others, express my deepest appreciation for his life and ministry in the Church of the Nazarene and at Nazarene Theological College."

—MARK MADDIX, pastor, San Dieguito United Methodist Church

The Holy People of God

Identity, Contexts, Challenges

Edited by
Svetlana Khobnya, Arseny Ermakov,
Deirdre Brower Latz, Peter Rae,
and MiJa Wi

PICKWICK *Publications* • Eugene, Oregon

THE HOLY PEOPLE OF GOD
Identity, Contexts, Challenges

Copyright © 2024 Wipf and Stock Publishers. All rights reserved. Except for brief quotations in critical publications or reviews, no part of this book may be reproduced in any manner without prior written permission from the publisher. Write: Permissions, Wipf and Stock Publishers, 199 W. 8th Ave., Suite 3, Eugene, OR 97401.

Pickwick Publications
An Imprint of Wipf and Stock Publishers
199 W. 8th Ave., Suite 3
Eugene, OR 97401

www.wipfandstock.com

PAPERBACK ISBN: 978-1-6667-7271-5
HARDCOVER ISBN: 978-1-6667-7275-3
EBOOK ISBN: 978-1-6667-7276-0

Cataloguing-in-Publication data:

Names: Khobnya, Svetlana, editor. | Ermakov, Arseny, editor. | Brower Latz, Deirdre, editor. | Rae, Peter, editor. | Wi, MiJa, editor.

Title: The holy people of God : identity, contexts, challenges / edited by Svetlana Khobnya, Arseny Ermakov, Deirdre Brower Latz, Peter Rae, and MiJa Wi.

Description: Eugene, OR : Pickwick Publications, 2024 | Includes bibliographical references.

Identifiers: ISBN 978-1-6667-7271-5 (paperback). | ISBN 978-1-6667-7275-3 (hardcover). | ISBN 978-1-6667-7276-0 (ebook).

Subjects: LCSH: Brower, K. E. (Kent E.). | Holiness. | Holiness—Biblical teaching. | Social justice.

Classification: BS2555.6 H6 H61 2024 (print). | BS2555.6 (epub).

03/11/24

This volume is dedicated to honoring the work of Dr. Kent Brower and his long-standing contribution to both theological education and ecclesiological conversations on living as the holy people of God. His lifetime research, love for the church, and voice for those who are not heard have inspired hundreds of readers, including academics, students, and practitioners within and beyond the Wesleyan-holiness tradition.

Contents

List of Contributors | xi

Preface | xv

INTRODUCTION

Biography | 3
  Derek Brower

For Such Is the Kingdom of God: A Heart for the Marginalized | 6
  Francine Brower

PART I | FINDING VOICE

John Wesley, George Herbert, and the Anglican "Line of Holiness" | 13
  Loveday Alexander

Recovering Sexual Holiness in 1 Corinthians 6: Spiritual, Theological, and Missional Implications | 22
  Michael J. Gorman

"Made Holy by the Holy Spirit" in Galatians? | 35
  Peter Oakes

What Does the "Spirit of Holiness" in Rom 1:4 Have to Do with Jesus, Paul, and All Who Are Called by Jesus? | 42
  Svetlana Khobnya

Holiness Then and Now: Principles of the Holy Life from the Fourth Century | 54
  Carla Sunberg

PART II | IN THE TIME OF CRISIS

Bringing the Kingdom: The Beatitudes as the Matthean Jubilee | 69
  Dwight D. Swanson

Ostensive Ethics and the Environmental Crisis | 79
  Andrew Brower Latz

Dangerous Bodies and Scandalous Touch: Reading Gospel Impurity Stories in the Time of Pandemic | 90
  Arseny Ermakov

"Present Your Bodies as Living Sacrifices or as a Living Sacrifice?" The Case for a Communal Sacrifice in Romans 12:1–2 | 101
  Christopher G. Foster

PART III | WALKING WITH THE MARGINALIZED

Personhood and Authentic Friendships: A Wesleyan Theological Reflection on the Relational Challenges Often Faced by People Living with Moderate to Severe Intellectual Impairment | 115
  David B. McEwan

Embracing the Ongoing Challenges of Intersectional Identities and Identifying: A Re-reading of Acts 16:16–18 | 124
  MiJa Wi

Wisdom for Marginalization (Acts 6:1–7) | 137
  Ezekiel Shibemba

Holiness in the Margins: The Ethiopian Eunuch as an Example of the Spirit Being Poured out "on All Flesh" (Acts 2:17), in Fulfillment of Joel's Prophecy (Joel 2:28), and the Relevance to Gender Non-conforming Christians | 148
  Kate Bowen-Evans

PART IV | CONFRONTING SOCIAL INJUSTICE

Justification, Sanctification, and Systemic Racism: Reflections on Romans | 161
  Andy Johnson

Holiness and a Life Reflecting Justice: Where Do We Go from Here? Wesley's "Thoughts on Slavery" for the Twenty-First Century | 179
  Deirdre Brower Latz

The Interplay of Spiritual and Economic Aspects of *Metadidōmi* in Paul's
   Writings and the Implications of Economic Justice in Africa | 188
   Gift Mtukwa

"You are Asked to Witness": Liturgical Use of Scripture as Mission in Sʼólh
   Temexw | 200
   Matthew Francis

PART V | REIMAGINING THEOLOGICAL EDUCATION

The Theological Curriculum | 213
   Thomas A. Noble

Mapping the Landscape of Theological Education in the UK | 223
   Peter Rae

African Communalism as a Paradigm for Theological Education | 234
   Samantha Chambo

List of Contributors

LOVEDAY ALEXANDER, Professor Emerita of Biblical Studies, University of Sheffield, and Canon-Theologian Emerita, Chester Cathedral.

KATE BOWEN-EVANS worked as a Humanitarian Aid worker. She is a PhD student in the field of biblical studies, focusing on sexuality and disability.

ANDREW BROWER LATZ (PhD, Durham University) is Head of the Religion and Philosophy Department at The Manchester Grammar School, Manchester, UK.

DEIRDRE BROWER LATZ (PhD, University of Manchester) is Principal and Senior Lecturer in Pastoral and Social Theology at Nazarene Theological College, Manchester, UK.

DEREK BROWER is the US political news editor and oversees the Financial Time's Washington DC bureau and the 2024 presidential election coverage. Based in New York, his role also includes reporting on foreign and military affairs, economic and monetary policy, and business regulation.

FRANCINE BROWER was previously a headteacher in an ASD specialist school and worked as a Team Leader for the National Autistic Society for over two decades. She is currently a consultant working with schools and individual children. Author of two books with Bloomsbury press, she has been married to Kent Brower for 56 years.

SAMANTHA CHAMBO (PhD, Nazarene Theological College/ University of Manchester) is the Regional Education Coordinator for the Church of the Nazarene in the USA/Canada region.

ARSENY ERMAKOV (PhD, Nazarene Theological College/ University of Manchester) is a Senior Lecturer in Biblical Studies at Eva Burrows College, University of Divinity, Melbourne, Australia.

List of Contributors

CHRISTOPHER G. FOSTER (PhD, Nazarene Theological College/ University of Manchester) is Associate Professor of Biblical and Theological Studies and Chair, Department of Undergraduate Theology at Oral Roberts University, USA.

MATTHEW FRANCIS serves as the parish priest of the Holy Apostles Orthodox Church in Chilliwack, British Columbia, Canada. He is also the Regional Director for British Columbia and the Yukon with the Canadian Bible Society.

MICHAEL J. GORMAN holds the Raymond E. Brown Chair in Biblical Studies and Theology at St. Mary's Seminary and University in Baltimore, Maryland, USA.

ANDY JOHNSON is Professor of New Testament at Nazarene Theological Seminary in Kansas City, MO. He holds the Willard H. Taylor Chair in Biblical Theology.

SVETLANA KHOBNYA (PhD, Nazarene Theological College/University of Manchester) is a Senior Lecturer in Biblical Studies at the Nazarene Theological College, Manchester, UK.

DAVID B. MCEWAN (PhD, University of Queensland) is Director of Research and Associate Professor of Theology and Pastoral Theology at Nazarene Theological College, Brisbane.

GIFT MTUKWA (PhD, Nazarene Theological College /University of Manchester) is Chair of the Department of Religion and Christian Ministry and Lecturer in New Testament and Greek at Africa Nazarene University in Nairobi, Kenya.

THOMAS A. NOBLE (PhD, University of Edinburgh) is Professor of Theology at Nazarene Theological Seminary, Kansas City, and is a Senior Research Fellow at Nazarene Theological College, Manchester.

PETER OAKES is Rylands Professor of Biblical Criticism and Exegesis at University of Manchester. He is editor for the Journal for the Study of the New Testament Booklist.

PETER RAE (PhD, University of Manitoba) is Dean and Vice Principal of Nazarene Theological College, Manchester, and teaches in the area of Leadership and Theological Education.

EZEKIEL SHIBEMBA (PhD, Nazarene Theological College/University of Manchester) is Lecturer in Biblical Studies at Nazarene Theological College. He is also the lead pastor of All Nations Church in Oldham.

List of Contributors

CARLA SUNBERG (PhD, Nazarene Theological College /University of Manchester) has served as Professor of Historical Theology and President of Nazarene Theological Seminary in Kansas City. She currently serves as General Superintendent in the Church of the Nazarene.

DWIGHT D. SWANSON (PhD, University of Manchester) is Senior Research Fellow & Senior Lecturer in Biblical Studies, and Co-Director, Manchester Centre for the Study of Christianity and Islam.

MIJA WI (PhD, Nazarene Theological College/University of Manchester) is Lecturer in Biblical Studies and Global Missions at Nazarene Theological College, Manchester, UK.

Preface

THIS COLLECTION OF ESSAYS addresses aspects of Christian identity formation as God's holy people in a global context in the midst of various challenges. The contributors offer interdisciplinary explorations on what it means to live as God's holy people in different settings and consider challenging questions from biblical, historical, theological, missiological, and pastoral perspectives. The volume is divided into four sections.

The first section tackles the question of the identity of God's holy people in the challenges faced in history and in the early twenty-first century. Loveday Alexander draws readers' attention to a peculiar detail in Chester Cathedral where John Wesley is depicted in stained glass alongside Anglican divines from the sixteenth and seventeenth centuries. Is he there to represent the "high-church" and Non-Jurors movement of the time, or is there a deeper connection between him and other Anglicans? Alexander identifies a closer parallel between them, i.e., a "line of holiness." This line of holiness is marked by a commitment to a life of personal holiness and the formation of a praying people, based on a disciplined rhythm of common prayer. To explicate this connection, she examines some key themes in George Herbert's concept of holiness that find echoes in Wesley.

Michael J. Gorman develops the theme of sexual holiness. First, he affirms that early Christian teachings, including those of Paul, express a distinctive stance on sexual morality as part of transformation and unity with God and those who know God. Second, he engages with some contemporary practical theologians who place the question of human sexuality outside of the scope of Christian holiness as unity with God, godliness, and separation from fleshly folly. Gorman re-examines the question of sexual holiness in 1 Cor 6:12–20 drawing spiritual, theological, and missional implications in light of Paul's theology and praxis.

Peter Oakes begins his essay on the premises of his previous analysis of holiness in Romans as separation from the ordinary, closeness to other holy entities, especially the divine, and use of the culture's terminology for the holy. When these categories of holiness are applied to Romans it leads to fruitful implications not only about the status of Roman Christians as the holy ones but also about the work of the Spirit who makes them holy (Rom 15:16). In this essay, Oakes asks to what extent the same pattern is applicable to Galatians, and offers a comparative analysis between Romans and Galatians. Oakes concludes that the concept of holiness in relation to the status of the Galatians and the work of the Spirit as instrumental in producing holiness has familiar and traceable parallels to Paul's teaching in Romans.

In her essay, Svetlana Khobnya enters the long-standing debate about the role of the *hapax legomenon* ("spirit of holiness") in Romans 1:4. She explains why recent discussions about the "spirit of holiness" have been dominated by a focus on the Spirit, with the faithfulness of Christ only peripheral. However, focusing on Paul's unique usage of "holiness" as a descriptor for the "spirit" that points to the principle of obedience when analyzed in the immediate and wider narrative context of Romans as well as through the prism of the Jewish background opens a possibility to narrow Paul's message at the beginning of the letter to a more specific christological argument that has shaped Paul, and one which determines the nature of those who are called by Jesus Christ.

Carla Sunberg's essay emphasizes the need to return to the foundational principles of the fourth century's Cappadocian Fathers, mediated by John Wesley's relatively modern perspective. The extent of Wesley's engagement with the Cappadocians is opened to further discussions. More specifically, she focuses on the role of scripture, the incarnation, the need for imitation of Christ, and the potential for continuous growth toward our true identity in Christ, as well as how these may revitalize the life of holiness today, as practiced within the Wesleyan-holiness tradition.

The second section offer robust reflections on the role and place of God's holy people in times of crisis. Dwight Swanson addresses the questions that reappear repeatedly among modern Christians: "Where is the gospel in this? What is Good News?" He explores the answers to these questions from a Biblical perspective, with a focus on the Gospel of Matthew: against a background of literature from Second Temple Judaism, with an examination of the use of Scripture by the Evangelist; and as a disciple of Jesus, with faith seeking understanding of "the gospel of Jesus Christ."

Andrew Brower Latz explores the ways in which the ostensive approach to ethics could be applied to navigate the current environmental crisis. This approach suggests that ethical action is best "explained, grounded and motivated" by showing concrete examples rather than by theoretical frameworks. In application to the environmental crisis, that means that climate change action could be encouraged by finding and disseminating examples of both good environmental ethics and things that should not be done. It also argues that living a holy life in the Anthropocene does not only require individual ethical action (i.e., reduce or cease driving, flying, wasting, and using plastic, or shift to a plant-based diet) but demands a return to political holiness since only political action and economic changes will bring the scope and depth of changes needed.

Arseny Ermakov brings readers back to the issues of impurities that evoked concern, anxiety, and fear in the ancient world but were intentionally reinterpreted in Jesus and reconfigured through his actions. Similar fears are re-emerging now due to the ongoing COVID-19 outbreak. However, engagement with the ancient texts in current circumstances invites caution and resistance to being seduced by primitive "parallelomania" and settling for obvious and simplistic interpretations. The essay asks how we can navigate purity/impurity issues in today's context, reflect theologically, and learn from Jesus' attitude toward impurity in the time of the pandemic.

Chris Foster focuses on reading Romans 12:1–2 with the idea of a corporate sacrifice taking prominence. He asks whether the sacrifice as corporate in this passage could be a corrective, with the corporate sacrifice of God's people together forming reasonable worship. If so, then this has further implications for God's holy people including corporate reasonable worship and corporate discernment of God's will rather than merely individualistic ones.

The third section raises issues of economic depravity, disability, and mental health. The essay by David McEwan reflects on the challenge the people of God face when relating to people who live with moderate to severe intellectual impairment. He argues that for people living with intellectual impairment it is vital that personhood is no longer linked to a capacity to think or act in certain ways. Rather, personhood is recognized as an intrinsic value and worth simply by virtue of a person's very existence. His challenge is that the people of God need to be intentional to build "friendships" instead of "ministries."

MiJa Wi explores what might have happened to the slave girl who had a spirit of Python in Philippi in Acts 16 when her ability to prophesy (and hence, to make profits for her owners) was gone. She employs intersectionality as "a hermeneutical prism" to examine the slave girl's intersectional realities within structural, interpersonal, and spiritual domains of power. She concludes that the fate of the slave girl remains unresolved and hence continues to challenge the people of God who encounter the unnamed girl today in their own context.

Kate Bowen-Evans examines the baptism of the Ethiopian eunuch in Acts 8:26–40 as an invitation to reconsider how radically disruptive it was and is to the holy people of God today. She argues that the account of the Ethiopian eunuch is most relevant to those who identify as gender-nonbinary, that is, not conforming to normative definitions of gender roles and identities; meaning those who are transgender, intersex, gender different or gender queer. Her reading of Acts 8:26–40 places the experience of those whose bodies have been regarded as "false, unreal or unintelligible" at the center of the interpretative process and challenges the church today to reconsider the parameters of holiness and membership among the holy people of God.

Ezekiel Shibemba examines Luke's use of overlooking (*paratheōreō*) and the solution to the complaint (*gongysmos*) in Acts 6:1–7 while employing Critical Race Theory to yield insight and wisdom that is relevant to contemporary issues such as racism, marginalization, and international justice. He argues that Luke uses "complaint" (*gongysmos*) to note the concern within the community and describes how the apostles extend the leadership to the marginalized and include them in the decision-making process. He concludes that the inclusion of the marginalized released a forward movement in the ideals of the community and suggests that genuine inclusion in international and ecclesiastical arrangement of the marginalized will open possibilities for an equitable world.

Andy Johnson's essay opens the fourth section on holiness and social justice. He identifies the problem of the systemic racism embedded in societal structures in the US. Unfortunately, many White Christians fail to see the continuing effects of racial biases on a bigger scale, interpreting injustices as isolated incidents. In theological terms, this problem can be defined as a refusal to recognize the way sin functions as a power to sculpt social structures in racialized ways. Johnson suggests acknowledging the scope of the power of sin and reconsidering the framework of justification beyond individual actions or choices. Paul's teaching in Romans on sin and especially on justification and sanctification serves Johnson as a framework for finding a way forward in dealing with this problem.

Deirdre Brower Latz recalls Wesley's approach to justice and wrestles with current issues in this area. She develops trajectories from Wesley's approach that enable Wesleyan-holiness theological heirs to consider their context and advocate for justice within it. Looking particularly at Wesley's theological framework through the lens of "Thoughts upon Slavery," acknowledging its limitations and the historical realities, Brower Latz takes themes that emerge and develops them as trajectories for practice today, ones which are both methodological and substantial.

Gift Mtukwa raises the issue of economic justice as desperately needed in Africa today where wealth is concentrated in the hands of a few, and most ordinary people lack basic necessities. He offers a proper example of economic justice from the teaching of Paul. For Paul, sharing among the people of God is more than just spiritual (distributing of the spiritual gifts or imparting the gospel message)—the people of God are to share economic resources (that includes exchange of goods and services) with one another and especially those who are in need. The essay examines Rom 1:11; 12:8; Eph 4:28 and 1 Thess 2:8 where Paul uses the word *metadidōmi* urging his audience not to have to choose one set of sharing against the other and offers some conclusions for the African context.

Matthew Francis reflects on a complicated history and of Christian mission among people who have traditionally lived in S'ólh Temexw, in Northern Canada. He specifically focuses on how Christian missionaries, embodying the traditional liturgical praxis of the Orthodox Church, and inspired by the missiological principles of the eighteenth century Valaam mission to Alaska, perennially engage people of this area with Scripture in the complex realities of twenty-first-century life.

The fifth and final section on reimagining theological education offers three essays. Tom Noble explores the concept of "theology" as key to the curriculum of the theological college or seminary—but not in the limited sense of systematic theology, and not only in the sense of theologia as an academic Wissenschaft or "science," as Edward Farley might define it. Instead, working from T. F. Torrance's perspective on theology and its method (Theological Science), he brings together the subjective and objective dimensions (spiritual formation and academic "science") as a way to understand the unity and diversity of the theological curriculum: "to know the Lord, to speak of the Lord, to walk with the Lord."

Peter Rae discusses the impact and implications of the transformation in the landscape of theological education in the UK over the past decades. As Alice Hunt writes, "Almost everything about theological education has changed and faces continual change. The basic assumptions of theological education . . . no longer function." These decades have seen a move from a system where theological education was overwhelmingly delivered within public universities, and where theological colleges were unvalidated and on the margins of the Higher Education sector, to a current scenario where Religion and Theology is in decline within the university sector, and theological colleges occupy a much more prominent place. Rae tracks this sea-change and discusses its significance.

Samantha Chambo starts with an observation of college education as a transitional space between childhood and adulthood, as a period of self-discovery and preparation to be a valuable, contributing member of society. Subsequently, she examines how the African concept of vital participation can advance the objective of holiness transformation in theological education and to what extent it may privilege spirituality and communalism instead of focusing only on cognitive aspects of theological education.

These essays, and their authors, represent something of the scope of Dr. Brower's influence—as colleague, friend, mentor, supporter of women's voices and the influence of someone whose life has been captured by a preoccupation with what it means to live in the Spirit and become who we are—the holy people of God.

Introduction

Biography

Derek Brower

EACH OF YOU READING this Festschrift will know Kent Brower, or his name, for your own reasons. For many, it will be his mastery of the subject matter. Kent has dedicated his adult life to the study of the Bible, especially the New Testament, especially the Gospels, and especially Mark. And the fruit of this endeavor has been precious to many: a long and distinguished lecturing career; a deeply enriching and still ongoing role as a PhD supervisor; the work, over decades, as an editor and author of countless articles and reviews; and the five books.

Others will know Kent for a different side of his academic life: as an accomplished and experienced administrator, including while lecturing at Canadian Nazarene College in Winnipeg and then in the UK, where he played a seminal role in securing Nazarene Theological College's accreditation by the University of Manchester. This was a gift to NTC, but also to the Church of the Nazarene at large. And so it has used Kent's expertise as an educational administrator in deployments across Africa, in particular, as well as in Asia and the US. Writing books is important. But building, strengthening, sustaining, defending and enriching institutions where they and other books will be taught long into the future is a different—often unseen, but no less significant—way to leave one's mark. Kent has excelled in the role. And part of his heart will always remain in Manzini, in the small apartment he and his wife Francine occupied periodically over the years on the campus of the South African Nazarene University in eSwatini—a home away from home.

Kent will have taught many readers of this Festschrift, too. Students of Dr. Brower are scattered around the world. I've met enough of them over the years to know the esteem they bestow on Kent. By repute, he was fair. "Always prepared," said one student. "Ever-ready." But, lest a Festschrift be mistaken for a paean to its subject, he could also be stern and demanding.

But he must have done something right. Many students remained friends long after graduating. Almost all of them will have been entertained in Kent and Fran's house, or at the annual barbeque—rain or shine—in the Brower home in Didsbury, Manchester.

Others would know Kent for different reasons. Maybe as "coach": the ice hockey teams Kent coached during his Winnipeg days—as a bearded, brooding presence prowling behind his bench of tightly drilled young warriors—brought back much silverware for Canadian Nazarene College. Discipline was a hallmark of those teams.

There's also simply Kent the churchman: like his father, loyal and devoted to his congregation, always. He has preached countless sermons, of course, and led even more house gatherings. On one occasion that comes to mind, he even volunteered to play the piano for the congregation: a memorable musical event, but not for the right reasons.

I also know Kent in a different way, unrelated to the books and lectures, and indulge me while I list some ways. I know him as a hapless—though never hopeless—golfer. I know him as a friend to dogs (dogs know this too). I remember him as the man who, with David McCulloch, would stand amid a throng of other Manchester United fans as the players warmed up reading his folded-up copy of the Independent.

I never sat through one of Kent's NTC lectures. But he did teach me how to ride a bicycle, ice skate like a good Canadian, and how to use both my feet equally to kick a ball so I would thrive in England. He passed on a sense of direction and fascination with maps to me; a love of birds; a skepticism about authority; an impatience for other drivers; and a passion for debate. Some say there are physical resemblances too. It makes sense: I'm proud to say Kent is my dad. I tell my own children that too.

And so for those of you who know him for all the other stuff, let me flesh out some of the other details.

I know him as a man who marched into a police station in Manchester with fury in his eyes when my friend Leon had been apprehended on utterly spurious grounds. Leon was black. Kent can sniff out racial injustice from a distance.

Kent wasn't born to the academic world; far from it. He was a farmer, raised outside Wainwright, a small town on the colossal Canadian prairie, to ride horses, throw footballs—the oval kind—to drive, break and fix tractors, put up silage for feed, and milk the cows that ate it.

Then he met a city girl at college: Francine. She wasn't keen on farmers, but she was keen on Kent. And Kent has doted on her for decades. After a stint in Boston, where Kent earned a Master's degree, and then some more time back on the farm, Kent sent a wildly speculative letter to the renowned

New Testament scholar F. F. Bruce, asking to come study the Gospel of Mark under him at the University of Manchester.

That was in 1973. And over the next two decades, Kent and Fran and their two children—Deirdre and I—moved back and forth across the Atlantic, between Manchester and Winnipeg, five times. In the Winnipeg days, when term time ended, we and our black Labrador Sport would cram into a VW Rabbit and drive 14 hours to the family farm. Kent would put down his spectacles, put on a battered old hat and his work clothes and dive into the job of harvesting crops. I would perch in the cab of the huge John Deere tractor next to him while he drove, up and down the field. We would watch for red-tailed hawks diving for prey.

It was in Wainwright too that Kent lost control of a chainsaw that ate through much of his leg above the knee. Denim grew from his flesh for years after.

Quite how this rugged prairie farm boy settled so comfortably in Manchester remains a puzzle. Much credit goes to my mother, Francine, who not only tolerated but endorsed dad's trans-Atlantic wanderlust, repeatedly altering her own career path to support his. It worked out. She became not just an author and expert on autism and education along the way, but the ever-reliable host as Kent opened the doors of their home to everyone in the NTC orbit (often with little advance notice to Francine).

Along the way, they became stalwarts in first the Didsbury then the Longsight Nazarene churches and active members of their neighborhood. The family broadened too, including the O'Briens and eventually some grandchildren, and then a vast extended network—from southern Spain to Belarus, from China to Lebanon and South Korea—of men and women to whom Kent and Fran became mentors, allies, supporters, and guides.

What else can I say?

What stands out to me—as someone who has been carried by Kent, taught by him, and fed by him; as someone who has celebrated with him on the best days, and been picked up and shielded by him on the darkest ones—is Kent's sense of justice and compassion; of sacrifice and discipleship.

For him, this comes directly from the New Testament. And no wonder: my father has spent almost a lifetime reading and seeking to understand the Scriptures. And yet for all the monographs and lectures, studying the New Testament has never been solely an academic exercise to Kent, but always a way to understand the Gospels—and seek to live them.

For Such Is the Kingdom of God: A Heart for the Marginalized

Francine Brower

EACH OF US HAS life experiences that influence our attitudes, interests, relationships, and choices. Hindsight provides clarity in explaining how we have changed, matured, and developed to become who we are today. I have had the privilege of being part of, walking beside, observing, challenging, and encouraging Kent for more than half a century.

In the 1940s and 1950s, it was customary for mothers to stay at home and raise their children. In the Brower family, carving a farm out of virgin land, living in poverty, dependent on what could be grown and raised to put food on the table, Kent's mum, a registered nurse, continued in her profession to help pay the bills, build the house, and clothe the family. It is common in this century, but not so in that era and it was often frowned upon. Within this context, the Brower family followed the biblical mandate to tithe 10 percent of their earnings regardless of the financial constraints they faced. Their generosity went beyond the monthly check to the church. When we were students together at Canadian Nazarene College, Kent's parents donated meat from the farm to help feed the students! This may seem unusual to many, but when you consider that some of our meals consisted of thin soup with a stack of white bread on the table, you will understand that any protein was a celebration! I attribute this sense of care for others, sacrificing for the ministry of the local church, and recognizing the needs of others, as a legacy that has been followed in good times and bad.

In the small western Canadian town of Wainwright, Kent's family worked with others to build and establish the Church of the Nazarene. In his early years, a team, Miss Prior and Miss Claire, pastored the church. Kent has often commented that at a young age he did not realize that men could be pastors! How much of an influence did these early years have on Kent's drive to value, affirm and encourage females to answer the call of God and to have a voice at the table?

Life's experiences shape who we are and the way we respond to ideas, to individuals, as well as carving out our beliefs and priorities. Living in Boston in our first years of marriage exposed Kent to the ugliness of racism for the first time in his life. There were, no doubt, situations he had not recognized or grappled with previously, in part related to his upbringing in a small rural community with limited diversity. Having a roommate at Canadian Nazarene College who was from British Guiana forged a strong and lifelong friendship. Going on to study together in Boston, the opinions of others attempted to create a divide of black and white. Kent addressed the situation and made it perfectly clear that discrimination, prejudice, and racism had no place in the heart, mind and actions of Christian friends. This has been and continues to be a strong matter of principle in the consistent acceptance, respect, and embracing of others.

I have at times commented on Kent adding to our family. Across the world there are many who refer to him as "dad," reflecting the support and encouragement he has provided over many years. A beloved leader in South Africa affectionately called him "my brother from another mother." Kent has actively encouraged others to share their stories to help him understand oppression, poverty, prejudice, and injustice from those experiencing it. Reaching out in love, listening, finding ways to support materially, enabling education, offering advice and guidance, and standing against discrimination have all contributed to the dignity and self-confidence of many.

Sharing life with another demands flexibility, negotiation, communication, mutual respect, and support. That in many ways sums up the relationship we have had throughout our marriage. I have always pursued my own career. This is in part due to family finances, supporting Kent as a farmer on an extremely low income and as a student in his calling to roles within Nazarene higher education. Of course, that means sharing responsibilities on so many levels, picking each other up when one is down, compensating when the burdens grow, recognizing the importance of parenting, and nurturing children. Kent always supported my career path and perhaps it began to have more influence on him when I entered the world of autism and became totally committed to the children, young people, adults, and their families who crossed my path. Through my growing understanding and empathy with those I worked with, Kent developed a growing awareness of the obstacles, anxieties, and pressure individuals with disabilities face day after day. For many, judging incidents perceived as unusual and observing behaviors that are confusing brings a quick and negative reaction. Rather than considering what the problem is and offering support, we turn our backs or cross to the other side of the road. We give disapproving looks and think critical thoughts. Kent changed from being dismissive or impatient to recognizing the multifaceted reasons for what we see in public settings. He began asking me, "Do you think he might be one of yours?" By this, he recognized that a crying or upset child may have autism, that an adult may be struggling with the environment and that confusion was causing undue stress. When we begin to respond in this sensitive way, we begin to demonstrate compassion and offer support rather than criticism and judgment.

How does this extend to a deepening understanding of theology and inclusion? I believe it is in response to life's experiences that Kent's world was opened up to individuals who were left behind, rejected, discriminated against, and denied the opportunities to be part of the kingdom of God as equal partners. Whether this be through race, culture, gender, economic status, disability or position, the encounters in life shone a lens on the absolute necessity that every individual has the right to be fully embraced by God's people. A question that arose and helped Kent to grapple with inclusion was the Eucharist. To make communion a test of understanding and the ability to explain surely limits those who are welcome at the table. As Kent met many of my pupils and recognized the complex needs of communication, relationship, and learning, he began to realize that all have not been welcome to partake of the bread and wine. In order to truly invite all to participate fully in this sacrament there must be true inclusion, not organized by the elders who complete a checklist of who is in and who is out. It is Christ who welcomes us to his table and the invitation is for absolutely everyone.

How do we evaluate the understanding of an individual with a learning disability, child or adult? An example that moved me was a school visit to the Liverpool Cathedral on St James Mount. The occasion was a large gathering of children from the diocese schools. One of my young pupils with autism participated in the event. She was nonverbal aside from very few one-syllable, basic words. Some had questioned the value of her attending, but I strongly believe in inclusion and away we went. On entering the cathedral, she stared at the light streaming through the magnificent windows, the vaulted ceiling and colorful banners. Her eyes widened as she took it all in and she uttered, "Aww, beautiful." That moment, those words of wonder, demonstrated an understanding beyond words and made the experience everything I longed for it to be.

What do we mean when we talk about inclusion in the body of Christ? This topic has long been neglected and has become a matter for concern in the twenty-first century: not before time! ABC Religion and Ethics defines it in this way:

For Such Is the Kingdom of God: A Heart for the Marginalized

> It means sharing in worship in a way that recognizes that we all bring different things to the table but receive back the same. It means seeking to help others while being constantly aware of the ways in which they are helping you. It means never doing things for people that they can perfectly well do for themselves, because affirming another person's humanity and agency is the first form of compassion.[1]

How often do we approach inclusion as if we are the benefactors and providers, positioning ourselves as "doing good" without recognizing the value and contribution of others? How often do we make decisions for others, failing to give them ownership in the process? It is worth reading the definition above again, concentrating on "receive back the same and affirming." When we begin to understand the breadth of what it means to open our personal lives and our worshiping communities to ALL, we will be modeling what Christ has taught us in Scripture. I am not, in any way, a biblical scholar or theologian. I am, however, a committed Christian and spend my life with a growing awareness and interest in biblical teachings. This will hardly be surprising given the family I am part of and influenced by!

Throughout the New Testament, Jesus demonstrates the principles of acceptance and inclusion. He welcomes and affirms those he meets, demonstrates compassion and acceptance, showering them with love. Looking briefly at some of these passages, we see example after example of the life and love of Christ modeled for us. We too often fail to have ears to hear and eyes to see. In Kent's book, *Holiness in the Gospels*, he ends by asking a series of questions, including, "Have we forgotten the simple truth that Christian holiness is nothing more nor less than single-minded and whole-hearted love of God and neighbor?"[2] This rings so true in the discussion of inclusion, acceptance, reaching out to, and loving all. This love extends to the marginalized, the "other" those we may not easily relate to or understand. Breaking down barriers, sharing our faith, our respect, our wealth and embracing others is what we are called to do. What an amazing world we would live in, what amazing churches we would have if we lived these values out in our daily lives, exemplifying Christ's love in our every thought and deed.

> Those who are judged by the color of their skin, by their gender, by their faith or their lack of faith, by their looks, by their orientation, by their abilities or by some people's perception of disability, need to remember—all of us—that we already are the way God would have us be, with one exception: God cannot

---

1. Wells, "'Inclusive' Church."
2. Brower, *Holiness in the Gospels*, 133.

force us to love ourselves or each other. We have to do that ourselves.[3]

Writing in *Living as God's Holy People*, Kent emphasizes throughout the book the importance of covenant relationships. He highlights the "contagion" of holy living. What an exciting thought that our lives, in obedience to Christ, with the indwelling of the Holy Spirit, living the resurrection life of Christians, squandering our love on others, is *contagious*! Individually and collectively, we are called to be "counter cultural in terms of unity in diversity, affirmation of the importance of the least in their society."[4] Kent points out, "Paul's readers are to let the mind of Christ be at work in their midst, fostering unity, mutual concern and support. Paul's desire is for community health that creates corporate solidarity and identity."[5] As the book comes to an end, once again referring to Paul's ministry, Kent points out, "Compassion for the lost, healing for the diseased, rescuing the dispossessed, reintegrating the excluded—these define the mission of the Holy One of God and his people."[6]

As I have journeyed with Kent, I have been so very aware of these themes running through his academic work and his daily life. We have learned to challenge each other as we have shared experiences and made mistakes, always with the goal of understanding and living out who we are called to be. Long may this continue!

WORKS CITED

Artson, Rabbi Bradley Shavit. "The Bible Is a Book of Inclusion and Love." *Open Horizons* (June 6, 2012). http://www.open horizons.org/.

Brower, Kent. *Holiness in the Gospels*. Kansas City: Beacon Hill, 2005.

———. *Living as God's Holy People: Holiness and Community in Paul*. Milton Keynes, UK: Paternoster, 2009.

Wells, Samuel. "What It Means to be an 'Inclusive' Church." *ABC Religion & Ethics* (August 9, 2019). https://www.abc.net.au/.

---

3. Artson, "Bible is a Book of Inclusion and Love."
4. Brower, *Living as God's Holy People*, 85.
5. Brower, *Living as God's Holy People*, 97–98.
6. Brower, *Living as God's Holy People*, 106.

PART I

Finding Voice

John Wesley, George Herbert, and the Anglican "Line of Holiness"

Loveday Alexander

IT IS A PLEASURE and an honor to be invited to take part in this tribute to Kent Brower. Kent, you know far more than I shall ever do about the Wesleyan-holiness tradition: so I am taking a more Anglican starting-point, in the cloisters of Chester Cathedral.

Chester Cathedral is not the obvious place to find John Wesley depicted in stained glass. But there he is, in the south-east corner of the cloisters, framed by a collection of Anglican divines from the sixteenth and seventeenth centuries (windows 56–59). This is very much an Anglican gallery, with a focus on bishops, the established church, and the Book of Common Prayer. The cloister windows date from Dean Bennett's restoration in the 1920s. As we might expect, they echo Chester's high-church and royalist connections, including Archbishop Laud and "king and martyr" Charles I himself. Eight of the fourteen are bishops: Matthew Parker, Lancelot Andrewes, William Laud, John Cosin, John Pearson, William Sancroft, Thomas Ken, and Jeremy Taylor, together with that great defender and architect of Anglicanism, Richard Hooker. So what is John Wesley doing in this august—but very Anglican—company?

Wesley himself of course was a high-church Anglican who declared himself to his dying day a loyal son of the Church of England. And one rather unexpected connection may lie in the fact that two of the bishops pictured here are identified as Non-jurors—that is, we might say, as bishops whose loyalty to God transcended their natural loyalties to the Crown. William Sancroft was imprisoned briefly in the Tower in 1688 for refusing to read James II's Act of Indulgence, and was then deprived of his living in 1689 for refusing to take the Oath of Allegiance to William III—along with

Thomas Ken and many other bishops and clergy.[1] Henry Rack points out that many of Wesley's associates in Manchester had Non-juror sympathies:

> Many high churchmen had remained within the Church of England after 1688 but with uneasy consciences and Jacobite sympathies, while Nonjuror devotional works were read well beyond their own circle. Wesley's Manchester circle of friends included Jacobite Nonjurors like Deacon, the layman John Byrom and others; but also conforming clergy like Clayton, close to Deacon in politics and theology.[2]

The Non-jurors had a special veneration for "primitive" usages such as station fasts on Wednesdays and Fridays, the mixing of water and wine at the Eucharist, and triple dipping in baptism.[3] This "high-church and near Nonjuror" influence played an important part in the development of Wesley's thinking, mixed eclectically with his later evangelicalism.[4]

But I want to suggest that there is a deeper and more subtle connection between Wesley and Dean Bennett's Anglican divines: a "line of holiness" marked by a commitment to a life of personal holiness and the formation of a praying people, based on a disciplined rhythm of common prayer. Thus Lancelot Andrewes, as well as being a powerful figure in the church of his day, was known for his holiness of life, and especially for his *Preces Privatae*, a collection of private prayers which was hugely influential on the spirituality of the Church of England. Laud, despite his controversial political role, was admired for his personal austerity and ecclesial integrity. Sancroft and Cosin were both deeply involved in the 1662 revision of the Book of Common Prayer, as was Pearson (Bishop of Chester 1673–86), also remembered for his commitment to the education of the laity through his *Exposition of the Creed*. Thomas Ken (1637–1711) wrote hymns (including the well-known Doxology) to create a practice of holiness for ordinary people. Jeremy Taylor (1613–1667) wrote two hugely influential books on *The Rule and Exercise of Holy Living and Holy Dying*. And Bishop Wilson, Bishop of Sodor and Man till his death in 1755, was described by Newman as "a burning and a shining light, as if a beacon had landed on his small island to show what his Lord and Saviour could do in spite of man."[5] Margaret Cropper, in a hagiographical but perceptive account of "Six Anglican Saints

---

1. Sancroft's window includes a roundel of the eight bishops in a boat on their way to the Tower.
2. Rack, "Wesleys and Manchester," 8.
3. Rack, "Wesleys and Manchester," 7.
4. Rack, "Wesleys and Manchester," 23.
5. Cited from Thomson, "Gallery of Saints."

of the 17th century" (which includes four of Bennett's saints), sums up their contribution as "a type of sanctity which grew to its perfectness in a special period when the Church of England was at a vigorous stage of her growth, with an ardour heightened by suffering, that stirred the hearts of men and women to reach forward towards holiness."[6]

It is this "disciplined corporate search for holiness" that James Thomson picks up as Wesley's contribution to this Anglican "line of holiness" in his online guide to the *Gallery of Saints*.[7] And that theme comes out most clearly in two figures in the cloister who are not bishops, not movers and shakers in the politics of church and Commonwealth, but were hugely influential in the development of the Anglican holiness tradition: George Herbert the priest and poet, and Nicholas Ferrar, the founder of the Little Gidding community. Both (like the Wesleys) were children of large families, shaped by the piety of strong-minded mothers. Both were university-educated royalists by birth and inclination, but united by a higher loyalty to the service of God. And both are celebrated for their commitment to a disciplined search for holiness, both as a rule of life and as an affair of the heart. Izaak Walton's description of their "holy friendship" sounds like a long-distance precursor of the Wesleys' "Holy club": "Mr. *Farrers,* and Mr. *Herberts* devout lives, were both so noted, that the general report of their sanctity gave them occasion to renew that slight acquaintance which was begun at their being Contemporaries at *Cambridge*; and this new holy friendship was long maintain'd without any interview, but only by loving and endearing Letters."[8]

Ferrar and Herbert appear side by side in another early twentieth-century window in the tiny church at Bemerton where Herbert ministered for three short years before his untimely death in 1633. What is extraordinary about this obscure parish priest, who served in a tiny and undistinguished parish just before the Civil War, is the way his inward spiritual struggles and his wry, self-deprecating wit seem to reach across the centuries in a way that is true of few seventeenth-century voices. The reason for that lies in the little book of poems which Herbert entrusted on his death-bed to his friend Nicholas Ferrar at Little Gidding, instructing him to publish it "if he think it may turn to the advantage of any dejected poor soul"—but if not, to burn it, "for it and I are less than the least of God's mercies."[9] Ferrar did not

6. Cropper, *Flame Touches Flame,* vii. Cropper's selection of "Six Anglican Saints of the Seventeenth Century" includes four of the figures in the Cloister windows (Herbert, Ferrar, Taylor and Ken) alongside Henry Vaughan and Margaret Godolphin.

7. Thomson, "Gallery of Saints."

8. Walton, *Lives,* 312.

9. Drury, *Music at Midnight,* 251.

burn it: the poems were published by the Clarendon Press within a year of Herbert's death, and have never been out of print since.[10] A note from the printers commends Herbert to the reader as "a companion to the primitive Saints, and a pattern or more for the age he lived in." Izaak Walton continues the theme in his *Life of Mr. George Herbert* (with a short memoir of Nicholas Ferrar), which first appeared in 1670, and continued to be popular throughout the eighteenth century.[11]

There is no doubt that the Wesleys knew and admired George Herbert. John Wesley "included no less than 47 poems from *The Temple* in his various collections of hymns and sacred poems," and published a considerable selection of the poems in their original form in 1773.[12] James Dale uses the phrase "the line of piety" to express Charles Wesley's debt to Herbert as part of "the tradition out of which he came and in which he worked: . . . he did not suddenly emerge out of a vacuum and start producing striking and effective hymns."[13] As well as poetic borrowings, Dale points out, there are theological affiliations: "Though assertions are sometimes made that Herbert's theology verges on Calvinism (despite his associations with the 'Arminian nunnery' of Little Gidding), one can see in several poems evidence of that seventeenth-century Laudian High Church Arminianism which reappeared and persisted in the Wesley family in the eighteenth century."[14] Against this backdrop, I want to explore some key themes in Herbert's concept of holiness as part of the Anglican tradition "out of which [John Wesley] came and in which he worked."

SEVEN WHOLE DAYS: HOLINESS AS A DAILY DISCIPLINE

"Seven whole days, not one in seven, I shall praise thee," says Herbert in one of his best-known hymns. Herbert was committed to modeling holiness as a disciplined way of life for all Christian people, lay and ordained alike. Like Ferrar, he set out to establish a rhythm of daily prayer for himself and his household, based on the Book of Common Prayer and the daily reading of the Psalms. "Days marked out by prayer were his inheritance from home and, particularly richly, from Westminster School. In his later years at Bemerton he was notably regular in his daily saying of Morning and Evening

10. Herbert, *Poems of George Herbert*; Hutchinson, *Works of George Herbert*.
11. Walton, *Lives*.
12. Hutchinson, *Works*, xlvii.
13. Dale, "Line of Piety," 55.
14. Dale, "Line of Piety," 58.

John Wesley, George Herbert, and the Anglican "Line of Holiness" 17

Prayer with his family in the church over the road."[15] It was said that when the ploughmen in the neighboring fields heard "Mr Herbert's Saint's bell" ringing, they would stop and take off their caps and say a prayer; and several of the local gentry took to coming down to Mr. Herbert's church to join him and his family at the appointed times of daily prayer.[16] Cultivating the habit of daily prayer was important for the laity as well as the clergy: praying "twice a day, every day of the week, and four times on Sunday . . . is so necessary, and essential to a Christian, that he cannot without this maintain himself in a Christian state."[17] But for the parson, "it is not enough to observe the fasting days of the church, and the dayly prayers enjoyned him by auctority . . . but [he] adds, out of choice and devotion, other days for fasting, and hours for prayers; and by these he keeps his body tame, serviceable, and healthfull; and his soul fervent, active, young and lusty as an eagle."[18]

A PRACTICAL PIETY AND DEVOTION

For Herbert, as for Wesley, piety and practical holiness go hand in hand. "And his most holy life was such, that it begot such reverence to God, and to him, that they [his parishioners] thought themselves the happier, when they carried Mr. *Herberts* blessing back with them to their labour.—Thus powerful was his reason, and example, to perswade others to a practical piety, and devotion."[19] Herbert believed that everybody should have a vocation, not just the working people of his parish: idleness is no calling for a gentleman, and riches should be treated as an active instrument of doing good.[20] A surviving letter to his friend Arthur Woodnoth, who was vacillating over a possible call to the priesthood, makes a firm but delicate case for the importance of doing God's work in a lay calling.[21] The life of the country parson was steeped in practical holiness: Herbert's time (and his wife's) was taken up with the relief of poverty, care for the church buildings, and hands-on involvement in the life of his parish as "not only a Pastour, but a Lawyer also, and a Physician."[22] Walton's story of the fastidious Mr. Herbert stopping on

---

15. Drury, *Music at Midnight*, 257.
16. Walton, *Lives*, 302.
17. Hutchinson, *Works*, 272.
18. Hutchinson, *Works*, 237.
19. Walton, *Lives*, 302.
20. Hutchinson, *Works*, 274.
21. Drury, *Music at Midnight*, 221–29.
22. Hutchinson, *Works*, 260. Cf. also Walton, *Lives*, 304–7.

the way to a musical soirée in Salisbury to help a carter to right his horse provides a nice example of a holiness that was not afraid to get its feet dirty:

> If I am bound to pray for all that be in distress, I am sure that I am bound, so far as it is in my power, to practise what I pray for. And though I do not wish for the like occasion every day, yet let me tell you, I would not willingly pass one day of my life without comforting a sad soul, or shewing mercy; and I praise God for this occasion. And now let us tune our instruments.[23]

HOLINESS ON THE HEAD

But discipline and good works are not enough: prayer must touch both mind and heart too. Walton describes Herbert's "diligence, to make his Parishioners understand what they pray'd, and why they prais'd, and ador'd their Creator."[24] The people should come to church on Sundays "with holy hearts and awfull minds, humbly adoring, and worshipping the invisible majesty and presence of Almighty God."[25] The parson should seek to encourage "all possible reverence on the people's part," ensuring that they say their prayers "not in a hudling, or slubbering fashion, gaping, or scratching the head, or spitting even in the midst of their answer, but gently and pausably, thinking what they say . . . not as Parrats, without reason."[26] To achieve this, the parson himself must show "all possible reverence in reading divine service" with "hearty and unfeigned devotion," as one who is "truly touched and amazed with the majesty of God . . . that being first affected himself, he may affect also his people."[27]

Prayer and preaching, to Herbert, were of equal importance, as is evidenced by his design for the church at Leighton Bromswold.[28] The pulpit is the parson's "joy and throne,"[29] and preaching requires diligent study of Scripture and the Fathers (*The Countrey Parson*, chapters iii and iv). But its object is not erudition or display: as a preacher, Herbert recommends drawing on homely images from everyday life to connect with his rustic

---

23. Walton, *Lives*, 305.
24. Walton, *Lives*, 302.
25. Hutchinson, *Works*, 235.
26. Hutchinson, *Works*, 231–32. Herbert's strictures apply equally to the "gentry and nobility."
27. Hutchinson, *Works*, 231–32.
28. Drury, *Music at Midnight*, 171–81 and plates 11 and 12.
29. Hutchinson, *Works*, 232.

hearers (*The Countrey Parson*, chapter vii). And the preacher's overarching aim is holiness: "the character of his Sermon is Holiness; he is not witty, or learned, or eloquent, but Holy."[30] The preacher must choose "moving and ravishing texts," texts of devotion, not controversy, "dipping and seasoning all our words and sentences in our hearts, before they come into our mouths ... so that the auditors may plainly perceive that every word is heart-deep," and "often urging of the presence and majesty of God, for such discourses show very Holy."[31]

This deep awareness of the majesty and holiness of God not unnaturally leads to a keen sense of the unworthiness of the minister. Herbert is acutely aware of this discrepancy: in "The Priesthood," he contrasts the "sacred and hallow'd fire" of the priesthood with the "earth and clay" of the minister; and in "Aaron," he contrasts the light and holiness of the biblical high-priestly garments with the "profaneness, defects and darkness" of his own "poore priest." The remedy in every case is the work of God's grace: it is God who chooses the unworthy clay vessel to carry the flame, Christ whose righteousness covers the inadequacies of the priest: *In him I am well drest*.[32] This absolute confidence in the prevenient and empowering mercy of God, which appears constantly in Herbert's writings (including his most famous poem, "Love III"), is surely something of which Wesley would approve.[33]

HEART-WORK AND HEAVEN-WORK: VULNERABLE HOLINESS

But that confidence was hard-won. Faith for Herbert is a running dialogue—an argument, even—with God. There is a serenity here, but it is a serenity that is "heart-deep." Holiness for Herbert is not a cozy or passive relationship: it is dynamic and vigorous, and searingly honest. "For Herbert it is quite OK to debate with God. God is big enough to take anything that might come up . . . He can adore and be impudent, be hostile and angry, and can also love and be speechless as one who is constantly reminded how much he is treasured."[34] Like St. Paul, he knows that nothing can separate him from the love of God.

---

30. Hutchinson, *Works*, 233.
31. Hutchinson, *Works*, 234.
32. Cf. "The Holdfast"; and the quietly self-mocking comments on "The Parson in Sacraments" in Hutchinson, *Works*, 257.
33. Wheeler, "Grace Bearing Fruit," 81–92.
34. Oakley, *Splash of Words*, 22–24.

This heart-stopping combination of adoration and impudence comes out particularly in the poems where he is struggling with his own vocation. *I know the ways of Learning*, he says in "The Pearl": *I know the ways of Honour . . . I know the ways of Pleasure . . .* daydreaming a series of alternative futures: *My stuff is flesh, not brasse; my senses live . . .* But each fantasy future is blown away by four simple words: *Yet I love thee.* In "The Quip," the poet is mocked by "the merrie world." All the delights he has given up parade before him—beauty, money, the delights of "quick wit and conversation," the whistling silks of a Van Dyck portrait: but the refrain is always, *But thou shalt answer, Lord, for me.* In "The Collar," anger and frustration build to a climax of outright rebellion: *I struck the board, and cried, No more!*—only to be blown away in the final quatrain: *But as I rav'd and grew more fierce and wild With every word, Methought I heard one calling, Child!—And I repli'd, My Lord.*

Herbert's ruthless honesty about his own temptations and doubts has always been appreciated by those who struggle with the demands of holiness. It was one of the reasons he hesitated about publishing the poems, entrusting them to Ferrar as "a picture of the spiritual Conflicts that have passed between God and my Soul, before I could subject mine to the will of Jesus my Master."[35] Yet (as he recognizes himself), this ability to record his own inward struggles as the raw material of the struggle for holiness is a powerful weapon in the hand of the preacher:

> The Countrey Parson's Library is a holy life: for besides the blessing that that brings upon it, there being a promise, that if the Kingdom of God be first sought, all other things shall be added, ever itself is a Sermon. For the temptations with which a good man is beset, and the ways which he used to overcome them, being told to another, whether in private conference, or in the Church, are a Sermon . . . so that the parson, having studied and mastered all his lusts and affections within, and the whole army of Temptations without, hath ever so many sermons ready penn'd, as he hath victories.[36]

"Being told to another, whether in private conference, or in the Church": perhaps a foreshadowing of the importance of what Wesley called "social holiness"—meaning not social ethics (though that of course has its place), but "something deeper and broader: that all true religion is lived out in relationships, and that Christians grow in holiness together, or not at all."[37]

35. Walton, *Lives*, 314.
36. Hutchinson, *Works*, 278.
37. Wheeler, "Grace Bearing Fruit," 91.

The holiness of a disciplined life; holiness that doesn't mind getting its feet dirty; social holiness; vulnerable holiness; holiness that is heart-deep. All of these Herbertian themes find echoes in Wesley—and perhaps especially the last, summed up in the admiring words of Richard Baxter the Puritan: "Herbert speaks to God like one that really believeth a God, and whose business in this world is most with God. Heart-work and Heaven-work make up his books."[38] Wesley would surely have endorsed Baxter's affirmation of this very Anglican—but also universal—tradition of holiness.

WORKS CITED

Baxter, Richard. *The Poetical Fragments of Richard Baxter*. London: Pickering, 1821.

Cropper, Margaret. *Flame Touches Flame*. London: Longmans, Green & Co, 1949.

Dale, James. "Charles Wesley and the Line of Piety: Antecedents of the Hymns in English Devotional Verse." *Proceedings of the Charles Wesley Society* 8 (2002) 55–64.

Drury, John. *Music at Midnight: The Life and Poetry of George Herbert*. London: Allen Lane, 2013.

Herbert, George. *The Poems of George Herbert*. World's Classics 109. Oxford: Oxford University Press, 1961.

Hutchinson, F. E. *The Works of George Herbert*. Oxford: Clarendon, 1941.

Oakley, Mark. *The Splash of Words*. Norwich, UK: Canterbury, 2016.

Rack, Henry. "The Wesleys and Manchester." *Proceedings of the Charles Wesley Society* 8 (2002) 6–23.

Thomson, James. "Gallery of Saints." https://chestercathedral.com/gallery-of-saints/.

Walton, Izaak. *The Lives of John Donne, Sir Henry Wotton, Richard Hooker, George Herbert, Robert Sanderson*. Reprint, World's Classics 303. Oxford: Oxford University Press, 1966.

Wheeler, Sondra. "Grace Bearing Fruit: John Wesley's Conception of Discipleship." In *The Meanings of Discipleship*, edited by Andrew Hayes and Stephen Cherry, 81–92. London: SCM, 2021.

---

38. Baxter, *Poetical Fragments of Richard Baxter*.

Recovering Sexual Holiness in 1 Corinthians 6

Spiritual, Theological, and Missional Implications

Michael J. Gorman

LARRY HURTADO MADE THE following claim about the earliest Christians and sex: "It is fair to judge that the impact of the distinctive stance of early Christian teaching involved a transformation in the deep logic of sexual morality."[1] Two texts expressing this distinctive stance are the following:

> For this is the will of God, your sanctification: that you abstain from sexual immorality (*porneias*); that each one of you know how to control your own body in holiness and honor (*en hagiasmō kai timē*), not in lustful passion (*en pathei epithymias*), like the gentiles who do not know God. (1 Thess 4:3–5; my trans.—mid-first century).

> For Christians are not distinguished from the rest of humanity by country, language, or custom . . . They marry like everyone else, and have children, but they do not expose their offspring. They share their food but not their wives. They are in the flesh, but they do not live according to the flesh (*Epistle to Diognetus* 5.1, 6–8—probably late second century).[2]

---

1. Hurtado, *Destroyer of the Gods*, 171.
2. The translation is from Holmes, *Apostolic Fathers*. It is likely that the text implies more than the rejection of the obvious (adultery, bigamy) and serves as a generic statement about sexual morality. On Jewish and Christian rejection of infanticide, exposure, and abortion, see Gorman, *Abortion and the Early Church*.

These texts raise various questions, but the principal point is clear: "Christians do human sexuality differently." What does that mean today in light of Paul's theology and praxis?[3]

SHAMELESS SEX?

Fast forward to 2019: the American Lutheran minister Nadia Bolz-Weber publishes her bestselling book *Shameless: A Case for Not Feeling Bad About Feeling Good (About Sex)*. Reacting against the Christian "purity movement" and similar approaches to sexuality, Bolz-Weber proposes a contemporary practical theology of sexual exploration and freedom. The first chapter of the book, "Sanctus" ("Holy"), begins by narrating the story of a young single woman whose Christian upbringing had led her to not have any sexual partners; that changed when she was twenty-nine. Writes Bolz-Weber:

> I thought, *You were robbed*. The church took away over a decade of her sexual development. All this time, she could have been gaining the kind of wisdom that comes from making her own choices, from having lovers, from making mistakes, from falling in love.[4]

When the young woman deals with the negativity of her first sexual relationship by next having a casual sexual encounter, Bolz-Weber advises her that such behavior will probably not help but adds, "There's nothing wrong with any of this."[5]

Bolz-Weber surmises that the church's obsession (as she sees it) with sexual purity is likely due to its desire for holiness. But she then raises the question of what holiness actually is: "Holiness is when more than one become one, when what is fractured is made whole."[6] Therefore, "when two loving individuals, two bearers of God's image, are unified in an erotic embrace, there is space for something holy. Two spirits, two bodies, two stories are drawn so close that they are something together that they cannot be alone. There is unity."[7] Holiness is distinct from purity, she then argues, "[b]ecause holiness is about union *with*, and purity is about separation *from*."[8] Real holiness, she insists, is on display in the Gospels, when Jesus

---

3. I am honored, with this essay, to express my gratitude to Kent Brower, both for his professional gifts and for his personal contributions to me.
4. Bolz-Weber, *Shameless*, 17.
5. Bolz-Weber, *Shameless*, 17.
6. Bolz-Weber, *Shameless*, 19.
7. Bolz-Weber, *Shameless*, 20.
8. Bolz-Weber, *Shameless*, 26.

touches bodies; thus, she implies, the richest form of holiness "is sensual and embodied and free from shame and deeply present in the moment and comes from union with God."[9]

When Bolz-Weber wrote a summary article of the book for *The Christian Century*, I responded with a letter to the editor, which was published in part. Here are some excerpts from the full letter:

> I am extraordinarily disappointed at an account of human sexuality that is blatantly pagan—in the name of "reformation."[10] Bolz-Weber records what she said to her own teenage daughter, a high school senior, after approving of her having sex with her boyfriend: "I want you to love sex, sweetie . . . I want you to be comfortable in your body and learn what it desires and how to communicate that to your lovers . . . And I hope for your faith to be a part of your sexuality and vice versa."

It is difficult to imagine an approach to sex that is more antithetical to New Testament teaching, especially about "fleeing" from sexual immorality because it is one of the marks of a culture that does not know the living God.

As every Christian denomination struggles with Christian sexuality, we deserve better than this. If a reformation is needed today, it is one of sexual sanctification, not sexual shamelessness.

HOLY SEX

Nadia Bolz-Weber's understandings of both holiness and human sexuality are seriously deficient, but her sentiments have been welcomed because they reflect—or elicit—a view that is increasingly common in the church: human sexuality is simply a matter of eroticism that is (allegedly) inherently "holy." Holiness in her definition lacks its most basic biblical content: that it involves being set apart and distinctive and, for humans, taking on the character of God. Holiness is what distinguishes the people of God from the not-people-of-God (e.g., Lev 20:26). In the words of Kent Brower and Andy Johnson, holiness has to do with a "publicly identifiable people who embody God's very character in their particular social setting."[11]

Furthermore, as we will see below, a simplistic sharp distinction between holiness as "union with" and purity as "separation from" is at odds with Paul (and the New Testament as a whole). Holiness as purity is an

---

9. Bolz-Weber, *Shameless*, 27.
10. The original title of the book was *Shameless: A Sexual Reformation*.
11. Brower and Johnson, "Introduction," xvii.

essential theme that emerges from the collection of essays on New Testament holiness edited by Kent Brower and Andy Johnson.[12] The New Testament, they write, "continues to affirm certain basic Jewish understandings of holiness as purity or difference from Gentiles, e.g., avoiding sexual immorality and idolatry."[13] Or in the words of theologian Beth Felker Jones, "Strange ideas about sex—odd ideas out of sync with those of the wider culture—marked Christians out from the very beginning."[14]

Paul's words to the Thessalonian faithful, "in holiness and honor, not in lustful passion," contain a pair of mutually exclusive phrases, in which the presence of one member (e.g., "holiness and honor") inherently excludes the other ("lustful passion").[15] Such a stark contrast between Christian and pagan sexual practices may be aspirational, even idealistic, but it was, and is, nonetheless to be taken seriously.[16]

Thus, I offer here a sketch of a Pauline perspective on sexual sanctification as seen in 1 Cor 6:12–20, which is essentially a theological elaboration of the 1 Thessalonians text. This sketch is an effort to contribute to "a fresh understanding of Christian holiness that addresses the 21st-century context" and that is "faithful to Scripture and tradition," to borrow two phrases from our honoree.[17] But before proceeding to that sketch, we must pause to consider a key word in this discussion: *porneia*.

WHAT IS *PORNEIA*?

There has been significant scholarly debate about the meaning of the Greek word *porneia*.[18] Space permits only a statement of what, to my mind, is its

12. See Brower and Johnson, "Introduction," xx–xxi.

13. Brower and Johnson, "Introduction," xx.

14. Jones, *Faithful*, 9.

15. Linguists call this phenomenon complementary, complete, non-graded, and/or negated antonyms. Such sets often take the form of "X not Y" or something similar.

16. However, not every pagan was guilty of "lustful passion," and pagan moralists often criticized such behavior. Paul is generalizing about a culture of sexual practices. Our situation today is analogous, though with far fewer critiques from pagan moralists.

17. Brower, *Holiness in the Gospels*, 9. I concur with Kent's fundamental assumptions about holiness named early in that book (15–16), three of which are relevant beyond the Gospels: (1) holiness is derived from God, the Holy One; (2) it is a theme throughout Scripture; and (3) its significance is not limited to a small list of words but is a much broader aspect of Scripture.

18. Prior to and apart from Jewish and Christian usage, *porneia* meant simply prostitution; see Wheeler-Reid et al., "Can a Man Commit πορνεία with His Wife?" But their conclusion that in Paul and other early Christian literature "anyone who has engaged in a sexual act and enjoyed it is guilty of πορνεία [*porneia*]" (398) misreads the evidence.

most plausible meaning, especially in 1 Corinthians 6. William Loader's thorough analysis concludes that *porneia* has "a wide range of meanings" in the New Testament[19]; "[c]ontext must determine meaning."[20] A suitable English gloss of Paul's usage is "sexual immorality," even if the particular form of *porneia* Paul addresses in 1 Corinthians 6 is some form of prostitution.[21] Kyle Harper similarly argues that the word signified "the chief vice in a [Jewish and then early Christian] system of sexual morality rooted in conjugal sexuality . . . [T]he term condensed the cultural differences between the observers of the Torah and Gentile depravity."[22] That is, *porneia* "could evoke the whole array of extramarital sex acts of which Greek and Roman culture approved."[23] For Paul, then, *porneia* means sexual activity outside

---

Similarly, Reno ("Pornographic Desire") argues that the term referred originally to all dimensions of "sex work" and then came to mean lack of sexual self-control; for Paul it signifies both, but especially the latter and not any particular "disoriented actions" (179). These sorts of arguments involve special pleading and contain internal contradictions. They are probably at least partially rooted in an attempt to say that specific activities today are not inappropriate, only certain attitudes. While Paul rejects lustful passion, it is not synonymous with *porneia* for him. The primary correlation he makes is to pair *porneia* with idolatry as two pagan practices to "flee" (see further below). The cognate verb *porneuō* in 1 Cor 10:8 (echoing 1 Cor 6:18) is likewise paired with practicing idolatry (1 Cor 10:7) and clearly signifies an activity, though Paul may also intend to suggest that practicing idolatry is practicing spiritual *porneia*. Space prohibits discussion of possible interpretations of *porneia* as signifying only acts of sexual violence. This position would rightly take sexual violence seriously but would again involve special pleading, likely motivated in part to imply biblical warrant for certain nonviolent sexual acts.

19. Loader, *New Testament on Sexuality*, 142n115; cf. 246. He includes pre-betrothal and premarital heterosexual sex (fornication) and homosexual relations as well as adultery, incest, and prostitution.

20. Loader, *New Testament on Sexuality*, 142.

21. Loader, *New Testament on Sexuality*, 168–69.

22. Harper, "*Porneia*," 374.

23. Harper, "*Porneia*," 383. Harper adds that a more specific meaning could also obtain: "the sexual use of dishonored women," especially prostitutes but also slaves. For our purposes, the critical point here is the more general one: *porneia* means all extramarital sexual activity. Harper's view that for Jews and early Christians forbidding *porneia* included prohibiting sex with their slaves has been challenged by, e.g., Glancy, "The Sexual Use of Slaves." Glancy's argument from silence (226–29)—that Paul does not condemn sex with one's slaves—is not proof that he accepted the practice. In fact, just the opposite is implied by texts like Gal 3:28 and the household codes in Colossians and Ephesians (whether written by Paul or by a disciple), for Christian masters are compelled by the texts themselves and by their co-texts to treat slaves with love and gentleness.

the marriage covenant, in that such activity embodies the works of the flesh rather than the fruit of the Spirit (Gal 5:19-23).²⁴

THE COVENANTAL, HOLINESS CONTEXT OF 1 COR 6:12-20

Fundamental to God's covenant with his people is love of God and love of neighbor, essential marks of God's holy, set-apart community. This double commandment appears implicitly and explicitly throughout the Old Testament, later Jewish literature, and the New Testament (including the teachings of Jesus). The antithesis of the double commandment—non-love of God (especially idolatry) and non-love of neighbor (especially injustice and sexual immorality)—are also regularly named throughout the same literature. For instance, Wisdom 12-15, echoed in Rom 1:18-32, pairs idolatry and sexual immorality, even portraying the latter as the result of the former (e.g., Wis 14:12).

This same pairing underlies 1 Thess 4:3-5: sexual immorality characterizes those who do not know God. It also underlies 1 Corinthians, where Paul instructs his audience to "flee" (*pheugein*) from two things: idolatry (10:14) and sexual immorality (*porneia*; 6:18).²⁵ Avoiding such fundamental sins and practicing their positive opposites—love of God and love of neighbor, reconfigured around the crucified and resurrected Messiah and the Spirit—constitutes the core of the holiness to which the Corinthians and we are called (1 Cor 1:2).²⁶

In 1 Cor 6:12-20, Paul builds on the two preceding passages: exhortations to community holiness in sexual matters (5:1-13) and to community justice, rather than injustice (*adikeō*; 6:7-8) in matters of dispute (6:1-11). His conclusion to 6:1-11 once again includes a set of antitheses: (1) the *adikoi* (6:9), practitioners of *adikia* who will not inherit God's kingdom (6:9-10), versus (2) those former *adikoi* ("you") who have been washed,

---

24. Dunn was right to think of a broad spectrum of acts ("unlawful sexual intercourse", *Theology*, 690), though "inappropriate sexual activity" might be a better descriptive phrase.

25. Unfortunately, translations do not always render the verb in these two texts consistently, so the connection may be missed. See also Acts 15:29.

26. In 1 Corinthians Paul does not specifically say "flee injustice/unrighteousness" (*adikia*), the broader term that includes *porneia*. But he clearly implies it, for *adikia* is the subject of the passage immediately preceding 1 Cor 6:12-20 (6:1-11), though (again) English translations often mask the presence of the "justice/injustice" word-family in that passage. See also the first two examples of *adikoi* in 6:9—*pornoi* and *eidōlolatrai*.

made holy, and made just (*edikaiōthēte*) by the working of God through the Son and the Spirit (6:11).[27]

As Paul approaches the new topic of Corinthians having (real or potential) sexual relations with prostitutes, he has these contextual factors at hand.[28] He also has a theological framework that has guided him throughout the letter: to examine everything by looking both back at Christ's first coming and all it entails (his death and resurrection and our resultant new life) and ahead to the second coming and all it entails (e.g., the general resurrection and the full establishment of God's kingdom).

THE STRUCTURE AND CONTENT OF 1 COR 6:12–20

As I have noted elsewhere and presented in a table,[29] 1 Cor 6:12–20 consists of two parallel parts, 6:12–18a and 6:18b–20, each with four main components: (1) Corinthian slogans; (2) Paul's counter-slogans; (3) Paul's theological corrections and claims, introduced by "Do you not know?"; and (4) a concluding exhortation. The following version of that table paraphrases these words from both the Corinthians and Paul:[30]

Paraphrased Parallels in 1 Corinthians 6:12–18a and 6:18b–20		
	6:12–18a	6:18b–20
Corinthian Slogans 12a, 12c, 13a // 18b	Christian liberty means I am free to do whatever I want. Sexual desire is a bodily appetite like hunger and must be satisfied; our genitalia are meant for sex, and vice versa.[31] One day our bodies will be destroyed, along with our sexual appetites, so now is the time to indulge!	Sin has nothing to do with our bodies.

---

27. Interestingly, the *adikoi* of 6:9–10 include the sexually immoral of various types and those who practice various forms of theft, in addition to those who mistreat others in the pagan courts (6:1–8).

28. For a full exegesis, see especially Loader, *New Testament on Sexuality*, 166–82.

29. Gorman, *Apostle of the Crucified Lord*, 299. Space does not permit an argument for this proposal.

30. The reader is advised to have the biblical text at hand.

31. That is, *eating : stomach :: sex : body*; or, "eating is to the stomach as sex is to the body." See also Jones, *Faithful*, 14–15: "The world we live in tells lies about sex that are analogous to" lies about food, such as "Food is a private matter," "Nobody gets hurt in the production of your food," and "Food should always make you happy. Pleasure is the only reason for eating."

Paul's Counterslogans 12b, 12d, 13b, 14 // 18c	Not all activity is beneficial to oneself or others in the Christian community; true liberty is the freedom to love, to put others' needs ahead of selfish desire (see, e.g., 8:1–13; 10:23; 13:5). No activity, including sex, should dominate or enslave us; sexual addiction is the opposite of freedom. Our bodies are intended to be in the service of the Lord, not in the service of sex as if sex were our god and master. The Lord has everything to do with our bodies. In fact, our bodies are not destined for destruction but for resurrection.	Actually, sin and the body are closely connected; lots of bodily actions can be sins. Those who engage in sexual immorality sin against their own bodies. (And, as I have said, these bodies are part of Christ's body.)
Paul's Theological Correction and Claims 15–17 // 19–20a	You should know that the gospel I preached clearly implied[32] that in baptism a person's body is joined to Christ and thus to his body (see chap. 12) and becomes one of his bodily parts, or members. It would be totally inappropriate to connect Christ with a prostitute! This is because, as you should also know, sexual union with a prostitute is a physical bond that is a pseudo-marriage, since Genesis tells us (Gen 2:21–25) that the sexual union makes one body out of two. There is a similar "spiritual marriage"—expressed in bodily acts—between believers and the Lord that creates a unity that should not be broken by uniting physically with a prostitute. (This does not rule out sexual relations in marriage, as I explain in chap. 7.)	You should know that the gospel I preached implied[33] that, contrary to your assumptions, your body does not belong to you! It actually belongs to the one who made it and redeemed it from the power of Sin. That's what God has done in Christ's death—liberated you/your body from Sin and made you/your body (they are inseparable) into a special entity for God's own presence—a temple of God's Spirit, a place for the worship and service of God. Your body is on loan to you from God, so to speak, but only so that you can acknowledge its true owner and do with it what it is meant to be. The liberation of you and your body from Sin was costly—it cost God the death of his beloved Son.

32. Paul may even have been explicit about this.
33. Paul may even have been explicit about this too.

Paul's Concluding Exhortation 18a // 20b	My practical, pastoral charge, therefore, is to run away from all forms of sexual immorality. With idolatry, it is one of the two great causes of spiritual disaster.	For all these reasons, you should not only flee from the negative—sexual immorality—but also practice the positive: use your body for activities that please, honor, and serve God. (See also Rom 6:12–23; 12:1–2.)

We see from these two tables that the Corinthian misunderstanding of human sexuality is rooted in a general misconstrual of a broad spectrum of Christian spirituality, ethics, and theology. Christian freedom has been severed from both self-control and neighbor-love, and reborn as total libertinism. Bodily activity has been disconnected from sin, on the one hand, and from God, Christ, and the Spirit, on the other. The body's telos has been disassociated from the future and the hope of resurrection, with the result that it is seen simply as a host for present desires to be fulfilled at will. This lack of eschatological perspective is complemented with a deficient understanding of salvation: there is no sense of liberation from Sin to serve a new master and to be in union with, and the holy locus of, a holy God. Human bodies have both a present purpose and a future destiny that some Corinthians' sexual behavior betrays. *Unholy sex is an existential denial of the reality and significance of the cross and resurrection of Christ, and of the transformation that this liberating, saving event is meant to effect in people, particularly in and to their bodies as vehicles of their participation in Christ.*

THEOLOGICAL REFLECTIONS

This brief analysis of 1 Cor 6:12–20 provides the opportunity for further theological unpacking of what Paul says.

Sexual Holiness and Justice: Love of Neighbor and of God

First Corinthians 5–6 presents us with two matters of human sexuality enveloping an issue of justice. These sorts of superficially different issues are actually interrelated, as signaled, for instance, by the presence of the words *adikoi* and *pornoi* in 6:9. There is therefore no necessary tension between being committed to sexual holiness and being committed to justice. They are, in fact, closely connected because both are rooted in the character of God; each is alter-cultural in both Paul's day and ours. In the Jewish and early Christian mind these two issues were naturally linked as fundamental aspects of neighbor-love.

Sexual immorality and cruciform love cannot co-exist, for *porneia* is at best a form of self-love and self-indulgence that harms others and radically diminishes the holiness of the individual, the so-called partner, and the community. At the same time, such self-indulgence is the opposite of what Christ displayed in his incarnation and death for us.[34]

Yet another connection exists between injustice (as seen in lawsuits, according to 1 Cor 6:1–11) and *porneia*: the abuse of power that derives from a sense of entitlement apart from grasping the implications of being purchased by, and having allegiance to, the triune God revealed on the cross. The cross establishes an inseparable connection between justification and justice, on the one hand, and between liberation and bodily self-control, on the other. *The context of 6:12–20 implies that paying for sex is an act of injustice toward another.* Christians with power over others—especially men—have a special obligation not to mistreat them sexually.

Furthermore, for Paul and other early Christians, love of neighbor and love of God were inseparable because Christ is and was the ultimate incarnation of both. There is an element of failure to love God in acts of injustice and sexual immorality.

"Not Your Own": Sexuality and Somatic Spirituality in Relation to the Triune God

In 1 Cor 6:12–20 we have a profound theology of the body and of the connection between sexuality and spirituality. This is not an erotic spirituality that says we experience God in sex, but a somatic (embodied) spirituality that says we must honor God with our bodies in all things, and in a special way in sex. It is thus the opposite of the "sex without shame" movement, whether secular or (allegedly) Christian.

Our sexual life is most fundamentally an expression of our spirituality, our relationship with the triune God: God the Father, to whom we belong through redemption (6:20); Christ the Lord, with whom we are in an intimate personal relationship of communion and commitment (6:13, 15, 17); and the Holy Spirit, whose indwelling makes us temples of the Spirit (6:19). Our sexual life must reflect this reality. We belong first and foremost to Another, who claims our bodies; our most fundamental spiritual connection

---

34. See Dunn's concise but insightful discussion in his *Theology*, 119–23.

is to this One, and that spiritual connection takes place in part, and never without, our physical selves, our bodies.[35]

The popular mantra "Our bodies, ourselves" is, for Christians, both profoundly true and profoundly false. It is true that we are embodied creatures who can serve God and others with our bodies. But we—our selves, including our bodies—do not belong to us. Paul's declaration that "you are not your own" (6:19) is arguably the most radical and most profound basis for Christian sexual ethics—and for much more. We are God's, and we serve God appropriately only when we recognize that it is God who has intended the human body for certain things and not for others in order for us to flourish sexually and otherwise. Whatever theologies of sexuality and gender we embrace or attempt to develop must start at this point—that our bodies are not our own, but God's—rather than at the point of self-discovery or self-realization, or they are doomed to go in the wrong direction.

Sexual "Freedom" as Slavery

What is sometimes thought of as sexual freedom can actually be a form of slavery, of being dominated by sexual desire, whether that is expressed in visiting prostitutes, having multiple partners, using pornography, or something else. This is another way in which sexual activity can become a form of idolatry, too: something other than God becomes the governing power in one's life. Bodily freedom is belonging—body, mind, soul, and spirit—to the right Lord (God, not self) and honoring that Lord in and through the Lord's temple, one's body. This biblical theology of the body and of freedom subverts ancient and modern claims that we have inalienable rights to the control and use of our bodies and to the sexual practices of our choosing.[36]

THE MISSIONAL DIMENSION OF SEXUAL HOLINESS

In his treatment of holiness in Second Temple Judaism, Kent Brower makes the claim that holiness required separation, though that separation "was never intended to be an end in itself" but to serve "God's mission in the

---

35. On the avoidance of *porneia* as necessary for participation in Christ and essential to Christian identity, see May, *Body for the Lord*.

36. However, as strong as Paul can be on matters of human sexuality, he never sees sexual sin in isolation. It is not the worst or only sin, neither in 1 Corinthians 6 nor in Romans 1. Christians who focus on Paul's teaching on human sexuality alone make a mistake nearly as serious as those who neglect it.

world."[37] But many Christians and churches today take a "laissez-faire" attitude toward sexual practices, motivated in part by a missional desire to reach out to everyone, especially those thought to have been abandoned, or even harmed, by the church.

These missional impulses are understandable and perhaps even laudable. But when they are left unchecked, or allowed to morph into a state of implicit or explicit approval, they are neither missional nor appropriate. For Christians, sexual practices are not matters that don't matter (*adiaphora*) or merely matters of private morality. So what is the contemporary church to do? A few suggestions:

1. Acknowledge, repent from, and make reparations for the church's own complicity in, and hiding of, sexual transgressions and violence.

2. Acknowledge the contemporary reality of many expressions of sexual behavior both inside and outside the church. This is no time to bury our heads in the sand.

3. Develop, teach, and practice a practical theology of sexuality grounded in the Scriptures, with particular emphasis on the inherent distinctiveness of Christian attitudes and practices and on the theology of the body articulated by Paul. Christians should not be "squeezed into the mold" (see Rom 12:2 Phillips) of our sex-obsessed secular age.

4. Treat persons struggling with sexual behavior with mercy and grace, but also with the good news of healing: liberation from attitudes and behaviors that are inappropriate for Christians.

It is this combination of repentance, honesty, holiness, hospitality, and healing that may be the most missional practice the church can now engage in with respect to human sexuality.

WORKS CITED

Bolz-Weber, Nadia. *Shameless: A Case for Not Feeling Bad About Feeling Good (About Sex)*. New York: Convergent, 2019.
Brower, Kent. *Holiness in the Gospels*. Kansas City: Beacon Hill, 2005.
Brower, Kent E., and Andy Johnson. "Introduction: Holiness and the *Ekklēsia* of God." In *Holiness and Ecclesiology in the New Testament*, edited by Kent E. Brower and Andy Johnson, xvi–xxiv. Grand Rapids: Eerdmans, 2007.
Dunn, James D. G. *The Theology of the Apostle Paul*. Grand Rapids: Eerdmans, 1998.
Glancy, Jennifer A. "The Sexual Use of Slaves: A Response to Kyle Harper on Jewish and Christian *Porneia*." *Journal of Biblical Literature* 134 (2015) 215–29.

37. Brower, *Holiness in the Gospels*, 25.

Gorman, Michael J. *Abortion and the Early Church: Christian, Jewish, and Pagan Attitudes in the Greco-Roman World*. Downers Grove, IL: InterVarsity, 1982. Reprint, Eugene, OR: Wipf & Stock, 1998.

———. *Apostle of the Crucified Lord: A Theological Introduction to Paul and His Letters*. 2nd ed. Grand Rapids: Eerdmans, 2017.

Harper, Kyle. "*Porneia*: The Making of a Christian Sexual Norm." *Journal of Biblical Literature* 131 (2012) 363–83.

Holmes, Michael W. *The Apostolic Fathers: Greek Texts and English Translations*. 3rd ed. Grand Rapids: Baker Academic, 2007.

Hurtado, Larry W. *Destroyer of the Gods: Early Christian Distinctiveness in the Roman World*. Waco, TX: Baylor University Press, 2016.

Jones, Beth Felker. *Faithful: A Theology of Sex*. Grand Rapids: Zondervan, 2015.

Loader, William. *The New Testament on Sexuality*. Grand Rapids: Eerdmans, 2012.

May, Alistair Scott. *"The Body for the Lord": Sex and Identity in 1 Corinthians 5–7*. Journal for the Study of the New Testament Supplement 278. London: T. &. T. Clark, 2004.

Reno, Joshua M. "Pornographic Desire in the Pauline Corpus." *Journal of Biblical Literature* 140 (2021) 163–85.

Wheeler-Reid, David, et al. "Can a Man Commit πορνεία with His Wife?" *Journal of Biblical Literature* 137 (2018) 383–98.

"Made Holy by the Holy Spirit" in Galatians?

Peter Oakes

KENT BROWER, ALONG WITH Andy Johnson, gave me one of my most stimulating writing commissions when they asked me to write the contribution on Romans for their book, *Holiness and Ecclesiology in the New Testament*.[1] My response to the commission was influenced by the social-scientific studies of scholars such as Jerome Neyrey[2] and by encounters, when teaching Roman history, with ways in which boundaries between the sacred and the ordinary tended to be constructed in Graeco-Roman societies. The resulting article ended up with a particular focus on Rom 15:16, in which Paul expresses the aim of his ministry as being that "the offering of the gentiles would be acceptable, having been made holy by means of the holy Spirit (*hēgiasmenē en pneumati hagiō*, my translation)."

The shape of the commission, together with the social-scientific and social history elements of my approach, led me to consider the issue of holiness in Romans under the rubric of studying ways in which, in that letter, Paul taught about Christian groups as belonging to the sphere of the sacred. The article took holiness as the status of someone or something belonging to the sphere of the sacred and/or as the culturally expected characteristics of a person, group or object that had that status. The article then focused particularly on holiness as a status. I divided talk about such status into three categories: separation from the ordinary; closeness to other holy entities, especially the divine; use of the culture's terminology for the holy. Applying these categories to Romans produced sections on *hagios* ("holy") terminology and on its application to Christian groups; on Christian groups as called by God; and on Christian groups as children of God.

1. Oakes, "Made Holy," 167–83.
2. Neyrey, *Render to God*.

The article concluded that Romans applied all three categories of expression of the status of holiness to Christians. They were called by God out of the sphere of the ordinary into that of the sacred (while still remaining involved in the efforts and trials of the world). They were made children of God, closely binding them to the sacred. They were described using the terminology of holiness, most notably in the general designation as "holy ones." In bringing all this about, the Spirit was a central actor, as Rom 15:16 indicated.

How far beyond Romans does this pattern go? A particularly sharp case to consider is Galatians. On the one hand, Galatians has the closest structural and thematic similarities to Romans of all of Paul's letters.[3] On the other hand, Galatians lacks the most central vocabulary that Romans uses on this topic. Is the topic absent from Galatians? Are the issues dealt with in sharply different ways? Does it make any sense to talk about being "made holy by the holy Spirit" in Galatians?

THE ABSENCE OF THE *HAGIOS* (HOLY) WORD GROUP IN GALATIANS

The *hagios* word group does not occur at all in Galatians. The related *hosios* and *hieros* word groups do not occur either. The Spirit is not called *hagios*. The Galatians are not called *hagioi*. The verb *hagiazō* is not used.

Some scholars argue that Abraham is discussed in Galatians because Paul's opponents made Abraham central to their argument.[4] One could argue, conversely, that the absence of *hagios* suggests that it was not a term at issue between Paul and his opponents. On the other hand, one could argue that Paul was nervous that use of the characteristically Jewish term, *hagios*,[5] gave an argumentative advantage to his opponents, so he avoided it. However, given Paul's extensive deployment of the term in Romans, and in view of his apparently "head-on" argumentative style in Galatians, this seems an unlikely reason for him to avoid the term. Either way, the absence of the term makes the question of our article very acute: does Galatians express at all the idea of his mission having the aim that "the offering of the gentiles would be acceptable, having been made holy (*hēgiasmenē*) by means of the holy (*hagiō*) Spirit"? How can we proceed?

We will use two starting points. First, Paul does write a good amount in Galatians about his understanding of his mission to the gentiles. We can

---

3. Parallels and differences are explored in Oakes, "Galatians and Romans," 92–118.
4. E.g., de Boer, *Galatians*, 186.
5. Oakes, "Made Holy," 175.

consider the extent to which this matches the aspirations of Rom 15:16 and related texts in Romans. A second way in is that Galatians talks at length about functions of the Spirit in relation to Christians. We can ask how that relates to the idea of the Spirit functioning among the gentiles in making them holy, in line with Romans.

PAUL AND HIS MISSION TO THE GENTILES

In Galatians, Paul certainly makes clear that he has a mission to *ta ethnē*, the gentiles. The purpose of God's revelation to Paul was that he should "gospel" God's Son *en tois ethnesin*, "among the gentiles" (1:16). In 2:8, Paul's apostleship is *eis ta ethnē* ("to the gentiles"). In 2:7, he has been entrusted with the gospel *tēs akrobustias* ("of the uncircumcision"—in the sense of "the state of not being circumcised").

Another point of similarity to Romans is that, in speaking and then writing to the Galatian gentiles, Paul stresses *pistis* ("trust," "loyalty": 2:16; 3:2–14, 23–26). This presumably gave his apostleship to the Galatians the same sense as in Rom 1:5, "I received grace and apostleship for obedience of faith (*pistis*) among all the gentiles" (cf. Rom 15:18; 16:26). The terminology of obedience, like the terminology of holiness, is absent from Galatians, again in striking contrast to its pervasive presence in Romans (1:5; 5:19; 6:12, 16; 10:16; 15:18; 16:19, 26). However, we do find in Galatians Paul's keenness that "Christ would be formed" in his hearers (Gal 4:19). We should set the contrast in frequency of "obedience" and "holiness" language alongside the contrast in frequency of language of *hamartia*, "sin." In Galatians this only occurs at Gal 1:4; 2:17; 3:22, whereas it is ubiquitous in Romans (Rom 2:12; 3:9, 20, 23, 25; 4:7, 8; 5:12, 13, 14, 16, 20, 21; 6:1, 6, 7, 10, 12, 13, 14, 15, 16, 17, 18, 20, 22, 23; 7:5, 7, 8, 9, 11, 13, 14, 17, 20, 23, 25; 8:2, 3, 10; 11:27; 14:23).

A factor in common between Romans and Galatians, as Paul writes about his work in seeking to bring *pistis* to the gentiles, is that this *pistis* leads to righteousness (*dikaiosunē*). The letter to the Galatians may lack *hagiōsunē* and *hupakoē* ("obedience") but it makes much of *dikaiosunē*. The letters link "faith" and "righteousness" in very similar ways, even both citing Gen 15:6 and Hab 2:4 in support of the juxtaposition, while using Ps 143:2 and Lev 18:5 against an alternative linking of law and righteousness. The common use of scriptural fulfillment extends to other areas too. In particular, the hearers' community life is due to fulfill the law as expressed in Lev 19:18, "You shall love your neighbor as yourself" (Gal 5:14; Rom 13:9). In both letters, *pistis* leads to *dikaiosunē*. That *dikaiosunē* appears to be some kind of status before God (esp. Gal 3:6 and Rom 4:3 on Abraham). However, given both the term's usage in Greek more broadly, and its usage in the Septuagint, it looks unreasonable to exclude the term also having some moral sense. In that case, the similar prominence of ethics of neighbor love in the two letters suggests that Paul sees the gentiles of Galatians being in a similar situation to those of Romans. The topics of sin, obedience and holiness have not come up in Galatians in the same way as in Romans but the related shared triangulation between *pistis*, *dikaiosunē*, and ethics suggests that Paul sees the Galatians as part of the same mission to the gentiles that he later enunciates, in terms of holiness, in Romans.

Having said that, Galatians does not include either the idea of Paul seeking to make the gentiles an acceptable offering to God or the holiness language associated with that. Of course, many topics happen not to come up in any given letter. However, in this case, there may be a positive reason for Paul to avoid this topic in Galatians. In Rom 15:14–21, Paul is justifying writing to the Romans, doing so by describing the scope and significance of his mission to the gentiles, even going so far as to "boast" about a feature of it (15:17). In Galatians, it is his opponents who, according to Paul, wish to boast about the (physical) results of their mission among the Galatian gentiles (Gal 6:12–13). Paul eschews this, boasting only in the cross of Christ (6:14). In Galatians, Paul emphatically sets out the authority for his mission (1:1, 11–16; 2:7–9) but is not wanting to do anything that could constitute boasting about the results of his mission.

THE TRANSFORMATIVE SPIRIT

In Rom 15:16, the Spirit is instrumental in producing the holiness of the gentiles—or, possibly, is the location in which that transformation takes place (if *en* is read locatively ["in"] rather than instrumentally ["by"/"by means of"]).[6] To what extent does the rest of Romans indicate how the Spirit operates to bring this transformation about? Probably a great deal. Most of the activities of the Spirit in Romans are ones that look likely to be part of what Paul would have included in the idea of becoming holy. Many of the key descriptions in Romans of the transformative Spirit and its actions correspond closely with Galatians.

In Galatians, God specifically sends both "his Son" (Gal 4:4) and "the Spirit of his Son" (4:6). The latter is sent out "because you are sons," into "our hearts," "crying out, Abba father!" (4:6). In Romans 8, the Spirit is something

---

6. For a defense of the instrumental reading, see Oakes, "Made Holy," 170, 178–79. Compare also n7, below.

"received" (Rom 8:15) by "sons of God" (8:14), "by which we cry out, Abba father!" (8:15). A few verses earlier it is made clear that this is "the Spirit of God," which is also "the Spirit of Christ" (8:9). In the two letters, the Spirit has the same origin, the same identity as the Spirit of Christ, and the same related function of enabling the children of God to call out to God as father.

As well as the Spirit being "in" people, their motion relates to the Spirit. In both letters this happens similarly in two ways. First, in each letter the Christian is to "walk" "by" (Gal 5:16) or "in accordance with" (Rom 8:4) the Spirit, a motion that will be contrary to "the flesh":

> . . . walk by the Spirit and you will certainly not fulfill the desire of the flesh (Gal 5:16)

> . . . the righteous requirement of the law will be fulfilled in us who walk not in accordance with the flesh but in accordance with the Spirit. (Rom 8:4)

In both letters, Paul then expands on the flesh–Spirit contrast in the succeeding verses (Gal 5:16–26; Rom 8:3–14). In the passage in Galatians there is more sense of imperative than in the Romans passage. There is a fairly clear sense of a current problem in the Galatian community, set up in the warning about "bit[ing] and devour[ing] each other" in Gal 5:15 and reinforced in the warning on "provoking each other" (and so on) in 5:26, as well as in the general warning tone of the letter as a whole. However, there are probable elements of indicative in the Galatians passage. For instance, Paul is probably appealing to their experience of "the fruit of the Spirit" in 5:22–23. Conversely, the Romans text does have some degree of imperative sense seen, for instance, in Paul's argument that Christians "are not in debt to the flesh, so as to live according to the flesh" (Rom 8:12).

The second way in which the Christian's motion relates to the Spirit is that in both letters, the Spirit "leads" the Christian. In Romans, those who "are led by the Spirit of God (*pneumati theou agontai*)[7] are sons of God" (Rom 8:14). Galatians 5:18 has "If you are led by the Spirit (*pneumati agesthe*) you are not under law." We can see here a flexibility and potential interconnectedness among various expressions about the Spirit and its functions. Gal 5:18 takes us back to a point about the law related to the expression in Rom 8:4, quoted above. It also takes us to the ethical point, made earlier, about each letter heading towards love of neighbor. As Galatians has it, "For the whole law is fulfilled in one saying, in 'You shall love your neighbor as yourself'" (Gal 5:14, cf. Rom 13:9). The life of the Spirit is one of being a child of God, of contrast to "the flesh," of love and consequently of a type of

---

7. Note the sense of the dative here and in Gal 5:18.

fulfillment of the law. Some of this can also be seen in "the fruit (*karpos*) of the Spirit" in Gal 5:22–23 (cf. the "first-fruits" [*aparchē*] of the Spirit, Rom 8:23). The first three of the Galatians list of fruit are also linked with the Spirit in Romans: love (Rom 5:5), joy, and peace (15:13 [indirectly], 8:6).

The range of aspects of the Spirit and its actions in Romans and Galatians indicates how fully the Spirit is integrated into the transformative actions of God and Christ. Rom 8:9–11 makes this particularly clear and warrants comparison with Gal 2:19–20.

> You are not in flesh but in Spirit (*en pneumati*), if the Spirit of God dwells in you (*eiper pneuma theou oikei en humin*). If someone does not have the Spirit of Christ, they do not belong to him. If Christ is in you, the body is dead on account of sin, but the spirit is life on account of righteousness. If the Spirit of the one who raised Jesus from the dead dwells in you, the one who raised Christ from the dead will bring to life also your mortal bodies through his Spirit dwelling in you (Rom 8:9–11).

You in the Spirit; God's Spirit in you; having the Spirit of Christ; Christ in you. The coordination between these, and the relationship of these to death and life make the Spirit integral to the processes also seen in Gal 2:19–20:

> For through law I died to law, so that I would live to God. I have been crucified with Christ. It is no longer I who live: Christ lives in me. The life I now live in the flesh, I live by trust in the son of God who loved me and gave himself for me.

The Spirit being in the Christian, and the Christian being in the Spirit, is equivalent to Christ being in the Christian, and the Christian being in Christ, in both Romans and Galatians. If the Spirit brings holiness to the gentiles in Romans, it does so in Galatians too, via the same processes in both letters.

CONCLUSIONS

Even though the Greek terminology of holiness is absent from Galatians, Paul shows the Spirit acting in ways that match the holiness-bringing actions of Romans. From a social-scientific perspective, we can say that, in Galatians, Paul does not generally present the Christians as radically separated from the sphere of the normal, except maybe in the initial characterization of Christ as having rescued us from the present evil age (Gal 1:4). On the other hand, Paul strongly presents the Galatians as having a close relationship with the ultimate holy entity, God himself, and Paul links this child–father relationship closely to the action of the Spirit. In that way, in terms of status, the Galatians have been "made holy by the holy Spirit."

WORKS CITED

de Boer, Martinus C. *Galatians: A Commentary*. New Testament Library. Louisville: Westminster John Knox, 2011.

Neyrey, Jerome. *Render to God: New Testament Understandings of the Divine*. Minneapolis: Fortress, 2004.

Oakes, Peter. "Galatians and Romans." In *The New Cambridge Companion to St Paul*, edited by Bruce Longenecker, 92–118. Cambridge Companions to Religion. Cambridge: Cambridge University Press, 2020.

———. "Made Holy by the Holy Spirit: Holiness and Ecclesiology in Romans." In *Holiness and Ecclesiology in the New Testament*, edited by Kent Brower and Andy Johnson, 167–83. Grand Rapids: Eerdmans, 2007.

What Does the "Spirit of Holiness" in Romans 1:4 Have to Do with Jesus, Paul, and All Who Are Called by Jesus?

Svetlana Khobnya

THE INTERPRETATION OF THE role of the "spirit of holiness" (*pneuma hagiōsunēs*) in Rom 1:4 has a long history, perhaps most helpfully summarized by Schneider in the late sixties[1] and later picked up in most commentaries, especially extended by D. Moo[2] and R. Longenecker who admits that the "spirit of holiness" is the most difficult phrase in the opening of Romans.[3] Many answers and angles of interpretation have been suggested, more recently by Peerbolte,[4] but the questions of what Paul emphasizes at the beginning of Romans and what significance this *hapax legomenon* "spirit of holiness" plays in Paul's argument remain intangible. Perhaps, it is time to engage with the main scholarly discussions on this subject again and offer a way forward in understanding the role of the "spirit of holiness" in Paul.

SPIRIT OR spirit?

Traditionally, the "spirit of holiness" is understood in three ways: either (1) in reference to divine nature of Jesus, (2) as God's Spirit known throughout the Bible and being active in the whole life and especially at the resurrection of Jesus, or, finally, (3) as the spirit of Christ discernible in his obedient

---

1. Schneider, "Κατά Πνεῦμα."
2. Moo, *Romans*, 47–51.
3. Longenecker, *Romans*, 69.
4. Peerbolte, "Spirit of Holiness," 36–51.

faithfulness to the Father up to death on the cross. To sharpen this classification further, the interpretations circle around the identity of the Spirit or specific nature/activity of Christ.

All three interpretations make sense within the Pauline immediate context of Rom 1:1–5 if one pays attention to the pairing of "according to the spirit of holiness" with the phrase "according to the flesh," Jesus's descendance from David and his recognition[5] as the Son of God with power, as well as Paul's connection between the "spirit of holiness" and the resurrection from the dead. All three interpretations have strong supporters throughout the history of Christianity.

The first one most likely reflects an early church's christological discussion in relation to Christ's identity as both human and divine and, thus, is preferred by church fathers all the way up to nineteenth-century's commentators.[6] It is uncertain whether this discussion preoccupied Paul's mind, however. First, Paul was familiar with the Jewish understanding of divine sonship attributed to the whole of Israel, the righteous ones and to the Messiah or anointed one (i.e., Exod 4:22–23; Deut 32:5–6; Ps 2:1–7). Second, Jesus's special divine sonship has been already revealed to Paul (Gal 1:16), hence Paul refers to him as God's Son with power and as Lord, and he mentions both the resurrection as a decisive moment for Jesus's unique sonship and the invitation through him to include even the gentiles in the family of God (Rom 1:5). One may assume that Paul's emphasis was not on the divine/human nature of Christ as it was in the subsequent Christian debates but on the universal scope of Christ's action as God's promised Son and Messiah.[7] In other words, this first view does not fully take into account the continuity of the gospel promised beforehand concerning Jesus (vv. 1–3) and the fulfillment of the promise in Christ on a larger scale (vv. 5–6). It also does not register the significance of the connection between the "spirit" and declaring (*horizō*)[8] Jesus as God's Son with power by the resurrection from the dead, which marks generous (grace in v. 5) and transforming effects (apostleship and obedience of faith in v. 5) on Paul and other Jews and gentiles. The descriptor "holiness" in relation to the "spirit" is left unaccountable.

---

5. Paul's usage of the participle from *horizō* (to declare, to appoint, to designate or to recognize) is a subject of discussions, as it is evident later.

6. See comprehensive history of interpretation in Longenecker, *Romans*, 69–73.

7. Supported by Dunn, *Romans 1–8*, 23.

8. The meaning of the verb is also debatable as will become evident later.

The latter two interpretations are more favorable in modern scholarship because they fit not only the immediate context better but also Paul's wider context of Romans and other letters.

SIMPLY THE HOLY SPIRIT

Possibly, equating the "spirit of holiness" simply with the Holy Spirit or God's Spirit who indwells and sanctifies Jesus is the safest and logical way of interpreting this phrase. Many English Bibles follow this direction in their translations (the NIV, the NEB, also recognized as an alternative reading in the NRSV). The Spirit is known in the Scriptures, guiding the people of Israel, or indwelling specific individuals, particularly prophets. It is the Spirit who inspires them to speak up against sin, represent God and call people back into obedient relationship with God (to give a few examples, Gen 41:38; Ex 35:31; Num 11:16–30; 27:18; Deut 34:9; Judg 3:10; 1 Sam 10:10; Ps 51:10; Is 32:15–20; Ezek 37:14). Although neither Paul nor anyone else in the NT uses "the spirit of holiness," this phrase presents a literal translation from the Hebrew *ruach ha-kodesh* ("spirit of holiness"). It occurs in three instances in the OT (Isa 63:10, 11 and Ps 51:11 [LXX 50:13]) and is translated in Greek (LXX) as the Holy Spirit (*to pneuma to hagion*). In the T. Levi, the same phrase also signifies the Holy Spirit that will rest upon the anointed one (T. Levi 18:7) which, according to some scholars, alludes to the Spirit coming upon Jesus at the baptism.[9] The phrase appears more often in other Qumranic scrolls in relation to God's activity among his people (1QS 3.6–8; 4.18–21; 8.16; 9.3; 4Q504; 1QH 7.6–7; 9.32; 12.12; 14.13; 16.7, 12). Paul may be aware of this connection and uses the phrase to stress the continuity of the work of God's Spirit known in the past and in Jesus's life.

In this respect, the Holy Spirit was constantly present in Jesus's earthly life (in the flesh) but at the resurrection became the source of his power on a higher level.[10] This aspect of the higher or exalted level at the resurrection, however, leads to further theological discussions that address the question of whether the resurrection refers to epistemology (the moment when believers come to know about Jesus's status) or ontology (Jesus's actual status, known also as "adoptionist" Christology).[11]

---

9. Longenecker, *Romans*, 73.

10. Schneider, "Κατά Πνεῦμα," 370; Longenecker, *Romans*, 70.

11. This question has been recently discussed by Peerbolte, "Spirit of Holiness in Romans 1:4," 36.

Thus, Karl Barth explained the resurrection as secure objectivity about the person and work of the Spirit.[12] It is the moment of the revelation of Jesus's identity as the Son of God, translating *horizō* as declaring. Dunn took this step further, arguing that the resurrection inaugurated or enhanced Jesus's status as the Son of God translating *horizō* as "appointing."[13] Others, like Jensen, oppose Barth's overemphasis on Christology in defining the Spirit and propose to consider not only the resurrection but also the overall work of the Spirit, including the Pentecost.[14] Interestingly enough, Schneider's analysis of Rom 1:1–7 in light of the Spirit's work in the NT and Acts leads him to a similar conclusion.[15] He turns his attention to Paul's subsequent statements in Rom 1:5–7: the action of the Spirit in Christ leads Paul and others (Paul uses "we" here) to receive the grace and apostleship to bring the obedience of faith among the nations. So, the resurrection marks not only Jesus's lordship for Paul, according to Schneider, but it should be essentially seen as awakening for believers. Believers should be inspired by the same Spirit that caused Jesus's resurrection in order to grasp the meaning of the resurrection.

Some scholars challenge Dunn's explanation.[16] On the one hand, they claim (like Dunn) that "with power" modifies the title "Son of God" and not the participle *horisthentos* but, on the other hand, they disagree with the overemphasis on Jesus's status as the appointed Son at the resurrection. In the alternative reading, the Son of God was already the Son but was designated, marked out, or confirmed the Son of God with power by the resurrection. Jesus is both the Son of God in weakness and the designated Son of God with power by virtue of his obedience to the will of the Father to death that is evident throughout his life and confirmed by virtue of the resurrection. Resurrection is perceived as a witness to Christ's faithfulness to the Father all the way to the end. N. T. Wright sees here Paul's opportunity to affirm Christ as the promised and acknowledged Messiah (as interplay between the descendant of David and the Son of God with power) and the beginning of the fulfillment of the promised restoration of Israel.[17]

---

12. Barth, *Church Dogmatics*, 283–84.
13. Dunn, *Romans 1–8*, 13.
14. Jenson, *Systematic Theology*, 146.
15. Schneider, "Κατὰ Πνεῦμα," 381.
16. Fitzmyer, *Romans*, 235; Moo, *Romans*, 49.
17. Wright, *Challenges of Jesus*, 108; Wright, "Romans," 747; Wright, *Climax of the Covenant*, 34–40. This idea is also confirmed in Acts 2:36, "Therefore let the entire house of Israel know with certainty that God has made him both Lord and Messiah, this Jesus whom you crucified."

Some avoid speaking about the precise meaning of the resurrection by focusing on the contrast between the old and the new age inaugurated by Jesus.[18] Paul's contrast between "flesh" and the "Spirit" is part of Paul's salvation-historical framework in which "flesh" and "Spirit" represent the contrast between the present or old age and the age to come. Jesus as human Davidic descendent comes in flesh and represents the era still influenced by sin and death. Obedient Jesus empowered by the Spirit represents and brings the new redemptive era and eschatological reality for all (vv. 5–7; cf. 1:16).

Viewing the "spirit of holiness" as the Holy Spirit fits Paul's context on many levels and triggers further theological analysis, as discussed. Yet, this view still leaves some questions unanswered. Why does Paul use the "spirit of holiness" instead of directly referring to the Holy Spirit? Is the descriptor "holiness" significant for Paul in any way? Does the emphasis on the Holy Spirit shift the discussion away from Paul's christological interest at the beginning of Romans?

CHRIST'S OWN SPIRIT

It seems that the understanding of the "spirit of holiness" as pointing to Christ's own spirit of holiness may resolve these questions. Although recognized in scholarship,[19] this understanding needs further examination to sway the consensus. My PhD research,[20] carried out under Kent Brower's careful supervision and to whom we express gratitude with this volume, contributes further to the understanding of the "spirit of holiness" in relation to Christ's obedience. There are several reasons that have been overlooked in the past that support this reading.

Jesus's Faithful Obedience

This reading fits Paul's narrative sub-structure in the whole letter. It is implied by R. Longenecker although without giving it proper attention.[21] Paul starts with the story of God finally revealed in Christ (1:1–7). Christ is the direct object of the first seven verses. Paul is the slave of Christ (1:1). God's

18. Moo, *Romans*, 50. More recently, Pate, *Romans*, 20; Thomas, *Living in the Flesh*.

19. It is supported by Longenecker, and a number of contemporary scholars discussed by him. See Longenecker, *Romans*, 72–77. Translated as such by Wright, *New Testament*. It is a preferable reading in the NRSV.

20. Khobnya, *Father*.

21. Longenecker, *Romans*, 69–73.

promised gospel is the gospel of God concerning his Son (1:2–3). Christ is the reason for grace and apostleship for Paul and others (1:5). Christ is behind the mission to the nations (1:5–7). The Spirit is not in Paul's view yet. In this unusually long greeting of the letter Paul skillfully incorporates the good news (gospel) about the fulfillment of God's story of redemption in the action of Christ that sets the tone of the whole letter. And what did Christ do? The rest of Romans as well as other of Paul's letters elaborate on this issue further. Christ fulfilled God's promises of redemption to the Jews and extended God's blessings to the gentiles because of his faithfulness to the Father (15:8–9).

While the story of God in Christ includes many stories below the surface of Paul's argument, as pointed out by K. Grieb,[22] Christ's faithful obedience, expressed through *hupakoē* ("obedience" in 5:19), *pistis christou* ("faith of Christ" in 3:22, 26), *dikaiosunē* ("righteousness" in 3:25, 5:17, 18), *ilastērion* ("sacrifice" in 3:25) and in other expressive ways (for example, 5:12–21, 8:3) is pivotal in Romans.[23] Christ's faithful obedience is the expression of God's faithfulness and fulfillment of God's redemption for the Jews and gentiles. If Paul sets the tone of the letter by announcing the good news concerning God's Son, then it is more than plausible that he includes the reason behind the good news, namely Christ's faithfulness to the Father that is most likely expressed in 1:4. Christ has always been God's Son but because of his complete faithfulness to God the Father, even to death, God exalts him as the Son of God with power and as the Lord because of his obedience (cf. Phil 2:5–11) which is evident after the resurrection (temporal explanation) or because of the resurrection (causative explanation). Both temporal (although less evidently) and causative interpretations would supplement the meaning of Christ's empowerment based on his faithfulness to God here. Moreover, the argument of the pre-existence of Christ and his obedience (namely, he was God's Son but is recognized as God's Son with power after demonstrating complete obedience) corresponds with Paul's fundamental identity between God himself and his Son. The pre-existence of Christ reflects the key convictions: Jesus's agency in creation and redemption (cf. 1 Cor 10:1–4) and, consequently, his significance and unity of divine purpose that he fulfills for humanity as the second Adam (5:12–21) and for Israel as their Messiah and representative (for example, 8:3; 10:4; 15:8).[24]

---

22. Grieb, *Story of Romans*, xvii.
23. On Christ's faithfulness see Khobnya, *Father*, 149–63.
24. Hurtado, *Lord Jesus Christ*, 118–26.

The Invitation to Obedience

One should not overlook that Paul's call to the "obedience of faith" next in 1:5 presents a logical connection to Christ's obedience expressed in the "spirit of holiness." Jesus's obedient act opens the way to obedience and life for others who believe in Christ. The call to the obedience of faith (or faithful obedience as in CEB, or believing obedience,[25] or even participatory and holy obedience to make human connection closer to Christ) builds the framework for Romans or *inclusio* between 1:5 and 16:26. In the Son and through his obedience Paul sees the fulfillment of the OT prophecies (1:2) that concern Israel and all the nations (1:5–7). The mystery that was kept secret for long ages is now disclosed to all who believe (16:25–26). Throughout the letter Paul would variously explain the good news of God's redemption through Christ acting faithfully to the Father and would draw the consequences for those who are justified and brought to the obedience of faith to God.[26]

The "Spirit of Holiness"

The unusual phrase the "spirit of holiness" requires special attention. Recognizing the atypical and rare usage of both the "spirit of holiness" and the verb *horizō*, as well as a fairly flowing and balanced structure of Rom 1:3–4, scholars suspect that Paul draws on a pre-Pauline tradition.[27] This opens a possibility of interpreting Paul's words outside of the context of Romans and to consider Paul's intentional adaptation of the common formula for his own purposes. Jewett is the proponent of early Christian pluralism of the whole letter. He sees at the beginning of Romans Paul's attempt "not to discern theological options" but "to find common ground in the faith for a variety of cultural, theological, and ethical alternatives."[28] Thus, Paul may satisfy Jewish Christian's affirmation of Jesus coming from the seed of David although later he will oppose their zealotism and pride (2:17–24; 10:1–4). He accepts the Hellenistic Christian dialectic of flesh versus spirit but will

---

25. See Wright, *New Testament*, 337.

26. This includes the unity with Christ; living in the sphere of Christ's rule freed from sin when the old self in Adam dies; living in one body of Christ; living as co-heirs with Christ and children of God in the newness of the resurrected life with the mind set on Christ and the Spirit of Christ; and living as holders of the eschatological hope of the final revelation when the whole creation will be liberated (see especially Rom 5–8; 12–15).

27. Jewett, *Romans*, 101–8.

28. Jewett, *Romans*, 108.

insist on moral transformation in Rom 6–8. Obviously, there is not sufficient evidence to verify Jewett's hypothesis.[29] But his research demonstrates that Paul's understanding of the "spirit of holiness" may differ from his audience's and that even his audience may perceive it in various ways. Yet it is methodologically wiser to deal with the phrase within Paul's immediate context that seems to have a clear line of arguments.

To reiterate, Paul (1) connects the idea of the "spirit of holiness" to the gospel of God that has its roots in Judaism, namely was promised beforehand in the Scriptures (1:2), (2) mentions the "spirit of holiness" in relation to the recognition of Jesus' sonship with power alongside (in parallel construction) Jesus's "fleshly" descent from a Davidic line (1:3), and (3) announces the results of Christ's action for the humankind (1:5–6). All of these arguments seem to point to Paul's initial announcement about the fulfillment of God's promises in Christ for the world and accordingly about Christ's action that fulfills his Father's will. Thus, the "spirit of holiness" is most likely Christ's obedient faithfulness.

Finally, what might also help shed light on the phrase is to consider it in Paul's wider context. "Holiness" is an ancient expression of God's very essence.[30] The word *hagiōsunē* occurs three times in the NT and only in Paul's writings. Otherwise, it refers to God's holiness in the OT.[31] Paul uses this word here in Rom 1:4 most likely to define Christ who embodies God's holiness through his holy living and dying and who is vindicated by the resurrection. Elsewhere Paul describes the divinely created condition of holiness that demands completion using the same word (2 Cor 7:1; 1 Thess 3:13). In 1 Cor 1:30 he explicitly refers to Christ who becomes God's wisdom and holiness and redemption for others although there he uses a variation of the word "holiness" (*hagiasmos*, which is usually translated in English as sanctification), perhaps emphasizing more the effect of holy living, already effected through Christ' work of redemption. If Paul wants to underline the work of the Spirit, he could simply say the "Holy Spirit" or "Spirit" as he does in many places in the rest of Romans. Perhaps the definition "holiness" in relation to the "spirit" means something different for Paul here.

The phrase "spirit of holiness" is Semitic and appears, as stated previously, in three places in the OT and in some instances in the Qumranic texts. In Isaiah passages (63:10–11), the phrase refers to God's relational activity

---

29. Criticized by Sampley and Schreiner, *Romans*, 40.

30. I am thankful to Kent for his persistent teaching and explanation of holiness in Scripture. For the purpose of this essay see "Holiness in the Second Temple Period" in Brower, *Holiness in the Gospels*, 21–37. On holiness in Paul see his *Living as God's Holy People*.

31. I.e., Ps 30:4 (LXX 29:5); 97:12 (LXX 96:12); 145:5 (LXX 144:5).

with Israel as remembered by the prophet. When God's grace toward Israel is overturned, his presence is lost because of sin and his holiness is wounded (his "spirit of holiness"). He changes into his people's enemy while once upon a time he was their friend (his "spirit of holiness" was among them) guiding and leading them through the times when they were listening to him.[32] In Ps 51:11 (LXX 50:13) the "spirit of holiness" is even more personal. It refers to the presence of God upon the psalmist who wants God to restore a relationship that was broken by sin. In all cases this "spirit of holiness" is God's Spirit but with a special twist implying God's holy presence that both requires and causes obedience, loyalty and surrender from his holy people so that God will continue his dwelling among them. The "spirit" in the OT is not expressed as a distinct third person as in the NT yet.[33]

In Qumranic texts the phrase gains further associations, carefully examined by B. Smith. While the phrase cannot be reduced to a single meaning, one distinctive use of the term as the "eschatological principle of obedience" seems to prevail.[34] For example, the Rule of the Community states that at the time of God's visitation, wickedness and injustice will be eliminated (1QS 4.18–21) and that God will purify people (the members of the community in the understanding of the writing) from deceit and evil by the means of a "spirit of holiness" setting the path of living in obedience to his truth (1QS 4.26–29). In 1QS 3.6–8, the author speaks about a "spirit of holiness" of the community that cleanses a person in God's truth. It seems that restoration occurs when a person enters the community and prevails in the community that is shaped by the "spirit of holiness." A person comes under the influence of a principle of obedience.[35] In T. Levi 18:9, 11 the righteous ones shall find rest in the anointed one (messiah). The spirit of holiness (T. Levi 18:11) will come upon him with a fatherly voice, as from Abraham to Isaac (T. Levi 18:6). All these discussions[36] may create a fresh illuminating point in understanding Paul if he is in some way aware of these overtones between the "spirit of holiness" and the principle of obedience.

Paul declares the fulfillment of God's promises in Christ Jesus whose life is the act of the "spirit of holiness." Through Christ's "spirit of holiness" Paul identifies him as God's obedient Son throughout his life and ministry and obedient representative of the Jewish nation and, as such, light to the

---

32. Westermann, *Isaiah 40–66*, 388–89.

33. Tate helpfully defines spirit as the transcendent realm of God. See Tate, *Psalms 51–100*, 23.

34. Smith, "'Spirit of Holiness.'"

35. Smith, "'Spirit of Holiness,'" 76.

36. A more detailed analysis could benefit with further implications but is outside of scope of this essay.

gentiles and the source of righteousness (10:4) and sanctification (1 Cor 1:30) for all. In Christ, the Jews and other nations are justified (are called holy) and invited into an obedient relationship with God. In him the unity with God and the disposition to obedience as indicative for holy transformation (especially Rom 6–8) is established. Paul will explain further that to be in Christ is also to have the Spirit of Christ (Rom 8) who enables believers to live as holy people. But Paul's pneumatology always follows his teaching on Christology.

IMPLICATIONS

So, it is possible that Rom 1:3–4 as a pre-Pauline formula may have appeared in a different setting and could have been perceived by some early followers in a different light, just as it is evident that the phrase "spirit of holiness" played a role in the subsequent discussions about the human/divine nature of Christ. It is possible that in light of the established doctrine on Trinity and Paul's insistence that the Holy Spirit that has been given to us (Rom 5:5) is nothing less than the Spirit of God, which is the Spirit of Christ (Rom 8), the "spirit of holiness" has become associated simply with the Spirit.

But in Paul's immediate context of Rom 1:1–7 the phrase characterizes Christ and his act of faithful obedience as the fulfillment of God's gospel to bring not only the Jews but also the gentiles through Christ into an obedient relationship. The theological questions of whether God's Spirit concerns believers' awakening or Jesus's exalted status and to what extent, or whether God's Spirit acts in contrast to flesh, although significant, are irrelevant in such reading: they are of no concern to Paul at the beginning of the letter. Paul opens his letter not with a debate but with testimony. He simply captures his readers with the story of God's triumph in Christ made possible through his obedience and its consequences for the world. If Paul relies on his Jewish traditions (as he usually does) to explain God's fulfilled promises in Christ, then the Semitic origin of the phrase and its meaning also needs to be taken seriously even if he borrows it from the existing formula. The "spirit of holiness" helps Paul underline the fundamental identity between God and his Son who is the embodiment of the holiness/the very character of God marked by Jesus's obedient action, and in whom those who are called holy (1:6–7) are also called to bring nations to faithful obedience which is the key to holy transformation that has been the goal of God's redeeming and righteous activity all along.

So, Rom 1:1–7 can be translated this way in light of this discussion:

1Paul, an [obedient] servant of the Messiah Jesus, called to be an apostle, set apart for the good news of God, 2which he promised beforehand through his prophets in the holy scriptures—3[and which is] about his Son, who was descended from David's seed in terms of flesh, 4and who was marked out powerfully as God's Son in terms[37] of the spirit of holiness [his holy/faithful obedience to the Father] by the resurrection of the dead, Jesus the Messiah, our Lord. 5Through whom we now received grace and apostleship to bring about the obedience of faith among all the nations for the sake of his name, 6among whom are also you, who are called by Jesus the Messiah. 7Finally, this is the good news for all of you who are in Rome [and everywhere], beloved of God and called to be holy. Grace to you, and peace, from God our Father, and from the Lord Jesus our Messiah!

WORKS CITED

Barth, Karl. *Church Dogmatics*. Part IV, 3.1. Edinburgh: T. & T. Clark, 1962.
Brower, Kent. *Holiness in the Gospels*. Kansas City: Beacon Hill, 2005.
———. *Living as God's Holy People: Holiness and Community in Paul*. Milton Keynes: Paternoster, 2010.
Dunn, James D. G. *Romans 1–8*. Word Bible Commentary 38a. Dallas: Word, 1988.
Fitzmyer, Joseph A. *Romans: A New Translation with Introduction and Commentary*. New York: Doubleday, 1993.
Grieb, A Katherine. *The Story of Romans: A Narrative Defense of God's Righteousness*. Louisville, KY: Westminster John Knox, 2002.
Hurtado, Larry W. *Lord Jesus Christ: Devotion to Jesus in Earliest Christianity*. Grand Rapids: Eerdmans, 2003.
Jenson, Robert W. *Systematic Theology, Volume 1*. Oxford: Oxford University Press, 1997.
Jewett, Robert. *Romans: A Critical and Historical Commentary on the Bible*. Hermeneia. Minneapolis: Fortress, 2007.
Khobnya, Svetlana. *The Father Who Redeems and the Son Who Obeys: Consideration of Paul's Teaching in Romans*. Eugene, OR: Pickwick Publications, 2013.
Longenecker, Richard N. *The Epistle to the Romans*. New International Greek Testament Commentary. Grand Rapids: Eerdmans, 2016.
Moo, Douglas J. *The Epistle to the Romans*. The New International Commentary on the New Testament. Grand Rapids: Eerdmans, 1996.
Peerbolte, Bert Jan Lietaert. "The Spirit of Holiness in Romans 1:4." In *The Spirit Is Moving: New Pathways in Pneumatology*, edited by Gijsbert van den Brink et al., 36–51. Leiden: Brill, 2019.
Schneider, Bernardin V. "Κατά Πνεῦμα Ἁγιωσύνης (Romans 1:4)." *Biblica* 48 (1967) 359–87.

37. I borrowed N. T. Wright's translation "in terms of" for *kata*.

Schreiner, Thomas R. *Romans*. The Baker Exegetical Commentary on the New Testament. Grand Rapids: Baker Academic, 1998.

Smith, Barry D. "'Spirit of Holiness' as Eschatological Principle of Obedience." In *Christian Beginnings and the Dead Sea Scrolls*, edited by John J. Collins and Craig A. Evans, 75–99. Grand Rapids: Baker Academic, 2006.

Tate, Marvin E. *Psalms 51–100*. Word Bible Commentary 20. Dallas: Word, 1998.

Westermann, Claus. *Isaiah 40–66*. Philadelphia: Westminster, 1969.

Wright, N. T. *The Challenges of Jesus*. Downers Grove, IL: InterVarsity, 1999.

———. *The Climax of the Covenant: Christ and the Law in Pauline Theology*. Minneapolis: Fortress, 1991.

———. "The Letter to the Romans: Introduction, Commentary, and Reflections." In *The New Interpreter's Bible*, 10:395–770. Nashville: Abingdon, 2002.

———. *The New Testament for Everyone*. London: SPCK, 2011.

Holiness Then and Now

Principles of the Holy Life from the Fourth Century

Carla Sunberg

THE CAPPADOCIAN FATHERS, BASIL of Caesarea, his brother Gregory of Nyssa, and his best friend Gregory of Nazianzus, wrote within the theological climate and context of the fourth century. This was a period of rapid change within society as the attitude toward Christianity shifted dramatically. After Constantine's vision of the cross, Christianity found itself in a more favorable position with the Empire. Whether out of genuine concern for the theological constructs of Christianity, or to bring about greater unity within the Empire, Constantine called the first ecumenical council, held in Nicaea in AD 325. By this time, the Arian controversy was already rife and creating a divide within Christianity. While it seemed that the heresy was dealt with at Nicaea, there continued to be a ripple effect until the Council of Constantinople in 381. It was in the intervening years, between Nicaea and Constantinople, that the Cappadocian Fathers engaged in theological discourse and in documenting the theological trajectory of what would become orthodox Christianity. The result was a faith encompassing a strong Christology, Pneumatology, and Trinitarianism, which provided a pathway for the Christianization of the Greek concept of *theosis*, or holiness. It is this emphasis on the holy life, practiced by the Cappadocians, that has provided foundational principles for the holy life today. One heir of this theology was John Wesley, an eighteenth-century theologian whose modern descendants include the Methodist world and its offshoots. He embraced Cappadocian *theosis*, confident that humanity was created in the image of God, and could, through striving to live as Christ modeled and taught, attain that likeness to the Savior for which we were meant.

As contemporary society continues to de-emphasize Christianity, there is a need to return to the foundational principles of the fourth century, perhaps as mediated by John Wesley's relatively modern perspective. In his study on "*Theosis* and Sanctification," Michael Christensen notes, "what Wesley envisioned as Christian perfection, holiness, or entire sanctification is based in part on his personal vision of what his sources taught about *theosis*."[1] In this essay, I will explore the role of Scripture, the incarnation, the need for imitation of Christ, and the potential for continuous growth toward our true identity in Christ, as well as how these may revitalize the life of holiness today, as practiced within the Wesleyan-holiness tradition.

ROLE OF SCRIPTURE

The Cappadocians' theological understanding of *theosis* was undergirded by Scripture. They frequently utilized Pauline language of "knowing Christ" and this created an understanding of unity with Christ. Knowing Christ was understood as a process, an ascent towards God that came with a growing maturity in Christ.[2] To know Christ was to be "in Christ" (Phil 2), who is "all in all" (1 Cor 15:28).

The Petrine epistles also provide guidance for the Cappadocians. Here, they conclude that to combat false teaching, Christians must be making progress, not only in their understanding of the faith, but in living out that faith. The key passage is found in 1 Pet 2:2–4:

> His divine power has given us everything needed for life and godliness . . . so that through them you may escape from the corruption that is in the world . . . and may become participants of the divine nature (NRSV).

These words were originally written for ordinary people, those Christians of the diaspora in the first century. The Cappadocians adapted and contextualized this passage for the fourth century. Nyssen saw the goal for humanity present from the moment of creation: "The Logos created humankind 'in the superabundance of His love . . . in order to make them partakers of the

---

1. Christensen, "Theosis and Sanctification," 91.
2. Nazianzen wrote, "Paul found no way through, no stopping-place in his climb, since intellectual curiosity has no clear limit and there is always some truth left to dawn on us." *Or.* 28.21 (Patrologia Graeca 36:54) (Sources chrétiennes 250), trans. Wickham, 53. Later he says, "This is the "maturity" towards which we speed. Paul himself is a special witness here. What he predicates of "God" without further specification in this passage, he elsewhere assigns clearly to Christ. I quote: "Where there is neither Greek nor Jew, circumcision nor uncircumcision, Barbarian, Scythian, bond nor free; but Christ is all in all." Nazianzen, *Or.* 30.6 (Patrologia Graeca 36:110) (Sources chrétiennes 250), trans. Wickham, 98. 1 John 3:2; 2 Pet 1:4; Col 1:28; 3:11.

divine benefits."³ This understanding of participation in the Triune God, escape from corruption that was the result of sin, is made possible through the presence of divine power. Therefore, this passage becomes fundamental in the early church fathers' understanding of *theosis*.

What the Cappadocians also found in the Scriptures was a tension between the divine power of God, and the ensuing synergy arising out of humankind's participation with the divine nature. It was this on-going unity with Christ, God at work, energizing the intentional human interaction, which would lead to *theosis*, and all of this available to ordinary humanity. All believers have at their disposal the necessary resources to enable them to work out the process of *theosis*, or holiness, which is visible by growth into the likeness of Jesus Christ.

The Cappadocians were able to work out their understanding of orthodox Christianity because of their deep commitment to the authority of Scripture. John Wesley was able to embrace the teachings of the Cappadocians in large part because he shared the same commitment to Scripture. While this understanding/interpretation may remain unchanged in Wesleyan theology, one might discover that larger society's belief in the authority of Scripture has shifted. The message of holiness loses the divine tension between love of God and love of neighbor when not founded on the word of God seen through the lens of *theosis*. Instead, there can be an over-emphasis on either social justice, or personal holiness, at the expense of the other. The beauty of Scripture is reflected in the mature Christ-follower who exhibits a life filled with love of God, and love of neighbor.

THE INCARNATION OF CHRIST

If *theosis* is revealed in Scripture, with an emphasis on unity through participation in the divine nature, then we must examine what makes that participation possible. Nyssen inevitably draws our attention to the incarnation of Christ:

> [Christ] became the image of the invisible God because of his love for mankind, in order to make you again the image of God. By his own change which he assumed, there was a change effected in you so that you also might be refashioned through him to the beauty of the Archetype into the character which was from the beginning.⁴

3. Nyssen, *Oratio Catechatica* 5 (Patrologia Graeca 45:21c) (Nicene and Post-Nicene Christian Fathers, Series 2 5:476) from Onica, *Divinization of the Christian*, 177.

4. Nyssen, *De Perfectione* (Patrologia Graeca 46:269c–d) (Gregorii Nyseni Opera III.I), trans. Keenan, "De Professione Christiana," 195.

In the incarnation, Christ assumed human flesh, thereby restoring the image to humanity that had been lost or corrupted because of the sin of Adam and Eve. At the same time, Christ's humanity provided a pathway for human flesh to be united to our holy God. Therefore, the potential exists for all of humanity to be restored in the image and likeness of God.

For the Cappadocians, *perichoresis* became the basis for the "believer's experience of the indwelling Trinity."[5] Nazianzen took up the use of the word *perichoresis* as a christological term, and, F. W. Norris tells us, he filled it with the meaning of "interpenetration," describing how the divinity and the humanity in Jesus could coinhere.[6] Because of the interpenetration of the human and divine in Jesus Christ, humanity is invited to participate in the relationship of holy love found in the Triune God. As one desires this communion, Nyssen affirms, "I and the Father will come and we will make our abode with him (of course, the Holy Spirit had already been dwelling there)."[7] Therefore, it is through the incarnation that the invitation to become partakers of the divine nature is extended, and through this participation there is transformation. And this, for all of humanity.

Nazianzen made it abundantly clear that the assumption of human flesh was for all of humanity, men and women alike. Both had sinned, and both were in need of restoration and a pathway for participation, through the life and work of the Savior. It was Christ who modeled a new way of ministering to and interacting with women that would impact the Cappadocians, and Wesley as well. Throughout his earthly ministry, Jesus intentionally healed men and women. He elevated the status of women through his own personal engagement, whether conversing at a well, or challenging accusers when a woman was caught in adultery. At his resurrection, Mary was the one to become the first to share the good news.

This affirmation of the full image of God in both men and women has implications for holiness and restoration. The woman is not of lesser status, nor does she simply receive the image because of the man. God's design is for her to be uniquely reflective of the image of God from the moment of creation. Only the fall corrupted this image, which is in need of divine healing.

> The Woman sinned, and so did Adam. The serpent deceived
> them both; and one was not found to be the stronger and the

---

5. Stramara, "Gregory of Nyssa's Terminology," 257. Nazianzen, *Epistula* 101.6 (Sources chrétiennes 208:38).

6. Norris, "Deification," 416. He is referring to Nazianzen, *Or.* 18.42; *Or* 22.4; *Epistula* 101.31; and, finally, Athanasius, *Discourse Against the Arians* 3.1, 17, 19, 24–25.

7. Nyssen, *Homily 6, On the Beatitudes*, 129 (*De Beatitudinibus* 4 [Gregorii Nyseni Opera VII.2 122, 23–25]).

other the weaker. But dost thou consider the better? Christ saves both by his Passion. Was he made flesh for the Man? So he was also for the woman. . . . He is called of the seed of David; and so perhaps you think the Man is honoured; but he is born of a Virgin, and this is on the Woman's side.[8]

This perspective on the "Woman's side" presented by Nazianzen leads to an egalitarian understanding of the relationship between men and women. Basil specifically portrayed women in his writings as equal to men in the image of God, in the practices of virtue, "firmness, vigour, and endurance."[9] This perspective has serious implications for practice. Macrina the Younger, older sister of Basil, was the leader of the family monastery at Anessi. The practices of her monastery informed "Basil's Rules," which were used for centuries in Eastern monasteries.[10] This fourth-century understanding of holiness as recognizing and celebrating the full humanity and worthiness of women can be seen in Wesleyan-holiness churches of the twenty-first century where, in many instances, women are welcomed into all levels of leadership including pastoral, episcopal, administrative and other roles historically understood by Christianity as available only to men, who have been interpreted by most Christians as more closely embodying the image of God (because they are male). Interestingly, of the 180 institutions represented by the Council of Christian Colleges and Universities (CCCU), the only schools with female presidents are of a Wesleyan theological background.

One can see that this emphasis upon the incarnation and assumption of human flesh becomes vital to the Cappadocians' understanding of the possibility of living the holy life for all people, female and male. Much of contemporary evangelical Christianity places almost exclusive emphasis upon the atonement, and the saving work of Christ. However, when this is done without examining the entire life of Christ, one becomes bounded by the corruption of the life of sin. One can see the gift given by the Cappadocians with this broader understanding of the life and work of Christ and the implications for holy living in this present generation. God's intention is for the restoration of humankind in the image of God, and for that likeness to be filled with God's holy love. Wesley, just like his theological forbearers, the Cappadocians, believed that God could bring this work to *perfection*, in this present age, and this is only possible through the incarnation of Christ.

---

8. Nazianzen, *Or.* 37.6–7 (Patrologia Graeca 36:262) (Sources chrétiennes 318) (Nicene and Post-Nicene Christian Fathers, Series 2 7:340).

9. Sunberg, *Cappadocian Mothers*, 158.

10. Stramara, "Double Monasticism," 282.

IMITATION OF CHRIST

The synergy created through the divine and human found in Christ becomes the model for all of humanity. Through the imitation of Christ, one would become more like Christ, and this is the goal of *theosis*.

The Cappadocian community chose to live out its theology through the practice of virtue, or imitation of Christ. The Petrine passage speaks of the divine power, or *dunamis*, which empowers the life of the believer, but then goes on to speak of the nature or character of the one who does the calling. God calls his people through his own "glory and goodness" or *areté*—better known as "virtue." John Wesley referred to Christian virtue as the means to reach humanity's intended end, which is "eternal glory."[11] This practice of virtue is to be embodied in the life of the believer.

At times, the life of holiness has been called a "distinctive." Wesley's followers were "distinctive" from those in their society because of the ways in which they chose to live their lives, or adopt particular "methods." The Cappadocians would have called this choice the practice of virtues. Both found ample support for this understanding of virtue (*areté*) in the Scriptures. One well-known example is found in Paul's letter to the church in Philippi in which he writes, "Finally, beloved, whatever is true, whatever is honorable, whatever is just, whatever is pure, whatever is pleasing, whatever is commendable, if there is any excellence (*areté*—virtue) and if there is anything worthy of praise, think about these things" (Phil 4:8-9 NRSV).

Earlier in the letter to the Philippians, Paul encouraged the believers to "work out your own salvation with fear and trembling" (Phil 2:12 NRSV). This is not a works theology, but it is a call to develop a genuinely Christ-like character that bears witness to our Christian identity status in this world. Even when we fail, we press on, for we are to be known by the fruit we bear (Matt 7:16-21; Gal 5:16-25).

Nyssen saw these practices of virtue as molding our lives on the pattern laid out before us, Christ, and in this way "we are to become the image of the Image."[12] He used Plato's metaphor of the painter to clarify his teaching.[13] The greatest artists of the Empire were employed to create portraits of the emperor. In doing so, they were to represent the image and the character of

---

11. Wesley, *John Wesley's Notes on the Whole Bible*.

12. Nyssen, *De Perfectione*, Patrologia Graeca 46:269D-272A (Gregorii Nyseni Opera III.I).

13. Nyssen, *De Perfectione*, Patrologia Graeca 46:269D-272A, (Gregorii Nyseni Opera III.I). "Wherefore, if we also are to become the image of the Image of the invisible God, it is fitting that the form of our life be moulded to the pattern of life presented to us."

the ruler. Imitation of Christ results in the creation of a beautiful portrait of the Image. Nyssen says, "so that we may become the Image by true imitation of the beauty of the Archetype, as Paul did, who by his virtuous life became an imitator of Christ."[14] The dominant colors to be used in our embodiment of the Image include humility and patience, virtues that are revealed in the passion of Christ.[15]

This intentional practice of virtue may be a descriptor of Wesley's understanding of social holiness. "Directly opposite to this [the approach of the desert mystics] is the gospel of Christ. Solitary religion is not to be found there. 'Holy solitaries' is a phrase no more consistent with the gospel than holy adulterers. The gospel of Christ knows no religion, but social; no holiness but social holiness."[16] God's dynamic work in and through the believer is united with the intentional practice of virtue, and this creates a synergy that catalyzes the life of the individual so he or she is transformed from "glory to glory" (2 Cor 3:16–18). Imitation of Christ leads the believer into greater participation with Christ, and this participation leads to ministry within the community. As a result, the Cappadocians rejected the monastic life of the desert fathers and, instead, believed that the practice of virtue had to occur within a community, which might be defined as a family, spiritual community, or an urban center. Basil moved his male monastery to the outskirts of the city of Caesarea and established soup kitchens, which he named *Basileidos*.[17] Without the deliberate imitation of Christ, and this within community, there is no holiness.

The similarities between the holiness of the fourth century and the Wesleyan-holiness movement are noticeable. As a result, the individual is left with a choice; either the Christian works to develop these qualities or characteristics in increasing measure, or the individual ignores this possibility and is left with a short-sighted view of salvation. This practice of holiness is to be visible to the world, not in a legalistic manner, but in a way that engages the justice of Christ among those on the margins of society. Imitation of Christ involves a daily journey in which self is denied and the individual and community willingly submit fleshly desires to those of Christ (Luke 9:23). This submission involves a life of prayer, scriptural reading, fasting, and service to others. In doing so, the master molds his disciples into his divine image.

---

14. Nyssen, *De Perfectione*, Patrologia Graeca 46:272A–B, (Gregorii Nyseni Opera III.I).

15. Nyssen, *De Perfectione*, Patrologia Graeca 46:272A–B, (Gregorii Nyseni Opera III.I).

16. Wesley, *Works of John Wesley*, 14:321.

17. Tredget, "Basil of Caesarea," 4.

CONTINUOUS GROWTH

The Cappadocians further emphasized that imitation of Christ is to be continuous and on-going, extending beyond our initial achievement of the "image of the Image of God." If humanity is invited into participation in the divine nature, and if God's nature is infinite, then there remains the possibility of continuous and infinite growth. Gregory of Nyssa wrote about this life of continual growth and transformation in *The Life of Moses*. He used the language of Paul, referring to Moses's transformation "from glory to glory" (1 Cor 3:18). Here Nyssen calls us ever upward on this journey:

> This is the reason why we say that the great Moses, moving ever forwards, did not stop in his upward climb. He set no limit to his rise to the stars . . . He constantly kept moving to the next step; and he continued to go ever higher because he always found another step that lay beyond the highest one that he had reached.[18]

In his *Commentary on the Canticle*, Nyssen would compare this *glory to glory*, "proceeding, as the Prophet says, from *virtue to virtue*."[19] Therefore, the fourth-century church embraced the practice of virtue, empowered by God, that resulted in the individual continually growing in Christlikeness.

This continuous growth was referred to as "perfection," and Nyssen encouraged followers to go on to this perfection in their Christian walk:

> This, therefore, is in my judgment the perfection of the Christian life, that in thought, in speech, and in all the pursuits of life there be a participation in all the names by which the name of Christ is made known so as to preserve perfectly in the entire body, mind, and spirit, without admixture of evil, the holiness praised by Paul.[20]

Those who were a part of the Christian community were to be completely and entirely devoted in service to God. According to the contemporary Wesleyan scholar, Paul Bassett, this perfection would continue from this life into the life to come. Through grace, we are able to participate in Christian service now, which is revealed in "absolute love to God and neighbor." However, he continues, "when this body is laid aside in death, we put on

---

18. Nyssen, *De Vita Moysis* (Patrologia Graeca 44:397d–405a), trans. Musurillo, 144.

19. Nyssen, *CC, Homily 5* (Patrologia Graeca 44:888c–893c) (Gregorii Nyseni Opera VI), trans. Musurillo, 200. Ps 83:38. Emphasis mine.

20. Nyssen, *De Perfectione* (Patrologia Graeca 46:285a) (Gregorii Nyseni Opera III.I), trans. Keenan, "De Professione Christiana," 205.

resurrected bodies and continue the service begun on earth."[21] Therefore, there is no end to this continuous participation, it remains on-going throughout eternity.

The natural course of this thought led the Cappadocians to expand their understanding of asceticism, including celibacy and the development of the monastic movement in their world.

"In the background of all [Nyssen] says stands the heavenly kingdom and its earthly manifestation, the Church—however battered. But he places in the foreground the question of the spirituality of the individual believer."[22] In Nyssen's day, the church had been battered by the persecutions. However, in the era of Constantine, the persecutions came to an abrupt halt. Previously, martyrdom and self-denial had been viewed as pathways to holiness. The combination of personal spirituality and the communal nature of ministry, with an eye for saving the church, resulted in a new understanding of holiness, which had to be lived out in community. The ascetics were to live in the midst of society so that they could become a model for true Christian living.[23] They were to be the image of Christ to society. As already noted, the Cappadocians often turned to Paul for clarity on the topic of holiness, believing Paul when he wrote, "Be imitators of me, as I am of Christ" (1 Cor 1:11 NRSV). This becomes the goal: "complete conformity to the will of God," with our aim "to be conformed to the image of Christ. Gregory's conviction is that, through the operations of the Holy Spirit, such conformity is possible in this life (especially through the means of grace offered by the Church), insofar as the individual is capable of it."[24]

Nyssen urged believers to move on toward perfection, not as a matter of skill or intellectual prowess, but by being in relationship with God and others. This is the call to perfection that remains for the holiness church of today. It is not a legalistic perfection, but one that responds to the upward call, leading to an on-going perfection through participation in the life of the triune God.

Wesleyans of the last few centuries have sometimes misunderstood Paul's exhortation, "Keep on doing the things that you have learned and received and heard and seen in me, and the God of peace will be with you" (Phil 4:8–9 NRSV). They have possibly focused too much on "you" in the

21. Bassett, *Holiness Teaching*, 125. Participation in an eternal God, means that there is no end to that participation, and for Nyssen, death was actually just the restoration of humanity to the original relationship which God had intended. Therefore, spiritual growth was to continue throughout all of eternity.

22. Bassett, *Holiness Teaching*, 126.

23. Basil, *Ascetical Works*, viii–ix.

24. Bassett, *Holiness Teaching*, 126.

singular, over-emphasizing the crisis moment. Combined with an imperfect understanding of Christian perfection, it was quite possible that believers felt the need to testify to being "saved" and "sanctified," but never admit the need of growth following the experience of "entire sanctification." Instead of participation in an infinite God, the Christ-follower's growth would begin to stagnate.

CONCLUSIONS

There are notable similarities between the Christian theology of holiness of the fourth century, and that of John Wesley, and the Wesleyan-holiness movement. That said, there have also been times when this emphasis upon *theosis*, or holiness, has been de-emphasized within Christianity. Phineas F. Bresee, one of the founders of the Church of the Nazarene, used to say that the holiness movement existed to "Christianize Christianity." There are some who would argue that the fourth-century Fathers were simply Christianizing Platonic or Neo-Platonic thought. However, there are notable differences, both then, and now. Bassett reminds us, "Gregory begins not with Plato nor Plotinus nor their followers, but the Hebrew Bible, or the Septuagint, and the collection of first-century writings that would come to be called the New Testament."[25] This scriptural foundation led to the Christian life of holiness that developed in the fourth century and that was reclaimed and promoted by the Wesleys.

In April 1995, Keith Drury presented a paper at a breakfast meeting of the Christian Holiness Partnership entitled, "The Holiness Movement is Dead."[26] In his paper, he argued eight reasons for the demise of the movement:

1. We wanted to be respectable.
2. We have plunged into the evangelical mainstream.
3. We failed to convince the younger generation.
4. We quit making holiness the main issue.
5. We lost the lay people.

---

25. Bassett, *Holiness Teaching*, 126. The designation "Hebrew Bible" is an attempt to recognize the original audience and authors of what has historically been known to Christians as the Old Testament and, the Hebrew Scriptures were, by the fourth century, widely available in the Greek Septuagint, especially among Christians, and only rarely consulted in the original Hebrew version.

26. Drury, *Holiness Movement*.

6. We over-reacted against the abuses of the past.
7. We adopted church-growth thinking without theological thinking.
8. We didn't notice the battle-line moved.[27]

Both the Cappadocians and the Wesleys have taught us that by reflecting the life of Christ in the kingdom of God, the church, even when battered, can reflect the holy love found in the Triune God. The result is transformation into the likeness of Christ, something that the contemporary church can learn from Christianity of the fourth century. The concerns of Drury can be addressed by re-embracing the authority of Scripture. Only after re-embracing this authority will the theological understanding of the incarnation begin to reveal its power. This is "theological thinking" that could, and must, inform our kingdom practice.

For fourth-century Christianity, *theosis* was not an optional view of Christianity, it was *the* understanding of Christianity. At the same time, one cannot imagine the Wesleys embracing a Christianity without an understanding of the transformative work of holiness. Holiness must once again become our "main issue" for, without this emphasis, we have a powerless Christianity. A participatory life of holiness is authentic holiness, and in a post-Christian world, when we are transformed from "glory to glory," the world will take notice. The point is that the world needs to experience authentic representations of Christ. Without holiness, that is not possible. Therefore, a renewed emphasis upon imitation of Christ is necessary. This may include a revival of Methodist's classes and bands, where discipleship was truly a discipline that helped to mold the believer, clergy and lay alike, into the likeness of Christ.

Drury's last point is quite profound: "we didn't realize the battle-line moved." Not only did the church stop leading her people into the transformational life of Christ-like holiness, but the church failed to preach "transformational conversion." Instead of *dunamis* empowered believers, the pews have been filled with cultural Christians. Whether in the fourth century, or the early decades of the Wesleyan movement, there was always an emphasis upon continuous and on-going growth within the life of the believer. Without recognizing this vital need, the entire movement becomes stagnant, and everything grinds to a halt, including the invitation to join the journey. The continuous and on-going growth that comes from participation in an infinite God provides the impetus for movement.

---

27. He explained his final point, "Many of our people do not need to be sanctified—they need to be saved! The doctrine at risk in many holiness churches is not entire sanctification but "transformational conversion." We may need to stand at Luther's side awhile before we can rejoin Wesley." Drury, *Holiness Movement*, para. 8.

A return to these simple, but vital principles, found both in the fourth century, and in the theology of the Wesleys, may lead the church back to the life of holiness, and holiness may well be the answer to Christianity's current woes.

WORKS CITED

Basil of Caesarea. *Ascetica*. Patrologia Graeca 31:619–1305. English translation by M. Monica Wagner in *Basil of Caesarea: Ascetical Works*. Fathers of the Church 9. Reprint, Washington: Fathers of the Church, 1999.

Bassett, Paul M. *Holiness Teaching: New Testament Times to Wesley. Volume 1*. Great Holiness Classics. Kansas City: Beacon Hill, 1997.

Christensen, Michael. "Theosis and Sanctification: John Wesley's Reformulation of a Patristic Doctrine." *Wesleyan Theological Journal* 31 (1996) 71–94. https://wtsociety.com/files/wts_journal/1996-wtj-31-2.pdf.

Drury, David. *The Holiness Movement is Dead*. Paper delivered at the Christian Holiness Partnership, April 1995. http://www.drurywriting.com/keith/dead.footnoted.htm.

Gross, Jules. *The Divinization of the Christian according to the Greek Fathers*. Translated by P. A. Onica. Anaheim: A&C, 2002.

Irenaeus. *Against Heresies 3, 4, 5*. Patrologia Graeca 7:437–1224. English translation in *The Ante-Nicene Fathers* 1 Series 1. Edited by Alexander Roberts and James Donaldson. Repr. Peabody, MA: Hendrickson, 1994.

Merriam-Webster Dictionary. https://www.merriam-webster.com/dictionary/virtue.

Nazianzen. *Orations 27–31*. Patrologia Graeca 36:40. *Grégoire de Nazianze: Discours 27–31*. English translation by Frederick Williams (27) and Lionel Wickham (28–31) in *On God and Christ; St. Gregory of Nazianzus, The Five Theological Orations and Two Letters to Cledonius*. Popular Patristic Series. Crestwood, NY: St. Vladimir's Seminary Press, 2002.

Norris, F. W. "Deification: Consensual and Cogent." *Scottish Journal of Theology* 43 (1996) 411–28.

Nyssen. *Canticum Canticorum* [Commentary on the Canticle]. Patrologia Graeca 44:756–1120. English translation by Herbert Musurillo in *From Glory to Glory: Texts from the Gregory of Nyssa's Mystical Writings*. Crestwood: St. Vladimir's Seminary Press, 2001.

———. *De Perfectione* [On perfection]. Patrologia Graeca 46:249. English translation by Virginia Callahan in *St. Gregory Ascetical Works*. Fathers of the Church 58. Washington: Catholic University of America Press, 1999.

———. *De Vita Moysis* [The life of Moses]. Patrologia Graeca 44:297. English translation by Abraham Malherbe and Everett Ferguson in *The Life of Moses*. New York: Paulist, 1978.

———. *Homily 6, On the Beatitudes*. Patrologia Graeca 44:1264. English translation by Anthony Meredith in *Gregory of Nyssa*. London: Routledge, 1999.

———. *Homilies on the Song of Songs*. Translated by C. McCambley. Brookline: Hellenic College Press, 1987.

Stramara, Daniel F., Jr. "Double Monasticism in the Greek East, Fourth through Eighth Centuries." *Journal of Early Christian Studies* 6 (1998) 269–312.

———. "Gregory of Nyssa's Terminology for Trinitarian Perichoresis." *Vigiliae Christianae* 52 (1998) 257–63.

Sunberg, Carla D. *The Cappadocian Mothers: Deification Exemplified in the Writings of Basil, Gregory, and Gregory*. Eugene, OR: Pickwick, 2017.

Tredget, Dermot. "Basil of Caesarea and His Influence on Monastic Mission." EBC Theology Commission, Belmont, March 2005. https://www.scribd.com/document/45605259/Basil-of-Cesarea-and-Monasticism.

Wesley, John. *John Wesley's Notes on the Whole Bible* (*Wesley's Notes*). Christian Classics Ethereal Library. http://www.ccel.org.

———. *The Works of John Wesley*. Volume XIV. Peabody, MA: Hendrickson, 1991.

PART II

In the Time of Crisis

Bringing the Kingdom

The Beatitudes as the Matthean Jubilee

Dwight D. Swanson

INTRODUCTION[1]

The most recent release of census and survey figures for religion in the UK reveals that the numbers identifying as Christian have fallen below half the population for the first time, and that more than a third describe themselves as of "no religion."[2] These figures are mirrored across Europe and the US for those under the age of 40. The disaffection of the young stands alongside media portrayals (wrongly or rightly) of (mostly Evangelical) Christians as negative, reactionary, and angry—particularly when the subject is sexuality. These figures highlight the crisis of Christianity in the West. Responses from every side emphasize the division and polarization of society seen elsewhere in the "Culture Wars." The question that repeatedly comes to my mind amidst the babble is, "Where is the gospel in this? What is Good News?"

The simple answer for a Christian might be "Repent and believe the good news" (Mark 1:15), and this is the starting point for this essay. I approach the question from my academic discipline of biblical studies, with a focus on the Gospel of Matthew; from my specialism in Second Temple studies, with an examination of the use of Scripture by the Evangelist; and as a disciple of Jesus, with faith seeking understanding of "the gospel of Jesus Christ."

---

1. Kent Brower and I have shared an interest in intertextuality from our PhD studies, particularly the use of Scripture within Scripture; and, we have worked through the Sermon on the Mount together with students for many years. This essay continues in the same vein as in Swanson, "Insights from Qumran," 341–66.

2. Office for National Statistics, "Religion, England and Wales."

BEGINNINGS

The beginnings of books are very important; they give clues as to the narrative—plot, characters, conflict—that an author wants the reader to follow. These set the context, so it is worthwhile recalling the beginnings of each of the Gospels, and the first words of the Protagonist. In the case of the Synoptic Gospels, the shared opening narrative framework is most succinctly stated in the Gospel of Mark (1:1–15), as can be seen below, beginning with "The Gospel of Jesus Christ":

> John the Baptist/Baptism of Jesus—wilderness testing—ministry in Galilee—announcement of the kingdom of God.

All likewise share the Scriptural base of the prophet Isaiah. Mark begins his Gospel with a catena of Scripture (Exod 23:20; Mal 3:1; Isa 40:3); Matthew and Luke cite only the Isaiah passage. Whatever we make of the story of Jesus, it is grounded in Isaiah's good news of Israel's redemption, and end of exile.

If beginnings are important, first words are key for the Gospels. All three record Jesus's first public message following the baptism and wilderness testing with some variation of the teaser, "The time is fulfilled, the kingdom of God has drawn near, repent and believe in the good news" (Mark 1:15). We must read on to learn what these terms mean.

In Mark, the kingdom is described in Jesus's kingdom actions, and the gospel in his call to disciples to follow him (Mark 1:17), taking up their cross for the sake of the good news (Mark 8:35). In Luke, we first hear Jesus's voice at the synagogue in Nazareth,[3] reading from Isaiah 61, then simply saying, "Today this Scripture has been fulfilled in your hearing" (Luke 4:21). Thus, he announces the Isaianic Jubilee, the year of release, then moves on to the other cities of Galilee, proclaiming this "good news of the Kingdom of God" (Luke 4:43). In Matthew, Jesus calls disciples, travels through Galilee, sees the crowds, goes up "the mountain," and teaches.[4] It is Jesus's teaching that defines the gospel/good news of the kingdom.

THE SETTING OF THE BEATITUDES

We turn to the Sermon on the Mount (SoM) with two observations. First, this is the first of five discourses by Jesus, strongly evocative of the five books

---

3. The young Jesus's words in Luke 2:50, though the first recorded, are spoken to his father and mother, part of the Birth Narrative's linking of Jesus as a continuation of the Jewish Scriptures, and a Samuel typology.

4. Between the proclamation of Matt 4:17 and the conclusion of the SoM in Matt 7:28 Jesus is referred to only as "he."

of Torah. The physical setting of teaching on "the mountain"[5] evokes the giving of Torah on Sinai, and a "new," or renewed, covenant code.[6] I have argued elsewhere that Matthew draws particularly from Deuteronomy in his Torah citations.[7] With this in view, secondly, Deuteronomy may be seen to inform the significance of *dikaiosunē* (righteousness/justice) in Matthew. The noun appears only in the envelope of John the Baptist references (Matt 3:15 and 21:32) and five times in the SoM (Matt 5:6, 10, 20; 6:1, 33). The unique Matthean phrase heard from the mouth of Jesus at his baptism, "It is proper for us in this way to fulfil all righteousness" (Matt 3:15), may be seen as an allusion to Deut 6:25 ("If we are careful to do this whole command . . . it will be for us *tsedeqah*"). This, in turn, becomes essential for understanding the *dikaiosunē* that "exceeds that of the scribes and Pharisees" (Matt 5:17–20).

The focus of this essay, in keeping with the interest in beginnings, is the opening section of the SoM, the "*makarisms*" of Matt 5:3–10. The first task is to determine the delimitation of the set. Dale C. Allison's argument that this is a unit of nine, viewed as three triplets, is widely followed.[8] I will follow Betz's consensus of a set of eight with a ninth expansion,[9] based on these observations:

1. The envelope of "for theirs is the kingdom of heaven," vv. 3 and 10, alone includes the verb "to be" (in third-person present tense); and this is emphatic given that *estin* is not required grammatically, nor is used in vv. 4–9.

2. V. 11 turns to direct second-person speech, breaking the third-person pattern and setting it apart from the rest as an editorial comment.

3. The first group of four names the kingdom people with four Greek "p"s ("*pi*"s), all descriptive of people living under oppression: poor; mourners; humble; hungering and thirsting.

---

5. The setting of the fifth discourse on the Mount of Olives (chs. 24–25) provides an envelope (or *inclusion*) of Jesus's teaching. The bracketing of/in the Gospel by balancing terms and narratives is a common structural feature of Matthew.

6. Dale C. Allison argues for Jesus as the New Moses at book-length in *The New Moses*, expanding beyond W. F. Albright and C. S. Mann's Israel typology in *Matthew*. While Allison's case has not been widely adopted, the motif is sufficiently evident.

7. From a yet unpublished seminar paper. This can also be seen in the Temptation narrative, and in the closing triad of the pericope in Matthew 7: Matt 7:13–14//Deut 30:1–15; 7:24–27//Deut 31:12 (LXX); 7:28//Deut 31:1, 24 and 32:45.

8. Allison, "Structure of the Sermon on the Mount," 429n17. Cf. Morris, *Gospel According to Matthew*, 91; Morris, like others, is more focused on the questions of relation to Luke.

9. Betz, *Sermon on the Mount*, 108.

4. "Righteousness" appears twice in the protasis, vv. 6 and 10. These each may be seen to close a section of four sayings, vv. 3–6 and 7–10.

5. The second group of four is not described by social condition, but by virtues. These kingdom people balance the first group: merciful, pure in heart, peacemakers, and (surprisingly) persecuted for righteousness' sake.[10]

6. Overall, the SoM begins with a blessing of and to "the poor," and ends with a blessing on the persecuted. Of such is the Kingdom of heaven.

ALLUSION IN THE BEATITUDES

The citation of Scripture is a hallmark of the Gospel of Matthew and the source of lengthy studies.[11] There are some 40 explicit citations, often but not always with a formula like "As is written." The Prophet Isaiah is quoted some 12 times with a specific fulfillment formula such as "to fulfill what was spoken/written by the prophet";[12] four of these by ch. 5, including Isa 40:3. In the SoM, the antitheses of 5:21–48 are introduced with the formula "You have heard it said." But there are no such citations in the Beatitudes; instead, we hear Scripture in allusive echoes.[13] When we examine these, we are not surprised to find the influence of Isaiah.

5:3 "Blessed are the poor in spirit"

The SoM begins with a reference to "the poor" (*ptōchoi*), which resonates with Jesus's reading of the "good news to the poor" from Isa 61:1 in Luke 4:18. Of course, one word does not (necessarily) an allusion make, but in this instance, it serves as a "key-word link" that signals the coming use of a text.[14] The phrase "poor in spirit" cannot be found in the LXX, but there

---

10. We will not be able to examine these any closer in this paper.

11. Most notably, Gundry, *Use of the Old Testament*, with the subtitle "With Special Reference to the Messianic Hope."

12. The number 12 invites attention but cannot be discussed here.

13. There is a body of literature on the definition of an allusion. Gundry, *Use of the Old Testament*, 3, refers to the "interweaving of scriptural phraseology" in Qumran scrolls in his discussion of the term, which is richly illustrated in the *Hodayot*. The mosaic of the language of psalms and worship in these hymns indicates a mind saturated in the Scriptures, which reminds one of the hymns of Charles Wesley. Here the poet of the Beatitudes is saturated in the poetry of Isaiah and the Psalms.

14. One of the most common techniques of the Temple Scroll; see the summary of

is a cluster of Hebrew words that are used together with "the poor" which are sometimes translated by *ptōchoi*. The good news of Isa 61:1 comes to "the poor"/*ʿanawîm* (plural) and to the "broken of heart"/*nišberê lēb* (not of spirit). In Isa 66:2 the Lord gives close attention to "the poor"/*ʿānî* (singular) and "broken of spirit"/*nkh rwḥ*,[15] which is very close to the Matthean phrase (cf. Ps 109:16).[16] In Isa 57:15 the Lord, "the exalted one" who dwells in "the exalted and holy place," also dwells with "the crushed" (*dakkāʾ*) and "lowly in spirit" (*špl rwḥ*), and revives the "crushed in heart" (*lēb nidkāʾîm*). In this simple phrase, Matthew draws in this cluster of almost interchangeable terms—crushed, humbled, oppressed, weak, wretched—all of which focus on the economically and politically helpless. What is important to note here is that these allusions may be found in the second half of the Book of Isaiah.[17]

The Isaianic influence can be seen elsewhere in Matthew. In Matt 11:5 the "good news to the poor" of Isa 61 is explicit, part of a catena of Isa 29:18, 35:3, and 42:18; and 15:30, 31 which combines "the mountain" and the list of healings in Isa 35.

What are we to make of this? Comparison to Luke's Sermon on the Plain (6:17–49) has led to the frequent contention that, whereas Luke says "Blessed are the poor" in literal and stark terms of God's particular concern for the oppressed, Matthew speaks of the kingdom in spiritual, even individualist, terms by beginning, "Blessed are the poor *in spirit*."[18] Commentators often describe Luke's Jesus as expecting God's action in the present, "Blessed are those who hunger now," but the Jesus of Matthew as eschatological action—that is, it is to take place in the future.[19]

---

this in Swanson, *Temple Scroll and the Bible*, 228. Goulder, "Poor Man's Christology," 332, sees this same connection to Isaiah 61 in all three Synoptic Gospels, including Mark 1:15, "The time is fulfilled," as from Isa 60:22.

15. The two terms may be seen as hendiadys, "poor and broken" as "the shattered poor."

16. Gundry, *Use of the Old Testament*, 70, notes this but does not discuss it.

17. I purposely refrain from calling this "Second Isaiah," since the Gospel writer would not recognize the boundaries in the term. The evidence of Isaiah in the Dead Sea Scrolls indicates the final form was already extant (as per the Great Isaiah Scroll, 1QIsaa, where the "second half" begins with ch. 34), as well as excerpted MSS abounding for the second half; see Swanson, "Text of Isaiah at Qumran," 191–212.

18. E.g., Gundry says "in spirit" confirms the "religious sense" of the word, and in relation to Luke is a "spiritualizing interpretation," *Use of the Old Testament*, 70; and Rohr notes, Luke "leaves the hard words of Jesus as they were originally spoken" while Matthew "has chosen to soften it," *Jesus' Plan*, 130.

19. "[W]hile Luke's beatitudes describe what the disciples actually are, Matthew's stress is more what they ought to be," Marshall, *Commentary on Luke*, 246.

Many, I think, prefer Matthew's version. Spiritual poverty can be overcome by spiritual experience—we may be comfortable in our economic situation but lost inside, so we pray and receive the riches of God. While the personal and transformational work of God is not to be discounted, it is not where Matthew starts. That place, as in Isa 61 (cf. Luke 4), is with the utterly abandoned poor. Such are Jesus's first words about the kingdom; here, then, *is* the kingdom.

5:4 "Blessed are those who mourn, for they will be comforted"

The signal of Isa 61:1 introduces the address to those who mourn (Gk. *penthountes*/Heb. *'ablym*) in Isa 61:2–3 (used three times) and to the Anointed's role of comfort (*parakalein/naḥēm*) in response to Isa 40:1 (51:12–19, and 4x in LXX 66:12–13). This is Isaiah's theme of restoration following exile: comfort following judgment, joy in place of mourning, and redemption after repentance. Matthew's only other reference to mourning is in 9:15, where the guests are not able to mourn in the presence of the Bridegroom— it is in the absence of the Bridegroom that the disciples fast with tears.[20]

Matthew uses the passive "be comforted" here and in Matt 2:18—citing Jer 31:15, of the inconsolable Rachel. Otherwise, the Matthean occurrences are in the active voice of people "pleading," mostly to Jesus, for help (Matt 14:36; 18:29, 32; 26:53; but also for him to leave, 8:31, 34). In comparison, Luke's parallel (Luke 6:21) uses wholly different vocabulary ("those who cry will laugh"), and the corresponding "woe" (Luke 6:24, 25) reverses the Matthean sense (the rich will have already received their comfort, those who laugh will mourn and cry). In both, happiness is related to the presence of Jesus.

5:5 "Blessed are the meek, for they will inherit the earth"

Here is a clear allusion to Ps 37:11, "The meek shall inherit [the] land." How should this be rendered? The NRSV retains the familiar KJV "the meek," which sadly has lost its English force over recent centuries. These are the same poor, Heb. *ʿănāwîm*, we saw in Isa 61:1, with a sense of economic affliction or oppression; but here the LXX Psalms (followed by Matthew) translates with *praeis*. Matt 21:5 portrays Jesus as the victorious king of Zech 9:9, "coming to you *praus*," the Greek again translating the Hebrew "poor."

---

20. Blenkinsopp, *Isaiah 56–66*, 225, considers the mourning over the destruction of Zion here and in 66:10 to be a "characteristic feature of [the prophetic disciples'] piety."

Previously, in 11:29, Jesus described himself as *praus . . . kai tapeinos tē kardia*, "gentle and humble of heart" (NRSV), which is itself an allusion to Zech 9:9. The added "humbled," "*tapeinos* of heart," often has the sense of "humiliated" (cf. Ps 34:18 "crushed of heart and humbled in spirit" and Matt 5:3). *Praeis* gives the nuance of a bruised gentleness toward "the poor." The Zecharian king who comes in peace identifies with the poorest in the land; and Matthew twice portrays Jesus as such a king, one and the same as the poor who are the citizens of the kingdom of heaven.

Turning to Matthew's "inheriting the earth": both the Greek *hē gē* and the Hebrew *hāʾāreṣ* can be translated either as "land" or "earth." In Psalm 37, the possession (*yaraš*) of a particular portion of land is in view; the dispossessed poor (// the blessed, v. 22, and righteous, v. 29) will live in peace on their land in the year of release.[21] But we must look past Ps 37. In LXX Isa 61:7 the redeemed people of God "shall inherit (*klēronomēsousi*) *the land* a second time" (NETS).[22] Thus we can see how Ps 37 is drawn into our text under the influence of the shared Isa 61 terminology. In Isaiah, oppressed exiles are restored to the land of Israel; the Prophet makes the move from the particularity of Psalmist's "allotted land" to the land of promise. Matthew, however, makes a further move from the particular (of which there is no hint) to the universal; in the SoM the poor, the people of the kingdom of heaven, inherit the earth (and so the Father's will is done, 6:10).

5:6 "Blessed are those who hunger and thirst for righteousness, for they will be filled"

The word pair "hungry/thirsty" is common in the OT, but in Ps 107:4–9, in the litany of the Lord's steadfast love for the "redeemed of the Lord" (v. 2; and Greek Isaiah's *lelutrōmenoi*), the precise phrase *peinōntes kai dipsuōntes* (v. 4) is found, and the empty soul is filled/satiated, *sabaʿ* (v. 9). This recounting of Israel's wilderness experience joins that of the "redeemed of the Lord" returning to Zion from Exile in Isa 35:10 and 51:11.[23]

The hungry and the thirsty appear again in Matt 25:35–40—forming another Matthean envelope—where the righteous are commended for

21. The particularity of the "land" is highlighted by the absence of the article in both Greek and Hebrew.

22. The Hebrew has "in place of shame, a double [portion]"; "the land" does not occur in the Hebrew text, and the Greek does not include the second Hebrew "double." These indicate Matthew's preference for the Greek here.

23. There is an intriguing echo of the phrase in Sir 24:21, where those who eat and drink of Lady Wisdom will hunger and thirst for more. Any relation is unlikely, but this highlights the intense opposite found in Matt 5—yet both meaning the same.

giving food and drink because, "Just as you did it to one of the least of these, you did it to me." This is clearly speaking of literal hunger and thirst; as does Ps 107. In the wilderness the bread of heaven is provided; in the SoM, it is righteousness.

And so, lastly, we look at *dikaiosunē*. We have already signaled the importance of this word for the Gospel and the concentration of occurrences in the SoM. Its use in vv. 6 and 10 at the conclusion of each section of the Beatitudes heightens the central significance of the term. Multiple questions arise: does this carry the same sense here as at Jesus's baptism (Matt 3:15); if not, what does it mean?[24] We can also point to the importance of *tsedeqah*, righteousness/justice, in Isa 61 (v. 3, LXX "you will be called generations of *dikaiosunēs*," Heb. *tsedeq*; and v. 8, Heb "I love *mishpat*," LXX "I am the one who loves *dikaiosunē*"), and its surrounding context: 56:1; 58:2, 8; 59:9, 15–17; 60:17; 62:1–2; 63:1. How should we translate it here, righteousness or justice, given it is used for both *tsedeqah* and *mishpat* in Isa 61?

To this point, I have been largely descriptive of the intertextual conversations in the passage. From this point, there is space only to be indicative of the questions raised. What of the second set of four Beatitudes? It does not continue to bring in Isa 61; they do not continue to speak from Isa 61; rather, I suggest, these depictions of the people of the kingdom are descriptive of Jesus, they epitomize Matthew's presentation of the ministry and crucifixion of Jesus in the rest of the Gospel. The evidence for this can be found in the discussion above.

CONCLUSION

In conclusion, I offer two literary and two theological observations. First, Matthew effectively bases the SoM on a mosaic of allusions from Isa 56–63, esp. 61. These first four *makarisms* bring together the vocabulary of poverty and oppression—those crushed in spirit, oppressed in the land, inheritance denied, longing for justice—drawing in other texts, particularly from the Psalms, by key-word signals. They breathe in the air of Isaiah.

Secondly, Matthew utilizes envelope structures to tie his narrative to the SoM. Key-words of the Beatitudes are developed elsewhere in the Gospel. The Isaianic "good news to the poor" lies between the envelope of the first Beatitude (Matt 5:3) and the day of reckoning (Matt 25:34), from Jesus's first to his fifth "discourses." Everything included between (thus, an *inclusio*) is held together by this theme.

---

24. The question has been thoroughly discussed by Przybylski in *Righteousness in Matthew*, but is not the last word.

These observations lead, thirdly and theologically, to the conclusion that Matthew and Luke share the same message: the presence of Jesus brings in the long-awaited Isaianic Jubilee. The SoM is a call to Jesus's disciples to seek the kingdom and his *dikaiosunē* in the midst of the poor, where justice and peace may kiss (Ps 85:10)—or, in the words of the Beatitudes, where poverty and powerlessness meet mercy and peace-making, persecution and shame (vv. 7–10). Does this read too much into the text? Goulder, again, observes: "All three Synoptic Gospels suggest independently that the first Christian community in Jerusalem saw itself as fulfilling the prophecy of Isa 61.1."[25]

It is striking to consider that nothing in this opening poem, or in the Gospel as a whole, suggests that the poor in spirit are necessarily followers of Jesus, or are expected to become followers; there are no "undeserving" poor, no conditions attached, in this kingdom. Simply stated, "theirs is the kingdom." Having noted this, it is also important to note that theirs is not exclusively the kingdom. The poor and the merciful, together, consist of the kingdom. And except their *dikaiosunē* exceeds that of the professionally religious, they can "in no way enter the kingdom of heaven" (Matt 5:20). They must enter together.

It may have been noticed that I have studiously avoided mention of the Church. That, of course, is because the Church *is not* the kingdom of God. But, it *is* the community of God, and the SoM is the matrix in which the Church is nurtured and grows and finds her mission. For this reason the SoM cannot be thought of simply as about personal piety; nor can it be dismissed casually as an impossible ideal. It is the only way the Church knows what and how to be, and so must be the purposeful aspiration of the Church, and every local version of the Church, as the holy people of God—that is, the earthly expression of obedience to the command of Jesus: the perfecting of love, as "our Father in heaven is perfect."

Lastly, a reflection on the "no religion" generation. The causes and influences in this age's crisis of faith cannot be reduced to a single cause. The Church's marred and muffled witness to the world around is not the whole story, and any redemptive action on the part of the Church can address only a part of the loss. Nevertheless, when the Church lives out these kingdom values, while her proclamation of the gospel may not reverse the disillusion, it will surely be good news.

---

25. Goulder, "Poor Man's Christology," 333. This conclusion complements Mi Ja Wi's thesis that the rich cannot enter the kingdom without the poor; developed in full in *Path to Salvation in Luke's Gospel*.

WORKS CITED

Albright, William F., and Christopher S. Mann. *Matthew: Introduction, Translation and Notes*. The Anchor Bible 26. Garden City, NY: Doubleday, 1971.

Allison, Dale C. *The New Moses: A Matthean Typology*. Minneapolis: Fortress, 1993.

———. "The Structure of the Sermon on the Mount." *Journal of Biblical Literature* 106 (1987) 423–445.

Betz, Hans Dieter. *The Sermon on the Mount: A Commentary on the Sermon on the Mount, Including the Sermon on the Plain (Matthew 5:3–7:27 and Luke 6:20–49)*. Hermeneia–A Critical and Historical Commentary on the Bible. Minneapolis: Fortress, 1995.

Blenkinsopp, Joseph. *Isaiah 56–66: A New Translation with Introduction and Commentary*. 1st ed. The Anchor Bible 19b. New York: Doubleday, 2003.

Goulder, Michael. "A Poor Man's Christology." *New Testament Studies* 45 (1999) 332–48.

Gundry, Robert Horton. *The Use of the Old Testament in St. Matthew's Gospel: With Special Reference to the Messianic Hope*. NovTSup 18. Leiden: Brill, 1975.

Marshall, I. Howard. *The Gospel of Luke: A Commentary on the Greek Text*. The New International Greek Testament Commentary. Grand Rapids: Eerdmans, 1978.

Morris, Leon. *The Gospel According to Matthew*. The Pillar New Testament Commentary. Grand Rapids: Eerdmans, 1992.

Office for National Statistics, "Religion, England and Wales: Census 2021." https://www.ons.gov.uk/peoplepopulationandcommunity/culturalidentity/religion/bulletins/religionenglandandwales/census2021.

Przybylski, Benno. *Righteousness in Matthew and His World of Thought*. SNTSMS 41. Cambridge: Cambridge University Press, 1980.

Rohr, Richard, and John Feister. *Jesus' Plan for a New World: The Sermon on the Mount*. Cincinnati: St. Anthony Messenger, 1996.

Swanson, Dwight D. "Insights from Qumran for the Exegesis of Scripture in the Gospel of Matthew." *Semitica* 62 (2020) 341–366.

———. *The Temple Scroll and the Bible: The Methodology of 11QT*. STDJ 14. Leiden: Brill, 1995.

———. "The Text of Isaiah at Qumran." In *Interpreting Isaiah: Issues and Approaches*, edited by David G. Firth and H. G. M. Williamson, 191–212. Nottingham: Apollos, 2009.

Wi, Mi Ja. *The Path to Salvation in Luke's Gospel: What Must We Do?* LNTS 607. London: T. & T. Clark, 2019.

Ostensive Ethics and the Environmental Crisis

Andrew Brower Latz

WHAT IF ETHICS IS best *explained, grounded,* and *motivated* not by theory but by ostension, that is, by pointing to examples and/or events that serve as paradigm cases? We can point to, say, an act of kindness and state, "that was a good action;" or we could point to Auschwitz and say, "this ought not to be done;" or to a person and say, "this is a holy person."[1]

These events or examples *explain* ethics: *they* are what make sense of the ethical ideas we have, rather than a theory. This is J. M. Bernstein in *Adorno: Disenchantment and Ethics*: "the force of the imperative, via practical abhorrence, depends on its not being logically demonstrable: structures of material inference leave gaps from the perspective of rational demonstrability; from the inside, conversely, there is no sense of a gap to be filled: right reasoning, again, occurs only from within ethical understanding and is not a route to it."[2] Sophie Grace Chappell in *Knowing What to Do* cites Linda Zagzebski:

> A moral theory consists in part of a system of concepts. Some concepts in the theory are defined in terms of others. But . . . unless we are willing to accept conceptual circularity, some concept or concepts will either be undefined or will refer to something outside the domain. [For m]ost moral philosophers [the] basic evaluative concept in their theory is defined in terms of something allegedly non-evaluative, such as human flourishing in the biological sense. The alternative I am suggesting is to anchor each moral concept in an exemplar. Good persons are persons *like that*, just as gold is stuff like that. The function of

---

1. For one example of the latter, see Hendra, *Father Joe*.
2. Bernstein, *Adorno*, 389. "Material inference" is Bernstein's term for the way in which ethical reasoning works in contrast to intellectual rationalizing.

an exemplar is to fix the reference of the term "good person" or "practically wise person" without the use of any concepts, whether descriptive or non-descriptive. Reference to an exemplar then allows the series of conceptual definitions to get started. So the system . . . is linked to the world the system is about by indexical reference to a paradigmatically good person.[3]

In ostensive ethics, it is the persons and events that allow us to make sense of ethics—its concepts, motives, force, etc.—not least because such indexing involves emotions and bodily responses just as much as the intellect. These same features are why ethics is *grounded* by ostension: the events and examples—rather than a theory—justify the ethical values we hold. Bernstein again: ethics "has no source of origin other than our response to these events . . . what is a moral principle contains a proper name; it is indexically bound."[4]

And ostension *motivates* ethics: events and examples are what incline us to act ethically far more than a theory can. Think, for example, of the way in which a theoretical argument can be met with a shrug of the shoulders, whereas seeing a good person in action can be inspiring. Or, conversely, the way in which an argument against one's values can be relatively untroubling, but the revelation that a role model didn't live up to her/his/your values can be quite devastating. This is precisely because it is the person *qua* example who explains, grounds, and motivates ethical values and hypocrisy from the role model undermines all three.

Something like this has been argued recently[5] by, amongst others, J. M. Bernstein and Sophie Grace Chappell and, were it to be true, it would be good news for Christian theological ethics, which is based more on persons (Jesus, Paul's call to imitate him as he imitates the Lord, the saints, immediate role models) and paradigm events (Exodus, Resurrection, etc.) than on a specific ethical theory. These become the indexical references, the proper names, that illuminate and make sense of ethical values, that justify them and motivate us to follow them.[6]

    3. Chappell, *Knowing*, 253, citing Linda Zagzebski, "Admirable Life." Zagzebski is also an influence on Bernstein.

    4. Bernstein, *Adorno*, 389.

    5. For some antecedents, see Clarke, "Anti-theory in Ethics."

    6. One can of course generate rules of thumb from these persons and events, including familiar moral rules such as do not lie, do not steal, etc. This would roughly correspond to the Aristotelian idea of moral rules of thumb as condensations of many particular judgments. A similar thought applies to the rule-like remarks of wisdom literature. One could regard the giving of the law on Mt. Sinai as an event establishing a set of rules, but this would be to take the story literally and to sidestep the thrust of the ostensive approach, which is that persons and/or events exemplify a rule or value, rather than being the occasion for the delivery of a set of rules or commands.

The ostensive approach to ethics can be taken in both positive and negative directions, both of which are useful to theological ethics. Positive ostension would be to point to good examples of people, actions, states of affairs, etc.; negative ostension would be to point to examples of what ought not to be done, what should not be, ways we should not behave. Bernstein takes the latter route. He cites Ernst Bloch's idea that

> the West has two great visions of the moral hero: Aristotle's great-souled man and the suffering Christ on the cross . . . In the . . . victim-based approach, our interest is in the nature of moral injury, in what should not occur and why, in what moral boundaries must not be crossed, in what human suffering is, in what its causes are, and in how suffering means to sufferer and spectator. In considering particular and precise forms of suffering, we connect moral reflection to historically and socially conditioned moral experience, giving moral experience a voice in the construction of morality.[7]

Bernstein's contrast between Aristotle and Christ points up the fact that which examples and events are taken to be paradigms will depend on the person doing ethics and the tradition in which the person stands. Christians will take Christ's life, death, and resurrection as paradigm events, but they will at the same time consider, say, the Exodus and the Holocaust,[8] other episodes in history, the lives of certain saints, people known to them personally, and so on. Nor does the ostensive approach to ethics think we can dismiss ethical theory (it is the theories' tremendous insights that established them as canonical theories), or that we approach events or examples unmediated, without the influence of theory (and not only ethical theory) on our perception of them.[9] Theoretical tools can help us think through ethical issues, but they do not have the role assigned to them in most contemporary philosophy.

Where Bernstein looks at what must not be done, Chappell looks for positive examples.[10] One reason for this disagreement is Chappell thinks ethics is much influenced by epiphanies.

---

7. Bernstein, *Torture and Dignity*, 123.

8. On the implications for theological ethics of the Holocaust, see, e.g., Shanks, *God and Modernity*.

9. Biggar, *Behaving in Public*, 38, speaks of "the extent to which moral reason is shaped by its metanarrative hinterland."

10. And she thinks the possibilities for ethical action remain as present as they ever were, whereas Bernstein thinks disenchantment has diminished the existence of, our knowledge of, and our ability to perform the good in modern society.

> An epiphany is an overwhelming existentially significant manifestation of value in experience, often sudden and surprising, which feeds the psyche, which feels like it "comes from outside"—it is something given, relative to which I am a passive perceiver—which teaches us something new, which "takes us out of ourselves," and to which there is a natural and correct response. (At least one; possibly more.) Often the correct response is love, often it is pity, or again creativity. It might also be anger or reverence or awe or a hunger to put things right—a hunger for justice; or many other things. It may be something that leads directly to action or new knowledge, but it may also be something that prompts further contemplation or reflection; or other responses again.[11]

An obvious problem for ostensive ethics is epiphanies cannot be manufactured—people either have them or they do not—whereas arguments exist already, ready to be encountered or applied. Here is Kant's derivation of our duties. Here is a utilitarian reason not to drive a car. If ethics is motivated by epiphanies and I don't have any, don't I have an excuse not to be ethical?

This concern is a bit quick. First, although arguments do exist, they take a great deal of intellectual work to understand, which many people have neither the time nor the training to manage. Everyone, however, is socialized during childhood into values that feel external and real, whereas the issue of having epiphanies or not applies more to later, adult life. Further, epiphanies are not the only way we come by values. Second, the experience of having an epiphany or not is not so dissimilar from responses to arguments (nor, *mutatis mutandis*, revelation): people are either persuaded or they are not. An advantage for ostensive ethics over ethical theory is the range of materials on which it can draw: not merely rational arguments but people, institutions, arts, film, literature, relationships, biographies, and so on.

Another problem for ostensive ethics is that examples can be interpreted differently. This is not as bad a problem as it may first appear. Firstly, some cases are paradigm cases, precisely because there is (near) universal agreement about them (e.g., it is wrong to torture for fun).[12] Secondly, disagreement is sometimes due to the lack of a *real* encounter with the

---

11. Chappell, *Epiphanies*, 8–9. I am grateful to Sophie Grace Chappell for sharing the pre-publication draft with me. Conversion experiences would be one kind of epiphany.

12. The occasional person who does not agree with the paradigm cases need not necessarily be entertained. On the distorting effects on moral philosophy of attempts to persuade moral skeptics to be moral, see Bernstein, *Torture and Dignity*. On paradigm cases generally, see Jonsen and Toulmin, *Abuse of Casuistry*.

example, rather than a superficial conceptual one. For example, ticking time bomb scenarios are often used in thought experiments about utilitarianism to discuss the morality of torture. These, however, significantly lack all the relevant contextual information and, crucially, avoid the engagement of *moral imagination* needed to think-and-feel adequately about the reality of torture.[13] Although these responses scale down the problem, they do not solve it, because it is insoluble. To see why, something must be said about relativism and about controversy.

First, relativism. Some people worry an anarchic moral relativism can only be constrained by the theoretical certainty (putatively) provided by ethical theory or divine command. But, of course, these theories or commands too are interpreted differently and theorists within the same camp come to different conclusions about the same issues, so theory or commands/laws are not the solution to relativism. But nor is relativism as worrying as is sometimes made out. As Bernard Williams argues, it is "seriously confused" to take "relativism to issue in a nonrelativistic morality of universal toleration."[14] Williams develops his own idea of the "relativism of distance" in which only societies similar enough to our own pose real ethical challenges (his example: it is simply not a live option for us to take up the lifestyle and values of a Japanese samurai even if we wanted to), though he accepts questions of justice may transcend differences. This is related to Williams's idea of authenticity as the most important idea in ethics, that an agent "is identified with his actions as flowing from projects or attitudes which . . . he takes seriously at the deepest level, as what his life is about . . . *his* actions and *his* decisions have to be seen as the actions and decisions which flow from the projects and attitudes with which he is most closely identified."[15]

In short: theory cannot constrain relativism, so abandoning it for ostension is no loss on that front. Relativism is not as relative as it first appears since the cultural palette of options actually available is far more limited than the conceptual range we are aware of. And any ethics worthy of the name in modernity has to be reflectively embraced by the agent, which makes external attempts to remove the threat of relativism ultimately self-defeating. Relativism in the sense of deep disagreement about ethics is a permanent feature of human life. What we should expect of one another is not agreement but honesty and thoughtfulness in the values we do hold. Much of this can be argued from Paul's advice to the weak and strong in Romans 14 and 15.[16]

---

13. For an argument to this effect see Chappell, *Knowing What to Do*, 29–59.
14. Williams, *Ethics and the Limits of Philosophy*, 177.
15. In Smart and Williams, *Utilitarianism*, 116.
16. For helping me see this, I am indebted to Kent Brower and his paper "Am I My

Second, controversy. In light of Paul's seemingly contradictory advice in Rom 14 and 1 Cor 10, some Christians seek to avoid "giving offense," and as a result avoid controversy. Jesus and Paul, however, deliberately generated conflict. We should not seek conflict for its own sake but we should not shy away from it when it is necessary in its various forms, e.g., advocacy, protest, or even direct action, subversion, illegality, depending on what one is opposing and in what context.[17] Many of the moral advances we now take for granted exist only as a result of controversy. If it is the case that authenticity is what matters and a certain kind of relativism is unavoidable, then it should not be troubling to find a range of ethical and holiness styles within Christianity; that is, a range of ways of being dedicated to God's service and of being morally excellent. Holiness does not mean homogeneity, nor does it entail an absence of conflict; rather it means the construction of an ethical identity that has integrity, is as thoughtful as we can manage, and bodies forth and witnesses to the divine presence.

Dietrich Bonhoeffer can be read as a version of ostensive Christian ethics since he eschewed false moral certainty derived from theories, principles or traditions, and appreciated the necessity of both subjective integrity and hard thinking in ethical reflection. The lodestar of ethics becomes, for Bonhoeffer, responsibility, which means three things:[18]

1. To act on behalf of others, or to "stand in their place."[19] "Responsibility is based on vicarious representative action."[20] "Jesus . . . lived as our vicarious representative . . . Jesus was not the individual who sought to achieve some personal perfection, but only live as the one who in himself has taken on and bears the selves of all human beings."[21] As Rowan Williams puts it, "Goodness, self-defined and self-contained, is something which will be poisonous if we're not careful. Without the wound, the openness, the crack that connects us to reality, to one another and to God, healing doesn't happen . . . Understand our implicatedness in a sinful world, and we begin to understand why we are saved not by goodness, but by a new level of connection which we

---

Brother's Keeper?" I am grateful to Dr. Brower for allowing me to see the MSS and for discussions thereof.

17. See Delmas, *Duty to Resist*; King, "Letter from Birmingham Jail."

18. Bonhoeffer, *Ethics*, esp. 47–75, 134–45, 246–98. Here I use the interpretation of Johannes Fischer in *Leben aus dem Geist*, 126–29.

19. Bonhoeffer, *Ethics*, 258.

20. Bonhoeffer, *Ethics*, 257.

21. Bonhoeffer, *Ethics*, 258.

call the body of Christ."[22] We should seek to develop solidarity more than our own goodness. "Jesus is not concerned with . . . some kind of personal quality of being good . . . This is why he is able to enter into human guilt, *able to be burdened with their guilt*. Jesus does not want to be considered the only perfect one at the expense of human beings . . . He does not want some idea of a new human being to triumph over the wreckage of a defeated humanity. Love for real human beings leads into the solidarity of human guilt."[23]

2. To act according to reality, accepting its entanglements and contradictions, as God did in Christ.[24] "In any action that is truly in accord with reality, acknowledgement of the status quo and protest against the status quo are inextricably connected."[25] Life in Christ is "a living unity full of *unresolved* contradictions."[26] "The 'world' is thus the *domain of concrete responsibility* that is given to us in and through Jesus Christ. It is not some kind of general concept from which one could deduce a corresponding system."[27]

3. To act in freedom—no law, theory, or doctrine will tell you what to do or give you security: you have to decide, using judgment and imagination and taking responsibility for it before God.[28] "To act out of concrete responsibility means to act in *freedom*—to decide, to act, and to answer for the consequences of this particular action *myself* without the support of other people or principles . . . The point is not to apply a principle that eventually will be shattered by reality anyway, but to discern what is necessary or "commanded" in a given situation."[29]

What would the ostensive approach to ethics have to say about the environmental crisis?[30] It would encourage finding and disseminating ex-

22. Williams, "Beyond Goodness," 166–67.
23. Bonhoeffer, *Ethics*, 233.
24. Bonhoeffer, *Ethics*, 253–57.
25. Bonhoeffer, *Ethics*, 261.
26. Bonhoeffer, *Ethics*, 252. My emphasis.
27. Bonhoeffer, *Ethics*, 267.

28. This is good news because research suggest those who think of morality as debt and obligation feel more resentment, failure and bitterness around morality and are, as a consequence, less likely to act morally, whereas those who think of it as a positive contribution they can make in the context of the specific relationships they have enjoy moral action more and are more likely to act morally. See May, *Decent Life*, 51–53.

29. Bonhoeffer, *Ethics*, 221.

30. On the outlines of the crisis, see, e.g., Wallace-Wells, *Uninhabitable Earth* and "Other Environmental Emergency" from *The Economist* on the loss of biodiversity.

amples and stories of good environmental ethics, whether by individuals, organizations, companies, or governments.[31] These examples would serve as ways to motivate further ethical action with regards to the environment, justify it and explain it. It would encourage finding and disseminating examples of what should not be done (and perhaps what should be done less).[32] Both types of examples, narratives and (anti-)role models help the reality of the damage and danger of climate change sink in, whilst having a greater chance than theory of moving us from anxious or overwhelmed paralysis to taking action. In this area we know what to do (individually at least, and corporately in broad outline), it's doing it that's the problem, and seeing others do something is more helpful than a theoretical explanation of what we ought to do.[33]

An example of this sort could serve as an epiphany about the value of nature that alters our behavior. For example, in the UK, a BBC documentary *Blue Planet* seems to have galvanized anti-plastic sentiment, partly by showing footage of a whale carrying its dead baby around for days, which baby died by ingesting plastic in the ocean. By bringing viewers close to the whale, its attachment to its offspring, and the effects of viewers' behavior on them both, the documentary enabled the reality of plastic use to "sink in" and made it especially vivid. The epiphany showed an aspect of the world as having value, motivated action and justified it to the actors. Another example may be that after reading Jonathan Safran Foer's book *Eating Animals* we may think, "animals should not have to suffer like that," and cease eating factory farmed meat. Here, "practical abhorrence" does what mere logical rationality cannot, particularly in motivating what must not be done.

Almost daily the news grows worse, e.g., Carrington, "Amazon Rainforest."

31. E.g., Project Drawdown, The Club of Rome, Collaboration for Impact, Crowd Foresting, Ecobirmingham, Extinction Rebellion, Seeds of Good Anthropocenes, Intergovernmental Science-Policy Platform on Biodiversity and Ecosystem Services (IPBES), The Millennium Alliance for Humanity and the Biosphere (MAHB), Oroeco, Earth Overshoot Day, Population Matters, Center for the Advancement of the Steady State Economy, Steady State Manchester, We Mean Business Coalition. White's famous paper "The Historical Roots of Our Ecological Crisis" suggests Francis of Assisi as the main Christian example of ecological ethics. For a critique of White's thesis see Whitney, "Lynn White, Jr.'s 'The Historical Roots of Our Ecologic Crisis' after 50 Years."

32. As an example of what ought not to be done by companies see, e.g., Rich, "The Lawyer Who Became DuPont's Worst Nightmare," and the film version *Dark Waters*. For what we can all do less as individuals see Wynes and Nicholas, "Climate Mitigation Gap."

33. On some of the psychological barriers to action on climate change, see Ross et al., "Climate Change Challenge and Barriers to the Exercise of Foresight Intelligence" on suggestions for overcoming some of these barriers see The Climate Reality Project, "Four Lessons."

Following Bonhoeffer's points above, taking responsibility means facing up to our own contradictions and then reflecting on what we are willing to sacrifice to be more consistent and to act more on behalf of others. For example, it is common knowledge that the four most effective things an individual can do to reduce their climate footprint are: reduce or cease driving, flying, reproducing, and shift to a plant-based diet. Knowing this, am I willing to go without meat a day a week? Two days? Altogether? Will I fly less or am I not yet ready to sacrifice, say, my holiday for the global good? Would I say this to brothers and sisters in flooded Germany, burned British Columbia or sugarcane farmers dying of dehydration-induced kidney disease in El Salvador?[34] Here we meet the psychological barriers to action on such big problems: my action is a drop in the ocean, most people are not sacrificing their pleasure so why should I?, and so on. Without a universal theory to impress upon everyone, including myself, all I am left with is my own sense of responsibility, my own willingness to sacrifice for the good of others, to agitate and advocate for the common good.

In these examples we see the ascetic dimension of holiness repurposed for the Anthropocene. But that is insufficient. Only political action and economic changes will bring the scope and depth of change needed. For this reason, holiness in the contemporary world requires political action of various kinds to address the climate emergency. Put otherwise, the Anthropocene demands political holiness from us all. (Of course, in the first century, politics was not a separate dimension of human life, but we should not thereby miss the challenge to political life entailed in the practice of Jesus and the early church.) Whilst holiness does not mean homogeneity, it often does entail commonality of purpose and action (where commonality does not exclude diversity). Meditative self-reflection focused on such questions, with examples to hand, will show that my own contradictions require me to be humble and patient with others, to understand and even admire those willing to take urgent and direct action where I am not. Such reflection has a better chance than theory of allowing reality to sink in and thereby moving me a step further along the extra mile I am willing to go in living a holy life.

WORKS CITED

Bernstein, J. M. *Adorno: Disenchantment and Ethics*. Modern European Philosophy. Cambridge: Cambridge University Press, 2001.

———. *Torture and Dignity: An Essay on Moral Injury*. Chicago: Chicago University Press, 2015.

---

34. The latter example is from Wallace-Wells's original article, "Uninhabitable Earth."

Biggar, Nigel. *Behaving in Public: How to Do Christian Ethics*. Grand Rapids: Eerdmans, 2011.

Bonhoeffer, Dietrich. *Dietrich Bonhoeffer Works*. Edited by Clifford J Green. Translated by Reinhard Krauss et al. Ethics 6. Twentieth Century Religious Thought. Minneapolis: Fortress, 2009.

Brower, Kent. "'Am I My Brother's Keeper?' Reflections on Identity and Conflict in Romans 14:1–15:13." Paper presented at the NTC One-Day Theology Conference, Nazarene Theological College, Manchester, UK, 25 June 2021.

Carrington, Damien. "Amazon Rainforest Now Emitting More CO2 Than It Absorbs." *The Guardian* (July 15, 2021). https://www.theguardian.com/environment/2021/jul/14/amazon-rainforest-now-emitting-more-co2-than-it-absorbs.

Chappell, Sophie Grace. *Epiphanies: An Ethics of Experience*. Oxford: Oxford University Press, 2022.

———. *Knowing What to Do: Imagination, Virtue, and Platonism in Ethics*. Oxford: Oxford University Press, 2017.

Chappell, Timothy, ed. *Values and Virtues*. Oxford: Oxford University Press, 2006.

Clarke, Stanley G. "Anti-theory in Ethics." *APQ* 24 (1987) 237–44.

The Climate Reality Project. "Four Lessons Psychology Teaches Us about Inspiring Climate Action." https://www.climaterealityproject.org/blog/four-lessons-psychology-teaches-us-about-inspiring-climate-action.

Delmas, Candice. *A Duty to Resist: When Disobedience Should Be Uncivil*. Oxford: Oxford University Press, 2018.

"The Other Environmental Emergency." *The Economist: Technological Quarterly*, June 19, 2021. https://www.economist.com/technology-quarterly/2021-06-19.

Fischer, Johannes. *Leben aus dem Geist: Zur Grundlegung christlicher Ethik*. Zürich: Theologischer Verlag Zürich, 1994.

Foer, Jonathan Safran. *Eating Animals*. London: Penguin, 2009.

Haynes, Todd, dir. *Dark Waters*. Universal City, CA: Focus Features, 2019.

Hendra, Tony. *Father Joe: The Man Who Saved My Soul*. New York: Random, 2005.

Jonsen, Albert R., and Stephen Toulmin. *The Abuse of Casuistry: A History of Moral Reasoning*. Berkeley: University of California Press, 1988.

King, Martin Luther, Jr. *Letter from Birmingham Jail, April 16, 1963*. The Martin Luther King, Jr. Research and Education Institute. https://kinginstitute.stanford.edu/encyclopedia/letter-birmingham-jail.

May, Todd. *A Decent Life: Morality for the Rest of Us*. Chicago: Chicago University Press, 2019.

Rich, Nathaniel. "The Lawyer Who Became DuPont's Worst Nightmare." *New York Times*, January 6, 2016. https://www.nytimes.com/2016/01/10/magazine/the-lawyer-who-became-duponts-worst-nightmare.html.

Ross, Lee, et al. "The Climate Change Challenge and Barriers to the Exercise of Foresight Intelligence." *BioScience* 66 (2016) 363–70.

Shanks, Andrew. *God and Modernity: A New and Better Way to Do Theology*. London: Routledge, 1999.

Smart, J. J. C., and Bernard Williams. *Utilitarianism: For and Against*. Cambridge: Cambridge University Press, 1973.

Wallace-Wells, David. *The Uninhabitable Earth: A Story of the Future*. London: Allen Lane, 2019.

———. "The Uninhabitable Earth." *New York Magazine*, July 9, 2017. https://nymag.com/intelligencer/2017/07/climate-change-earth-too-hot-for-humans.html.
White, Lynn, Jr. "The Historical Roots of Our Ecological Crisis." *Science* 155 (1967) 1203–7.
Whitney, Elspeth. "Lynn White, Jr.'s 'The Historical Roots of Our Ecologic Crisis' after 50 Years." *History Compass* 13 (2015) 396–410.
Williams, Bernard. *Ethics and the Limits of Philosophy*. London: Routledge Classics, 2011.
Williams, Rowan. "Beyond Goodness: Gilead and the Discovery of the Connections of Grace." In *A Balm in Gilead: A Theological Dialogue with Marilynne Robinson*, edited by Timothy Larsen and Keith L. Johnson, 157–67. Downers Grove, IL: InterVarsity, 2019.
Wynes, Seth, and Kimberly A. Nicholas. "The Climate Mitigation Gap: Education and Government Recommendations Miss the Most Effective Individual Actions." *Environmental Research Letters* 12 (2017). https://iopscience.iop.org/article/10.1088/1748-9326/aa7541/.
Zagzebski, Linda. "The Admirable Life and the Desirable Life." In *Values and Virtues: Aristotelianism in Contemporary Ethics*, edited by Timothy Chappell, 53–66. Oxford: Oxford University Press, 2007.

Dangerous Bodies and Scandalous Touch

Reading Gospel Impurity Stories in the Time of Pandemic

Arseny Ermakov

INTRODUCTION

Decades of studies of ancient Mediterranean religious traditions unravel the world filled with anxiety about "ritual" impurity. That fear was deeply rooted in a widespread belief that *miasma* was contagious, detrimental to personal and communal well-being, and, most importantly, able to compromise divine presence. Often emerging out of the natural processes of human life and death, uncleanliness was predominantly transmitted by touch.[1] The ancients employed a variety of strategies to contain the spread of impurity: they separated, isolated, abstained from, warned about, scapegoated, and purified unclean bodies. In the world of the Scripture, the Greeks and Romans appear to be no less concerned about purity than the Second Temple Jews.[2] However, according to Herodotus, no one among the ancients could surpass the Egyptian obsession with cleanliness.[3] Indeed, there was "no Jew

---

1. In some instances, one could become impure by seeing, by family association, or by actions.

2. On purity in the Greco-Roman world see Parker, *Miasma*; Lennon, *Pollution and Religion*; Pertrovic and Petrovic, *Inner Purity*; Carbon and Peels-Matthey, *Purity and Purification*; Nihan and Frevel, *Purity*.

3. Herodotus, *His.* 2.37; Petrovic and Petrovic, *Inner Purity*, 26–27.

or Gentile" when it came to the recognition of the dangers of impurity, its contagious nature, and the central role the human body played in ancient purity "systems."[4]

Some striking similarities to the handling of the ongoing COVID-19 outbreak, emerged practices, discourses, and attitudes can't escape an attentive modern reader of the Gospels. The fear of the destructive coronavirus and its effects on human well-being penetrated almost all aspects of modern living: from matters of personal hygiene to state legislation. Suddenly, the human body—affected by the contagious virus—became the focus of media, public, and government attention. To limit the spread, a set of practices and policies, that echo the ancient ways of dealing with ritual impurity[5] were imposed on the society at large and the communities of faith. Purification in the forms of handwashing/sanitizing and disinfecting surfaces was prescribed and demanded; "social distancing," abstention, forced isolation, and timed self-isolation were enforced and policed. Touch and proximity became "toxic" and difficult to negotiate. In the early stages of the pandemic, these were often accompanied by shaming, stigmatizing, and scapegoating. Alas, body politics became apparent to all, even to "angry old men."

The pandemic and the seeming similarities in purity politics between the two worlds sounded to me like an invitation to reflect on the Gospel impurity stories in the current challenging context. Can we even draw on those similarities/parallels in a theological reflection? How can we navigate gospel purity/impurity discourse in today's context? How do we read stories of touch, inclusion, and restoration of "unclean people" in times of social distancing? What can we learn as modern holy people of God from Jesus's attitude toward impurity in a time of pandemic?

DANGEROUS BODIES: NEGOTIATING BODILY IMPURITIES

Among other sources of impurity, the human body takes the central stage in purity regulations and practices. Unlike modern theologians, the ancients often placed impurity on *the map of the body* rather than against the binary oppositions of cult and morality.[6] The sources of impurity lay outside or within the human body and crossing bodily boundaries by different substances on the way out (e.g., semen, menstrual blood) or on the way in

---

4. See Lemos, "Where There Is Dirt" for a discussion on the usage of the term "system" in the studies of purity.

5. However, vaccination and mask-wearing were not in the ancient repertoire.

6. Neyrey, "Idea of Purity," 102–3.

(e.g., food, unclean spirits) rendered people unclean. One's own body or the bodies of others could become a source of impurity, and different parts of the body could be contaminated. Sickness in some cases was connected to impurity as well.[7] Moreover, one can't ignore the gendered nature of purity regulations where female bodies were seen as creating impurity more often.

The treatment of the human life cycle and bodily functions is a prime example of bodily-generated impurities. An inscription from the sanctuary of Athena Nikephoros at Pergamon (133 BCE) reads:

> "[P]eople who enter the temple of the goddess shall be pure, having washed themselves clean from their own wife or their own husband for one day, or from another woman or another man for two days; similarly from a corps or from a woman in labour for two days."[8]

This impure tirade of sex, birth, and death often appears in Hellenistic (and beyond) temple purity norms also known as *leges sacrae*.[9] Giving birth, touching a corpse, or having sex with a partner or someone's partner rendered humans unclean and unfit for temple worship. Divine aversion to uncleanliness spills out into the regulations for priests and priestesses: they also must be free from the "taint of birth and death."[10] They cannot enter the house of death or the house of birth; they must abstain from sex before attending to priestly duties.[11] According to Plato and Aristotle, the ideal priests are those of ripe age who, supposedly, lost any interest in amorous activities.[12] For some reason, the ancient gods were quite prudish about the key aspects of the human life circle and YHWH was not an exception. Jewish purity laws were equally demanding; they required the highest levels of purity for the priestly cast as well. Purity regulations from Torah and other Second Temple texts, particularly the Temple Scroll, prohibit entry to the holy city after intercourse with a spouse (e.g., 11QT XLV:11–12), require a purification from touching a corps or death in a household (11QT XLV:17; XIV:1–15; XLIX:1–L:4), forbid priests from approaching corpses (apart from close relatives, Lev 21:1), designate mothers and their newborn babies

---

7. Parker, *Miasma*, 207–8, 216. On connections between healing and purity in incubation rituals, see von Ehrenheim, *Greek Incubation Rituals*.

8. Carbon, *CGRN* 212, lines 1–9.

9. Gunther, "Concepts of Purity," 257, after surveying Greek temple purity regulations notes "the concepts of purity, or impurity, remained constant through the centuries." Also see Parker, "Miasma," on the current discussion on the status of these norms.

10. Parker, *Miasma*, 52.

11. Finn, *Asceticism*, 15.

12. Parker, *Miasma*, 87.

as impure (11QT XLVIII:16; Lev 12), and treat unusual or natural genital discharges as extremely polluting (11QT XLV:7–10; XLVIII:16; Lev 15). The logic behind such regulations remains unclear; what is clear, however, is that the human body in its natural cycle of life is perceived as a source of impurity that is incompatible with the divine.[13]

But impurity was not only produced by things of natural occurrence; people's actions could generate impurity as well. A whole new level of abomination could be reached if one gave birth, made love, or spilled blood on a temple's sacred grounds thus committing sacrilege.[14] Murder and suicide were equally polluting.[15] According to Torah, minor inadvertent sins pollute and require both expiation and purification.[16] Moreover, Leviticus provides an impressive catalog of sexual practices, child sacrifices, idolatry, divination, and intentional consumption of non-kosher food that directly pollute the sanctuary (Lev 20). In Numbers, murder—the shedding of innocent blood—pollutes the holy land itself (Num 35:34). Those impurities are harder, if not impossible, to cleanse and often involve the most radical cleansing practice—the death of the perpetrator (Lev 20:6, 9–18; Num 35:30).

The ancients felt that to curb the spread of impurity, purity demands ought to be extended to the core of the human body and personality. Across the ancient world, worshippers were called to pay attention to inner purity; purity of heart or mind or thoughts.[17] The temple inscription from Lindos reads: "For those who wish to enter the temple auspiciously. First and most important is to be sound and pure in hands and thought, and not to have knowledge of dreadful [things]."[18] The worshippers of Asclepius at Epidaurus were instructed: "Pure must be the person who goes inside the sweet-smelling temple; purity is to think holy thoughts."[19] Cicero recognizes that purity of the mind is most challenging to achieve: "Physical impurity can be removed by a splash of water or the lapse of a fixed number of days, but a stain on the mind does not fade with time, nor can it be washed out by any river."[20] Here Jesus joins the chorus of ancient philosophers, sectarians, and

---

13. Chaniotis, "Greek Purity," 36.
14. On sacrilege see Parker, *Miasma*, ch. 5.
15. Parker, *Miasma*, 109–30.
16. Swanson, "Offerings for Sin," 19–20; Sklar, "Sin and Impurity," 23–28.
17. See Pertrovic and Petrovic, *Inner Purity* for a thorough study of inner purity in Greek traditions.
18. Cited in Blidstein, *Purity, Community, and Ritual*, 20.
19. Translation is taken from Bremmer, "How Old is the Ideal of Holiness," 16.
20. Cicero, *On Commonwealth*, 139.

religious legislators when he formulates his purity *halakha* by prioritizing the purity of heart over ritual cleansing in Mark 7.[21]

Purification was negotiated in different ways but there were a few key elements: the passing of time, washing/immersions in lustral water, using cathartic plants (laurel and squill; hyssop in Jewish tradition), and offering sacrifices. Depending on the severity of the impurity, one element or a combination of a few could be used. Impurity from lawful sexual intercourse lasted only one day, but birth, death, or abortion renders a person unclean for 40 days. Water purification took different forms as well: from hand-washing to sprinkling, from ablutions to full immersions.[22] While Greeks and Romans employed sacrifices sparingly in purification rites, Leviticus demands sin-sacrifices for all major impurities (e.g., Lev 12:6–8; 14:10–32; 15:14–15, 29–30). The best way of staying pure is to abstain and separate from the sources of *miasma*. Unclean persons with long-lasting impurity were commanded to isolate or keep their distance.

Different ancient religious traditions perceived and negotiated purity issues in a variety of sometimes mutually exclusive ways. But all would agree: a human body—living or deceased—is the primary source of dangerous *miasma*. Humans perpetually generate impurity and pass it on through contact and their actions. What transpires is that the human body from its core to its outer boundaries, from intentions to actions, from birth to death was wrapped in layers of purity concerns. These culturally and religiously constructed overlays held the human body impurified, labeled, and subjugated to prescribed patterns of behavior and locked in social status.[23] All of that is done in a bid to curb the spread of impurity and prevent it from reaching sacred places; since compromising divine presence and favor could lead to catastrophic consequences and undermine the prosperity, well-being, and security of a *polis* or a whole nation. Such an overwhelming danger forced the ancients to police their own bodies and the bodies of others.

SCANDALOUS TOUCH: JESUS AND BODILY IMPURITY

In the narrative worlds of the Gospels, the Pharisees—a Jewish purity sect—embody that ancient obsession with uncleanliness. Their relentless pursuit of purity guided all aspects of their individual and communal living;

---

21. Ermakov, "Purity," 105–9.

22. A good example of a variety of Greek purity practices could be found in *Characters* by Theophrastus.

23. E.g., sex workers, people with disabilities, funeral workers, etc.

Levitical purity laws and Mosaic regulations for priests had been extended into the lives of commoners.[24] Regular washing of hands, ritual immersions, purification of furniture and utensils, abstention from all things and people unclean, and eating *kosher* food in the state of ritual purity was an everyday occurrence in the life of a Pharisee and his family.

Set in this context, Jesus exhibits a seemingly *nonchalant* attitude towards uncleanliness. According to the gospel narratives, he did not participate in purification rites on a regular basis or follow purity protocols on his visits to the Temple or to Pharisees' houses. He traveled to unclean places: a graveyard, a house of death, or gentile territory. He confronted unclean spirits. He often found himself in the company of persons who are—to various degrees—deemed impure: disabled, sick, gentiles, and non-observant Jews (aka "sinners"). He received a touch from the woman with genital discharges (Mark 5:27) and "a sinful woman" (Luke 7:36–50). But most disturbingly, Jesus intentionally crossed invisible purity boundaries and touched bodies that were labeled as the primary sources of contagious impurity: little children (Matt 19:15), a dead girl (Mark 5:41), a bier with a male corpse (Luke 7:14), and a leper (Mark 1:41). In a world obsessed with purity and uncleanliness, Jesus's attitudes and practices appear disturbing and outright dangerous. Jesus's scandalous touch could have been perceived as perpetrating the spread of impurity and potentially undermining the sanctity of the Jerusalem Temple and compromising divine presence.

It is not surprising then to observe that Jesus clashed with the Pharisees over the purity norms and practices. In that confrontation, he exposed the seeming inconsistencies in their observances through ironic remarks and clever parables, castigated excesses of purity-observance in his speeches, and subverted their approach to impurity by crossing forbidden boundaries. He highlighted their over-emphasis on external sources of impurity and—in a twist—revealed who is truly unclean; they are "whitewashed tombs," whose hearts are filled with worse impurities (Matt 23:25–28). In Jesus's teaching, "a Pharisee" turns from a paragon of purity and righteousness into a synonym for hypocrisy. But Jesus wasn't the only one in the ancient world who expressed uneasiness with purity regulations, pointed out their inconsistencies, castigated obsession, or acted provocatively. Here he finds himself in a company of Jewish prophets, Greek and Roman philosophers, poets, and playwrights.

However, for the Gospel writers, provocation or subversion is not the point. Gospel purity narratives have a different purpose. They all have one thing in common—against the logic of contagious impurity—Jesus is

---

24. Neusner, *Idea of Purity*, 65–66.

never rendered unclean through direct contact. Touching unclean bodies and being touched by unclean people did not transmit impurity to Jesus. The opposite is always the case; the source of impurity is being removed and the unclean body—purified. Leprosy leaves the afflicted (Mark 1:42); persistent genital blood flow stops (Mark 5:29); the dead rise (Mark 5:42; Luke 7:15); unclean spirits are banished (Mark 5:12); and sins are forgiven (Luke 7:47, 50). Those stories unapologetically make a christological point, and the leper's statement in Mark 1:40 captures it well: "you [Jesus] can make me clean."

In the narrative worlds of the gospels, Jesus is "the Holy One of God" (Mark 1:24//Luke 4:34) and the source of contagious holiness that restores the purity of the people of God in the last days. He employs an eschatological posture that provides an alternative to traditional ways of dealing with impurity.[25] In Jesus's mission, the pharisaic body politics of withdrawal, separation, and exclusion is confronted by the logic of divine presence, hospitality, and solidarity. His scandalous touch restores and breaks the chain of impurity contamination. He is not putting the community in danger; the opposite is the case. The holy people of God are being restored. But what underpins those purity stories, to my mind, is the issue of dislocation and relocation of divine presence. What appears as Jesus's negligence in the matters of purity turns out to be an outworking of divine presence. Every touch turns into an epiphany.

Here the Gospels are trying to negotiate—maybe not always successfully—a tricky scenario. It's not only about the Holy One touching an unclean body but it's about the Holy One being a body that is culturally and religiously conceptualized through categories of im/purity. In this context, purity concerns underpin not only impurity stories but the whole Gospel narrative of Jesus's life: from birth to death on the cross, from bodily resurrection to ascension. In a time when human bodies were seen as sources of uncleanliness and hindrances to the divinely established order of things, the Christ event disrupted that logic and redefined the notion of divine presence itself. Birth impurity is purified by incarnation; death impurity is sanctified by resurrection. God in Christ does not shy away from bodily uncleanliness and transforms it. Perhaps, the totality of Christ's event starts the deconstruction of impurified bodies, peeling off the cultural layers of impurity logic and releasing the human body—that is "fearfully and wonderfully made"—from the tyranny of "ritual" purity anxiety.[26]

25. Ermakov, "Purity," 109.

26. Perhaps here lay some of the foundations of Pauline anthropology where in Christ, the human body—regardless of gender—is primarily conceptualized as a place of divine presence, a temple, and not as a source of impurity and danger. See recent

JESUS, IMPURITY AND THE PANDEMIC

This brief excursus into ancient purity practices and gospel Christology highlights the gap between the Western world engulfed in the pandemic and ancient realities. To my mind, similarities are very limited. Put simply, impurity and a virus—though seemingly dangerous and contagious—are not the same thing. The pandemic doesn't threaten divine presence; hygienic and distancing practices are dictated by modern scientific and medical reasoning and not by Levitical codes or temple regulations. Thus, engagement with the ancient texts in current circumstances invites caution, attention to the historical context, and resistance to being seduced by primitive "parallelomania" at any end of the theological spectrum. However, living through the pandemic helped me to sympathize with the ancients and understand some of their perceived dangers of *miasma*. Though most of their purity beliefs and practices might appear to some modern people as superstitious nonsense, that real feeling of danger, anxiety, disgust, and suspicion of others—generated by an uncontrollable, invisible force—became a shared reality between the two worlds. Perhaps, here is where some lessons could be learned.

First, the main thrust of gospel impurity stories is to reveal Jesus's identity. His touch and proximity to the sources of impurity reveal divine nature through the work of contagious holiness.[27] Thus, those stories simply don't provide a license for modern Christians to disregard "social distancing" or mask-wearing in face of a contagious virus. In the same way, one can't use the example of Pharisaic ritual handwashing and distancing from "the sinners" for dismissing (or imitating!) COVID-safe hygiene protocols.

Second, the purity stories unequivocally demonstrate that God in Christ is at work in unexpected ways and places; at a time when the majority believed that impure bodies are not worthy of divine presence. Striking images from the height of the pandemic showed the frontline medical workers—wrapped in protective gear—attending to dying patients affected by the contagious virus.[28] While relatives and friends had to stay away, doctors and nurses extended human touch and proximity, which are so crucial for humans, to people taking their last breath in isolation because their bodies are dangerous. As a Wesleyan, I can't help but see God at work in this world, and those medical workers—believers and non-believers—who sacrificed so much in this pandemic as those who exemplified Christ and showed divine grace in the darkest moments.

---

discussion on purity in Pauline tradition in Harrington, *Purity and Sanctuary*; Blidstein, *Purity, Community, and Ritual*; Whittle, "Purity in Paul."

27. Ermakov, "Purity," 109–10.
28. Al-Arshani, "Heartbreaking Photos."

Third, among many other anxieties of ancient life, impurity was an invisible, contagious, and dangerous force that people had to live with every day; it was a constantly present concern. Yet the ancients seemed to find the key to minimizing its spread—the notion of inner purity. Christians are quite familiar with the concept of purity of heart which is understood in terms of sanctification, sinlessness, complete devotion to God, righteousness, pure thoughts, intentions, etc. But in the context of the pandemic, perhaps, inner purity could be reconceptualized as personal integrity. COVID-19 with its variants (and other viruses for that matter) are here to stay and be part of our everyday lives. As a society and communities of faith, we have to find a way to live with that dangerous force. On a personal level, the notion of inner purity as integrity might be of help; particularly when we assess the wellness of our own body and read those symptoms. Here, honesty with oneself, transparency with others, and responsible action could minimize the risk of dangerous infection and curb the spread. Living with integrity—that is rooted in love for God and neighbor—in the time of the pandemic could be one of the learnings from ancient wisdom.

Finally, two particularly worrying societal responses—echoing the ancient world—to the pandemic stood out to me. First is scapegoating, labeling, and ostracism of those affected by the virus and unvaccinated people. In the early stages of the pandemic, people experienced shame, exclusion, and stigma for having COVID or passing it on to someone.[29] At the peak, othering—driven by fear and fueled by media—reached frightening proportions. Second is the damaging and long-lasting effects of pandemic policies on different social groups, particularly marginalized ones.[30] It becomes clear that the policies created and enforced by the privileged ruling class—without considering the voices and concerns of different groups—were damaging, leading to impoverishment and further marginalization. In contrast, there is something dignifying in the way Jesus treated "the unclean," seeing people behind labels and affliction. It was not coincidental that "impure people" of the day were also marginalized. Yet, according to the gospels, Jesus shattered the traditional everyday patterns of pollution and cleanliness and welcomed those who "threaten" the order of things by their bodily uncleanliness; this didn't only restore their purity but also removed the social stigma associated with impurity. He brought them to the center of God's kingdom and restored their dignity. And by doing so, he confronted religious elites' obsession with pollution and the overwhelming prejudices of the masses. Instead

---

29. E.g., Johnson, "I Bawled My Eyes Out."

30. E.g., see Begum et al., "How Inequalities Are Affecting the Response" (in the UK); Kantamneni, "Impact of Covid-19" and "Covid-19: Disproportionate Impact" (in the USA); Centre for Social Impact, "Fact Sheets" (in Australia).

of following human logic of othering and marginalization, Jesus extended embrace, hospitality, and solidarity. Is there still room for these attitudes of the kingdom of God when people feel threatened and scared in the time of the pandemic?

WORKS CITED

"COVID-19: The Disproportionate Impact on Marginalized Populations." *University of Illinois Chicago.* https://socialwork.uic.edu/news-stories/covid-19-disproportionate-impact-marginalized-populations/.

Al-Arshani, Sarah. "Heartbreaking Photos Show How Frontline Nurses Treating COVID-19 Patients Live in the Divide Between Home and the Nightmare of the Pandemic at Work." *Business Insider,* August 18, 2020. https://www.businessinsider.com/heartbreaking-photos-show-lives-of-frontline-healthcare-workers-coronavirus-2020-8#health-care-workers-don-gloves-an-n95-mask-a-gown-a-hairnet-and-a-face-shield-while-caring-for-coronavirus-patients-to-protect-themselves-from-infection-of-the-highly-contagious-virus-4.

Begum, Nasima, et al. "How Inequalities Are Affecting the Response to COVID-19." *The University of Manchester.* https://blog.policy.manchester.ac.uk/posts/2020/04/how-inequalities-are-affecting-the-response-to-covid-19/.

Blidstein, Moshe. *Purity, Community, and Ritual in Early Christian Literature.* Oxford Studies in the Abrahamic Religions. Oxford: Oxford University Press, 2017.

Bremmer, Jan N. "How Old Is the Ideal of Holiness (of Mind) in the Epidaurian Temple Inscription and the Hippocratic Oath?" *Zeitschrift für Papyrologie und Epigraphik* 141 (2002) 106–8.

Carbon, Jan-Mathieu, et al. *Collection of Greek Ritual Norms (CGRN).* http://cgrn.ulg.ac.be.

Carbon, Jan-Mathieu, and Saskia Peels-Matthey, eds. *Purity and Purification in the Ancient Greek World: Texts, Rituals, and Norms.* Krenos Supplement 32. Liège: Presses Universitaires de Liège, 2018.

Centre for Social Impact. "Fact Sheets: Addressing Social Issue Areas in the Context of Covid-19." https://www.csi.edu.au/research/covid-19-fact-sheets.

Chaniotis, Angelos. "Greek Purity in Context: The Long Life of a Ritual Concept, or Defining the Cs of Continuity and Change." In *Purity and Purification in the Ancient Greek World: Texts, Rituals, and Norms,* edited by Jan-Mathieu Carbon and Saskia Peels-Matthey, 35–48. Krenos Supplement 32. Liège: Presses Universitaires de Liège, 2018.

Cicero, Marcus Tullius. *On the Commonwealth and On the Laws.* Cambridge Texts in the History of Political Thought. Edited by James E. G. Zetzel. Cambridge: Cambridge University Press, 1999.

Ehrenheim, Hedvig, von. *Greek Incubation Rituals in Classical and Hellenistic Times.* Krenos Supplement 29. Liège: Presses Universitaires de Liège, 2016.

Ermakov, Arseny. "Purity in the Synoptic Gospels." In *Purity: Essays in Bible and Theology,* edited by Andrew Brower-Latz and Arseny Ermakov, 89–113. Eugene, OR: Pickwick, 2014.

Finn, R. D. *Asceticism in the Graeco-Roman World.* Key Themes in Ancient History. Cambridge: Cambridge University Press, 2009.

Frevel, Christian, and Christophe Nihan, eds. *Purity and the Forming of Religious Traditions in the Ancient Mediterranean World and Ancient Judaism*. Leiden: Brill, 2012.

Gunther, Linda-Marie. "Concepts of Purity in Ancient Greece, with Particular Emphasis on Sacred Sites." In *Purity and the Forming of Religious Traditions in the Ancient Mediterranean World and Ancient Judaism*, edited by Christian Frevel and Christophe Nihan, 245–60. Leiden: Brill, 2012.

Harrington, Hannah K. *The Purity and Sanctuary of the Body in Second Temple Judaism*. Journal of Ancient Judaism Supplements 33. Göttingen: Vandenhoeck & Ruprecht Verlag, 2019.

Johnson, Sian. "'I Bawled My Eyes Out': When 11 Friends Were Diagnosed With Covid, They Banded Together to Overcome the Stigma." *Australian Broadcast Corporation*. https://www.abc.net.au/news/2021-11-25/covid-exposure-warning-dinner-party-superspreader-risk/100624140.

Kantamneni, Neeta. "The Impact of the COVID-19 Pandemic on Marginalized Populations in the United States: A Research Agenda." *Journal of Vocational Behavior* 119 (2020).

Lemos, T. M. "Where There Is Dirt, Is There System? Revisiting Biblical Purity Constructions." *Journal for the Study of the Old Testament* 37 (2013) 265–94.

Lennon, Jack J. *Pollution and Religion in Ancient Rome*. New York: Cambridge University Press, 2013.

Neusner, Jacob. *The Idea of Purity in Ancient Judaism*. Leiden: Brill, 1973.

Neyrey, Jerome H. "The Idea of Purity in Mark's Gospel." *Semeia* 35 (1986) 91–128.

Parker, Robert. "Miasma: Old and New Problems." In *Purity and Purification in the Ancient Greek World: Texts, Rituals, and Norms*, edited by Jan-Mathieu Carbon and Saskia Peels-Matthey, 23–33. Krenos Supplement 32. Liège: Presses Universitaires de Liège, 2018.

———. *Miasma: Pollution and Purification in Early Greek Religion*. Oxford: Clarendon Press, 1983.

Petrovic, Andrej, and Ivana Petrovic. *Inner Purity and Pollution in Greek Religion. Volume I: Early Greek Religion*. Oxford: Oxford University Press, 2016.

Sklar, Jay. "Sin and Impurity: Atoned or Purified? Yes!" In *Perspectives on Purity and Purification in the Bible*, edited by Baruch J. Schwartz et al., 18–31. Library of Hebrew Bible/Old Testament Studies 474. London: T. & T. Clark, 2008.

Swanson, Dwight D. "Offerings for Sin in Leviticus, and John Wesley's Definition." *European Explorations in Christian Holiness* 1 (1999) 9–22.

Whittle, Sarah. "Purity in Paul." In *Purity: Essays in Bible and Theology*, edited by Andrew Brower-Latz and Arseny Ermakov, 134–52. Eugene, OR: Pickwick, 2014.

"Present Your Bodies as Living Sacrifices or as a Living Sacrifice?"

The Case for a Communal Sacrifice in Romans 12:1–2

Christopher G. Foster

INTRODUCTION[1]

In Rom 12:1, Paul says, "to present your bodies—a sacrifice living, holy, acceptable to God." Many scholars gloss over the abnormal combination of the plural "your bodies" (*ta sōmata hymōn*) with the singular accusative *thysian* "sacrifice." Some translate it in the plural.[2] Many, who retain the singular, do not highlight its significance nor recognize a possible corporate meaning.[3] Others make no mention of a possible corporate understanding.[4] Did Paul

---

1. An initial draft of this paper was presented at the Wesleyan Theological Society annual conference at Asbury Theological Seminary, March 3, 2017.

2. The 1984 NIV renders the phrase "living sacrifices" (Rom 12:1). The 2011 NIV corrects "living sacrifice." Of the scholars surveyed, the following translate it in the plural: Fitzmyer, *Romans*, 637–38; Longenecker, *Romans*, 917; Mounce, *Romans*, 230–33; Stott, *Message of Romans*, 321–22; Witherington, *Romans*, 283.

3. For example, see Bird, *Romans*, 414; Hultgren, *Romans*, 439–40; Keener, *Romans*, 143–44; Kruse, *Romans*, 460–63; Morris, *Romans*, 434; and Osborne, *Romans*, 318–20.

4. See Achtemeier, *Romans*, 195; Bruce, *Romans*, 213; Calvin, *Romans*, 451–52; Cranfield, *Romans 9–16*, 599–605; Dunn, *Romans 9–16*, 708–12; Käsemann, *Romans*, 327–29; Mohrlang, *Romans*, 184–85; Moo, *NIV Application Commentary: Romans*, 394–95; Murray, *Romans*, 109–16; Schreiner, *Romans*, 643–44; Stuhlmacher, *Paul's Letter*, 187–88; Despite Wright's ecclesiological and covenantal lens of Roman 9–11, he does not mention a corporate aspect here, "Romans," 10:704–6.

intend this to be read as a plural—meaning individual sacrifices—or as a singular—communal sacrifice?

Are there any scholars who do identify a possible corporate or communal aspect to the singular *thysian*? Sarah Whittle observes that these bodies are offered "as a corporate sacrifice."[5] George Smiga,[6] Robert Jewett,[7] both of whom Whittle builds upon, Mike Thompson,[8] Richard Hays,[9] and, more recently, Scott W. Hahn[10] also emphasize a possible communal aspect to the sacrifice.[11]

Since most scholars overlook the significance of the singular and only six of those surveyed suggest a communal sense, Paul's intended meaning warrants further investigation. Douglas Moo, in his extensive *NICNT Romans* commentary, mentions in a footnote: "The shift from the plural *sōmata* "bodies" to the singular *thysian* "sacrifice" could indicate that Paul thinks of this presentation as having a corporate dimension, involving the service of the entire Christian community together."[12] He then says, "But *thysian* is probably a distributive singular."[13] Moo does not explain how he arrives at that conclusion. Could this assumption be the reason most overlook a communal meaning? His syntactical claim needs closer inspection.

Consequently, the first part of this examination will consider what makes a clear grammatical case for a singular to be read in the plural (as a distributive singular) and if this fits with Paul's use of these words or similar phrases elsewhere in Romans. Second, a close read of the letter's immediate and broader context may help disclose how a corporate meaning of *thysian* fits the context best. With the gathered evidence for a corporate sense to this sacrifice, further implications from the parenesis for God's holy people will

---

5. Whittle, "Bodies Given for the Body," 104. This correlates with my research on 2 Cor 3:18, where the perfect passive dative singular participle singular (*anakekalymmenō prosōpō*) "unveiled face" is often translated in the plural as "unveiled faces," which overlooks and obscures the corporate context of the passage. See Foster, *Communal Participation*, 131–61.

6. Smiga, "Romans 12:1–2," 257–73.

7. Jewett, *Romans*, 724–30.

8. Thompson, "Romans 12:1–2," 121–32.

9. Hays, *Echoes of Scripture*, 206n58.

10. Hahn builds on Hays's footnote, *Romans*, 215.

11. Greathouse and Lyons acknowledge "the corporate nature of the Christian consecration and transformation" and note "their sacrificial offering is a community project," *Romans 9–16*, 127. This representative survey of scholarly literature on Rom 12:1–2 does not claim to be exhaustive.

12. Moo, *Romans*, 750n24. He cites Smiga, "Romans 12:1–2," as the source of this view.

13. Moo, *Romans*, 750n24.

be explored. This will include reasonable corporate worship and corporate discernment of God's will, as opposed to exclusively individualistic ones. Paul intentionally employed the singular *thysian* to correct the crisis of division among the beloved in Rome through an ecclesiological and communal sense.

A DISTRIBUTIVE SINGULAR IN ROMANS 12:1–2?

Linguistically, a plural subject linked with a singular object occurs frequently in Paul.[14] Often this appears with a plural possessive pronoun *hymōn* (e.g., Gal 6:18; Phil 4:23). Occasionally, the singular object is interpreted as a "distributive singular"[15] with little to no grammatical or syntactical explanation.[16] Sunny Chen notes that combining a singular object with a plural possessive is abnormal grammatically because it "violates the rule of agreement."[17] When the object is not a concrete noun but is abstract or a metaphor, it is not a distributive singular. Chen gives examples of abstract nouns, like hope, faith, character, and love, that always appear in the singular. Instead, these singulars can and should be explained by other grammatical designations.

In this case, if Paul is using the singular *thysian* metaphorically instead of concretely, then a distributive singular would be an inadequate category. For a distributive singular must be a concrete noun. If *thysian* is a standard concrete noun, then one would have to rule out a corporate essence to Paul's meaning first before it can be designated a distributive singular. The plain reading is in favor of a corporate meaning to the sacrifice.

So, how should *thysian* be understood? Surprisingly few call this sacrifice a metaphor.[18] This may be because, in the New Testament, Jesus is identified as a sacrifice, which is concrete. Moreover, the word sacrifice in various Second Temple Jewish texts is identified with the bloodless sacrifices of praise, prayer, thanksgiving, and God-pleasing actions.[19] Paul rede-

---

14. Possibly, this derives from similar constructions of Hebrew and Aramaic as reflected in the lxx. It is rare in classical Greek literature and does follow grammatical rules. See Turner, *Grammar*, 3:23.

15. Winer states that a distributive singular is "the use of the singular in reference to a plurality of objects" (*Treatise on the Grammar*, 218) in Chen, "Distributive Singular in Paul," 106.

16. This grammatical form is also known as a collective singular, Wallace, *Greek Grammar*, 400–406.

17. Chen, "Distributive Singular in Paul," 105.

18. Jewett calls this a "metaphor of personal devotion," *Romans*, 727.

19. Here are some examples: bloodless offerings of the angels (T. Levi 3:6), "sacrifice of praise" (Heb 13:15), sacrifice tied to service (Phil 2:15–17); "lifting up hands as an

fines sacrifice by calling it "bodily" and "living." This changes it from being metaphorical—a comparison to a dead animal—to concrete bodily action of the community. Rather than a "bifurcation of spiritual from physical," Paul brings these together.[20] Bird even suggests that the sacrifice could point to the priesthood of all believers.[21] This correlates with Paul's self-perceived priestly role in the offering of the gentiles (Rom 15:16), which may be the people themselves. This sacrifice is consistent with the rest of Romans, characterized by faithful bodily obedience (e.g., Rom 1:5; 16:26).

Since Paul is using it concretely,[22] the question remains whether it is meant to refer to individual bodies, each being a sacrifice, or whether Paul intended the singular to "denote corporate and relational dimensions of the community"?[23] Linguistically, either convention is acceptable in Koiné Greek and especially in the New Testament. If it is the latter, then "corporate essence," as proposed by Chen, might be a better category of explanation.[24]

Before examining whether Paul intended a corporate meaning for the sacrifice, does Paul use sacrifice in the singular or plural elsewhere, and could this usage determine Paul's intent in Rom 12:1? Pauline literature speaks of sacrifice in four other places. Two of these have the normal grammatical agreement and can be ruled out—other than to note that one is plural in 1 Cor 10:18. First, Paul refers to the people of Israel "who eat the sacrifices" (*hoi esthiontes tas thysias*). This plural noun has agreement grammatically. Second, in Eph 5:2, the singular sacrifice is employed to describe Christ's offering to God: "for us, a fragrant offering and sacrifice to God" (NRSV) (*hyper hēmōn prosphoran kai thysian tō theō eis osmēn euōdias*). This usage does not illuminate the singular necessarily. Still, it does point to how Paul in Romans 12 may be urging believers to follow Christ or participate in him in a similar "self-sacrificing" manner through their bodily worship.[25] Third,

---

evening sacrifice" (Ps 141:2); spiritual sacrifices offered from a soul and heart (*Corp. herm.* I:31; 13:18, 21; Philo, *Spec.* 1.209, 272, 277; *Sib. Or.* 8:408; *Odes Sol.* 20:1ff); praise replaces cultic sacrifice (1QHa), spiritual actions replace animal sacrifice (1QS 9.4–5; Pss 9:30–31; 50:14, 23). See Käsemann, *Romans*, 328–29, and Talbert, *Romans*, 283–84, for a full listing of spiritual sacrifices in Second Temple Judaism. Stuhlmacher argues the worship then is synagogue-like, *Paul's Letter*, 187–88.

20. Moo, *Romans*, 397.
21. Bird, *Romans*, 330.
22. While not many call it a metaphor, Jewett argues for metaphorical language. It is consonant with the definition of a metaphor by Richards with a vehicle and tenor, *Philosophy of Rhetoric*, 96. In this case the tenor is the bodies of believers and the vehicle is the sacrifice.
23. Chen, "Distributive Singular in Paul," 112.
24. Chen, "Distributive Singular in Paul," 109.
25. Campbell, *Deliverance of God*, 831.

Paul characterizes his service, in Phil 2:17, as a libation "being poured out over the sacrifice and the offering of your faith" (*epi tē thysia kai leitourgia tēs pisteōs hymōn*). Here, the singular sacrifice has a plural possessive pronoun *hymōn*. While faith is abstract and always takes a singular, the singular sacrifice grammatically corresponds to singular faith. Nonetheless, the context implies the faith and sacrifice of the whole community. The fourth place is in Phil 4:18, where Paul describes the gifts they sent as "a fragrant offering, a sacrifice acceptable and pleasing to God" (*osmēn euōdias, thysian dektēn, euareston tō theō*). The plural "gifts" are characterized as a singular sacrifice. Here, Paul employs the singular sacrifice to describe a plurality of subjects—gifts. In summary, Paul uses sacrifices in the plural intentionally in 1 Cor 10:18 and uses the singular on two other occasions in a collective sense (Phil 2:7; 4:18). In light of this review, one can reasonably conclude that Paul employed the singular in Rom 12:1 deliberately.

While these exhaust Paul's use of *thysia*, one can look at another use of the cultic term *paristēmi* (to present)[26] that will further support the intentionality of a singular. In Rom 6:13, Paul has a parallel expression: "no longer present your members to sin *as* instruments of unrighteousness" (*mēde paristanete ta melē hymōn hopla adikias tē hamartia*). The phrase maintains a plural predicate accusative, *hopla*, with the plural subject, *ta melē*. The fact Paul does not keep agreement between the subject and predicate in 12:1 as he does in 6:13 further indicates that Paul purposefully chose the singular "sacrifice" to highlight a corporate or communal aspect. Due to the concrete nature of the noun, he or his amanuensis, Tertius, could have easily chosen "sacrifices," but did not. So, the plain sense of what is written urges the reader to consider a corporate meaning. The burden of proof lies upon those who seek to make it a distributive singular.

THE CORPORATE CONTEXT OF ROMANS 12:1–2

Even with the four cases of *thysia* and the parallel passage that lean the argument in favor of a deliberate singular, the best place to discern Paul's intended meaning is the immediate context. So, what can one see from a careful reading? First of all, Paul's address is to *hymas, adelphoi*, a corporate audience, the beloved in Rome. Paul uses the genitive second person plural pronoun *hymōn* two times "your bodies" and "your worship" and refers to the second person plural pronoun *hymas* again concerning who discerns the will of God in v. 2.[27]

---

26. Hultgren rightly argues that the "verse contains cultic terminology," *Romans*, 439.
27. *hymōn* that occurs with "mind" is omitted by earlier texts 𝔓46, A, B, D*, F, G

The corporate context continues with exhortations in the proceeding verses regarding how one ought to behave within the community. These appear to be an outworking of the bodily sacrifice (somatic) and rational worship in Rom 12:1 and the renewal of their mind and discernment (noetic) in v. 2. In verse 3, the address concerns how each one is to think of themselves within the community *en hymin*.[28] In verse 4, Paul speaks of the corporate body of believers: "For as in one body we have many members" (NRSV). In verse 5, he continues by referencing the mystical union of the body of those *en Christō*. He writes, "so we, who are many, are one body in Christ and individually we are members one of another" (v. 5). After an explanation of differing charismata given "to us" (*hēmin*), according to grace in vv. 6–8, a series of appeals follow in vv. 9–21. These exhortations, mostly plural masculine participles, detail how community members should relate to one another inside and to those outside. In 13:8–10, more relational exhortations appear that fulfill the law of love and provide "mutual upbuilding" (14:19) for the community. These demands are "for the sake of unity" and "harmony of the community," contributing to reputation and witness.[29] The conclusion of section 15:7–13 reiterates the goal of hospitality that produces through the Holy Spirit hope, joy, and peace within the community between believing Jews and gentiles—a corrective to community divisions.

The context, which follows Rom 12:1–2, is predominantly a corporate one. This strengthens the case that a communal understanding of sacrifice was intentional and lends strength to "worship," "mind," and "discern" as having a corporate sense too. Does a corporate reading fit with the preceding context and theme of Romans from 9–11 or even 1–11?

Romans 12:1 begins with *parakalō oun*; "I appeal to you therefore, brothers and sisters, by the mercies of God" (NRSV), which draws upon the preceding context of 9–11. Paul answers the questions of whether God's word has failed (9:6) and whether God has abandoned/rejected his people (11:1) regarding the covenant and his promises. God remains faithful and merciful; he has not abandoned his people. The salvation of Israel will happen through God's great mercy (9:15–23; 11:31–32) and the witness of Gospel-believing gentiles (11:13–14). In addition, 9–11 has a pastoral goal to counter gentile arrogance and foster unity between believing Jews and believing gentiles/Greeks.

6, 630, 1739, 1881, and thus was also omitted for this paper—even though it would strengthen the case for a corporate understanding. Likely, it was added for parallelism and consistency.

28. For Longenecker, verses 3–8 address one's "attitude toward oneself vis-à-vis the body of Christ," *Introducing Romans*, 428.

29. Fitzmyer, *Romans*, 638.

Paul has a focus in 9–11 on corporate bodies: Israel, Jews, Greeks, gentiles, and "his people."[30] In some sense, he has, in Dunn's words, "redrawn the boundaries of the people of God" in Romans 1–11.[31] Thereby, Paul attempted to resolve tensions between believing Jews and gentiles and answer questions about Israel's place in God's plan.

Wright argues that "Paul applies the whole theology of Romans 1–11 to the church itself."[32] This ecclesiological emphasis becomes even clearer in 14:1—15:13, where Paul addresses the weak and the strong, judging, accountability, and hospitality. This ecclesiological focus also comes into play in 12:1-2, especially the combination of singular nouns with plural possessives. Hahn picks up on the context and ties Paul's ecclesial "vision of Christian living" to the singular "sacrifice."[33] Thus, Paul "envisions not a series of unconnected, individual acts but a collective effort of the Christian community to glorify the Lord in union with one another."[34] This vision avoids privatizing one's service to God and "calls for a sacrificial, communal commitment from the Church."[35]

A COMMUNAL READING OF ROMANS 12:1-2

What benefits come from understanding the sacrifice as corporate? First, a communal sacrifice addresses the particular tensions between Jews and gentiles in the Roman house churches that resulted from Claudius's edict (49–54 CE). Romans, as a contingent letter, seeks to redress and resolve the crisis of this division. This grounds the parenetic section ecclesiologically within the situation of the Roman believers.[36] If Paul wants to bring resolution, unity, and mutual upbuilding (14:19), then they, as one body in Christ, need to be unified in their sacrifice. Accordingly, Smiga argues, "The living, holy, and acceptable 'sacrifice' for which Paul calls is that of the community. This communal offering of self is their 'proper worship' (*tēn logikēn latreian*)

---

30. Israel=historic nation/people with the religious identity of the Jewish people before God. Jews=ethnic Israel. See also Staples, "Romans 11:25–27," 371–90.

31. Dunn argues this because "the covenant promise to all Abraham's seed" is "not determined by physical descent"; ethnic markers are set aside (705). The promise is open to anyone who believes, and mercy is extended to all, *Romans*, 716.

32. Wright, *Climax of the Covenant*, 251–57.

33. Hahn, *Romans*, 215.

34. Hahn, *Romans*, 215.

35. Hahn, *Romans*, 215.

36. Wright agrees: "In standard Christian theological language, it wasn't so much about soteriology as about ecclesiology; not so much about salvation as about the church," *What Saint Paul Really Said*, 119.

because it flows from who they are, one body in Christ (12:4–5)."[37] For Smiga, the singular sacrifice is "of the one body" as related to Rom 12:5.[38] However, one should not underemphasize the participation of individual bodies (*ta sōmata*) in the collective sacrifice as 12:1 indicates.[39] Moreover, Levitical sacrifices in the Hebrew Bible have social implications. Sacrifice procured "civil reconciliation and forgiveness in the eyes of the law, which allowed an *individual* to remain a member of Israel," and the day of atonement sacrifice brought about "corporate expiation" to maintain and protect the "corporate existence."[40] Likewise, sacrifice in the Greco-Roman context was often a collective and public affair. The general population of a city or village could participate "collectively" in the sacrifice by eating and celebrating together.[41] This played a key role in unifying the *polis* and cultivating a corporate identity.[42] Is Paul then advocating through a singular living sacrifice the formation of a corporate identity with the fruit of unification?

Whittle provides some helpful insight here and relates the corporate bodily sacrifice of many in one body to Christ's singular offering for a corporate body.[43] In a mirrored, corporate reversal of Christ's sacrifice, many bodies are given as a singular "corporate sacrifice."[44] Bird rightly notes that this sacrifice alludes to and builds upon Romans 1–11: "those who bear Christ's name will learn to walk in Christ's way."[45] This implies a cruciform (i.e., cross-shaped) community, where "self-giving deeds" lead to the "well-being of others."[46] Indeed the "living" designation points back to chapter 6, walking "in newness of life" (6:4), but also the union in Christ's death, being crucified, along with the simultaneous participation in his resurrection (i.e., anastiform—resurrection-shaped life). Again, Paul speaks of these aspects within the community context through the second person plural. Paul calls this ongoing presentation of yourselves (plural) "sanctification" (6:19, 22).

If the sacrifice was strictly individual or personal, then due to the problem of division along Jew/gentile lines, the people might work toward

---

37. Smiga, "Romans 12:1–2," 269.
38. Smiga, "Romans 12:1–2," 269.
39. Incidentally, Jewett suggests that the bodies are "sacrificed individually," *Romans*, 729.
40. Ribbens, *Levitical Sacrifice and Heavenly Cult*, 8.
41. Hurtado, "New and Mischievous Superstition."
42. Grijalvo, "Public Sacrifice in Roman Athens," 21–32.
43. Whittle, "Bodies Given for the Body," 104.
44. Whittle, "Bodies Given for the Body," 96.
45. Bird, *Romans*, 412.
46. Bird, *Romans*, 414.

"factional" sacrifice.[47] Instead, the communal sacrifice allows them to discern God's will, which in part appears to have already been revealed by Paul from 1:18—11:36, i.e., their oneness in Christ.

Does the mirrored, corporate reversal also imply a one-time sacrifice? Whittle and Jewett argue that the aorist present infinitive indicates a one-time act. The aorist infinitive, however, takes its cue from guiding verbs around it, which are in the present tense. Additionally, "the infinitive of indirect discourse," as is the case here, "retains the tense of the direct discourse and usually represents either an imperative or indicative."[48] Furthermore, the word "living" (*zōsan*) lends to a present continual aspect. Living cannot be a past or one-time event. In light of this contextual consideration and in agreement with the majority opinion, ongoing corporate participation in this bodily sacrifice fits the context best.

Second, when a communal bodily sacrifice has a collective sense, then "your rational worship" (*tēn logikēn latreian hymōn*) may also have a collective essence. This is more difficult grammatically since worship always appears in the singular as an abstract noun. As established earlier, this rules out a distributive singular for worship as individualized worship. Certainly, the plural subject with the corporate context and communal emphasis through the singular sacrifice would support corporate, rational worship.[49]

Third, "be transformed by the renewing of the mind" (*metamorphousthe tē anakainōsei tou noos*) could also hint at the singular mind of the community. It is often translated with the second-person plural pronoun *hymōn*, which does not appear in the earliest manuscripts.[50] Since Paul follows this with you plural, *hymas*, and the discerning of the will of God, he seems to have intended a communal understanding of the whole of verse two. Paul encourages both believing Jews and gentiles to be renewed in the mind so that they can collectively discern God's will. Discernment includes all of 1:18—11:36, especially discerning the body of Christ appropriately. One should not think too highly of him or herself within the community; instead, he or she should show hospitality, avoid judgmentalism on *adiaphora*, avoid factionalism, and seek unity between the weak and the strong.

The singular mind implies oneness of thought, like 1 Cor 2:16. Paul says, "we have the mind of Christ" (1 Cor 2:16 NRSV). The implication is communal; the mind of Christ is not exclusively personal. Indeed, Paul

---

47. Smiga, "Romans 12:1–2," 270.

48. Wallace, *Greek Grammar*, 604.

49. Worship is a "right-minded" "way of life" (127) that is "*corporate* and *united*" and incorporates a diversity of expression from believing Jews and gentiles, Thompson, "Romans 12:1–2," 130.

50. See n27.

says, "we know only in part" (1 Cor 13:9). Likewise, corporate discernment proves vital to the community of faith.[51] Thus, the discernment to know or prove God's good, pleasing, and perfect will comes from the community of believers, both Jews and gentiles together. Discernment does not come through factionalism or even the individualistic mysticism of Hellenism. Instead, Paul implies a communal mysticism. They, together, will prove God's will as they embody one sacrifice together in reasonable worship. This reading directly opposes a strictly individualistic understanding of the passage familiar to Western Christianity, which is often devoid of communal responsibilities.

CONCLUSION

In response to the factional crisis among the beloved in Rome, Paul calls believers to be a communal sacrifice. The corporate tenor of the grammar and context provides an ecclesiological corrective to an overly individualistic understanding of bodily worship. For Paul, the holy people of God have a relational and cruciform obligation to one another as participants in this living sacrifice. This corporate reflection of Christ's sacrifice acts as an ongoing, transformational witness to the world—a notion that communities of faith need in the face of crises today.

Paul's communal exhortation shows how to navigate several issues endemic to Western Christianity. Bodily participation in a unified, communal sacrifice of worship fosters unity and mutual upbuilding through regrounding one's identity within the body of Christ—a corrective to culturally-driven polarization (factionalism). Corporate renewal of the mind and discernment of God's will disclose that a cruciform body of believers truly needs one another. Therefore, renewal and discernment are not exclusively personal but ought to engender a healthy communal function that counters the pitfalls of hyper-individualism and the excesses of celebrity Christianity. A corporate, living sacrifice that is holy and pleasing to God will help fulfill Paul's vision for a unified transformative community of faith that exhibits a genuine Christlike example to the world no matter the crisis.

WORKS CITED

Achtemeier, Paul J. *Romans*. Interpretation. Atlanta: John Knox, 1985.
Bird, Michael. *Romans*. Grand Rapids: Zondervan, 2016.

---

51. Romano, "Discernment in First Corinthians," 59–67, esp. 63–67.

Bruce, F. F. *The Epistle of Paul to the Romans: An Introduction and Commentary*. Tyndale New Testament Commentaries. Grand Rapids: Eerdmans, 1985.
Calvin, John. *Commentaries on the Epistles of Paul the Apostle to the Romans*. Translated by John Owen. Grand Rapids: Eerdmans, 1959.
Campbell, Douglas. *The Deliverance of God: An Apocalyptic Rereading of Justification in Paul*. Grand Rapids: Eerdmans, 2009.
Chen, Sunny. "The Distributive Singular in Paul: The Adequacy of a Grammatical Category." *Journal of Greco-Roman Christianity and Judaism* 11 (2015) 104–30.
Cranfield, C. E. B. *Romans 9–16. Volume 2: A Critical and Exegetical Commentary*. International Critical Commentary 32. Edinburgh: T. & T. Clark, 1979.
Dunn, James G. D. *Romans 9–16*. Word Biblical Commentary 38b. Dallas: Word, 1988.
Fitzmyer, Joseph A. *Romans: A New Translation with Introduction and Commentary*. Anchor Bible 33. New York: Doubleday, 1993.
Foster, Christopher G. *Communal Participation in the Spirit: The Corinthian Correspondence in Light of Early Jewish Mysticism in the Dead Sea Scrolls*. Wissenschaftliche Untersuchungen zum Neuen Testament 2.575. Tübingen: Mohr Siebeck, 2022.
Greathouse, William M., and George Lyons. *Romans 9–16: A Commentary in the Wesleyan Tradition*. New Beacon Bible Commentary. Kansas City, MO: Beacon Hill, 2008.
Grijalvo, Elena Muñiz. "Public Sacrifice in Roman Athens." In *Empire and Religion: Religious Change in Greek Cities under Roman Rule*, edited by Elena Muñiz Grijalvo et al., 21–32. Impact of Empire 25. Leiden: Brill, 2017.
Hahn, Scott W. *Romans*. Catholic Commentary on Sacred Scripture. Grand Rapids: Baker Academic, 2017.
Hays, Richard B. *Echoes of Scripture in the Letters of Paul*. New Haven, CT: Yale University Press, 1989.
Hultgren, Arland J. *Paul's Letter to the Romans: A Commentary*. Grand Rapids: Eerdmans, 2011.
Hurtado, Larry. "A New and Mischievous Superstition: Early Christian Distinctiveness in the Roman World." https://www.youtube.com/watch?v=tb96kYfk628.
Jewett, Robert. *Romans: A Commentary*. Hermenia. Minneapolis: Fortress, 2007.
Käsemann, Ernst. *Commentary on Romans*. Translated and edited by Geoffrey W. Bromiley. Grand Rapids: Eerdmans, 1980.
Keener, Craig. *Romans: A New Covenant Commentary*. Cambridge: Lutterworth, 2009.
Kruse, Colin G. *Paul's Letter to the Romans*. Pillar New Testament Commentary. Grand Rapids: Eerdmans, 2012.
Longenecker, Richard N. *The Epistle to the Romans*. The New International Greek Testament Commentary. Grand Rapids: Eerdmans, 2016.
———. *Introducing Romans: Critical Issues in Paul's Most Famous Letter*. Grand Rapids: Eerdmans, 2011.
Mohrlang, Roger. *Romans*. Cornerstone Biblical Commentary 14. Carol Stream, IL: Tyndale, 2007.
Morris, Leon. *The Epistle to the Romans*. Grand Rapids: Eerdmans, 1988.
Moo, Douglas J. *The Epistle to the Romans*. The New International Commentary on the New Testament. Grand Rapids: Eerdmans, 1996.
———. *NIV Application Commentary: Romans*. Grand Rapids: Zondervan, 2000.

Mounce, Robert H. *Romans*. New American Commentary 27. Nashville: Broadman & Holman, 1995.

Murray, John. *The Epistle to the Romans*. Grand Rapids: Eerdmans, 1968.

Osborne, Grant R. *Romans*. IVP New Testament Commentary 6. Downers Grove, IL: InterVarsity, 2003.

Peterson, David G. *Commentary on Romans*. Biblical Theology for Christian Proclamation Commentary. Nashville: B&H, 2017.

Ribbens, Benjamin. *Levitical Sacrifice and Heavenly Cult in Hebrews*. Berlin: Walter de Gruyter, 2016.

Richards, I. A. *The Philosophy of Rhetoric*. New York: Oxford University Press, 1936.

Schreiner, Thomas R. *Romans*. Baker Exegetical Commentary on the New Testament 6. Grand Rapids: Baker Academic, 1998.

Smiga, George. "Romans 12:1–2 and 15:30–32 and the Occasion of the Letter to the Romans." *CBQ* 53 (1991) 257–73.

Staples, Jason A. "What Do the Gentiles Have to Do with 'All Israel'? A Fresh Look at Romans 11:25–27." *Journal of Biblical Literature* 130 (2011) 371–90.

Stott, John R. W. *The Message of Romans*. Downers Grove, IL: InterVarsity, 1994.

Stuhlmacher, Peter. *Paul's Letter to the Romans: A Commentary*. Translated by Scott J. Hafemann. Louisville, KY: Westminster/John Knox, 1994.

Talbert, Charles H. *Romans*. Macon, GA: Smyth & Helwys, 2002.

Thompson, Michael B. "Romans 12:1–2 and Paul's Vision for Worship." In *A Vision for the Church: Studies in Early Christian Ecclesiology in Honour of J. P. M. Sweet*, edited by Markus Bockmuehl and Michael B. Thompson, 121–32. Edinburgh: T. &. T. Clark, 1997.

Turner, Nigel. *A Grammar of the New Testament Greek, Volume 3. Syntax*. Edinburgh: T. &. T. Clark, 1963.

Wallace, Daniel B. *Greek Grammar beyond the Basics: An Exegetical Syntax of the New Testament*. Grand Rapids: Zondervan, 1996.

Whittle, Sarah. "Bodies Given for the Body: Covenant, Community, and Consecration in Romans." *WTJ* 46 (2011) 90–105.

Winer, G. B. *A Treatise on the Grammar of New Testament Greek: Regarded as a Sure Basis for New Testament Exegesis*. Translated by W. F. Moulton. Edinburgh: T. &. T. Clark, 1877.

Witherington, Ben, III. *Paul's Letter to the Romans: A Socio-Rhetorical Commentary*. Grand Rapids: Eerdmans, 2004.

Wright, N. T. "The Letter to the Romans: Introduction, Commentary, and Reflections." In *The New Interpreter's Bible: A Commentary in Twelve Volumes*, edited by Leander E. Keck, 10:393–770. Nashville: Abingdon, 2002.

———. *What Saint Paul Really Said: Was Paul of Tarsus the Real Founder of Christianity?* Grand Rapids: Eerdmans, 1997.

PART III

Walking with the Marginalized

Personhood and Authentic Friendships

A Wesleyan Theological Reflection on the Relational Challenges Often Faced by People Living with Moderate to Severe Intellectual Impairment

David B. McEwan

IN A RECENT BOOK dealing with the impact of the COVID-19 virus on Australian society, Hugh Mackay asks the question, "Could we [Australia] become renowned as a loving country, rather than simply a 'lucky' one?"[1] The book makes the case for the vital importance of love if Australian society is to be truly transformed into a "kinder, more compassionate, more cooperative, more respectful, more inclusive, more egalitarian, more harmonious, less cynical" country.[2] As we continue to deal with the pandemic and its impact on every level of society, this sentiment is often raised in the light of the isolation and loneliness experienced by so many—and the answer given usually focuses on the idea of increased community. In other words, to quote the words of the famous Beatles' song: "All you need is love."[3] The words are so easy to say, but they often prove incredibly difficult to put into practice. Early in his ministry Jesus had said:

> Love your enemies, do good to those who hate you, bless those who curse you, pray for those who mistreat you . . . If you love those who love you, what credit is that to you? Even sinners love

---

1. Mackay, *Kindness Revolution*, 14.
2. Mackay, *Kindness Revolution*, 205.
3. Lennon and McCartney, "All You Need Is Love."

those who love them. . . . But love your enemies, do good to them, and lend to them without expecting to get anything back.[4]

The clear inference is that, on a purely human level, we find it relatively easy to love those who love us; the challenge comes when we are dealing with people who are not like us. Earlier in the passage (Luke 6:20–26), Jesus had addressed the blessings and woes related to the poor and the rich. Joel Green says that these are not just economic classes, but "socially defined constructs" contrasting those who are marginalized in society and those who are deeply embedded in its friendships and reciprocal relationships, with all the benefits that brings.[5] It is in this context that Jesus calls his followers to "form a community the boundaries of which are porous and whose primary emblematic behavior is its refusal to treat others (even, or especially, those who hate, exclude, revile, and defame you) as though they were enemies."[6]

Jesus intends to overthrow the old structure of society by the power of divine love. This is emphasized during the final meal that Jesus shared with his disciples before his crucifixion, when he said: "A new command I give you: Love one another. As I have loved you, so you must love one another. By this everyone will know that you are my disciples, if you love one another."[7] It is a command, and this implies it is not something we do automatically or easily. Human love by itself is unable to meet this requirement the moment the people we are asked to love are radically different to us—especially if they are also disregarded by the mainstream of our society. The nature of God's love is defined by his character and actions, particularly as they are revealed to us in the person and work of Jesus Christ. If we have experienced this divine love through a relationship with Christ, and we are serious about being followers of Jesus, then we need to pay attention to those to whom he paid attention. This kind of awareness enables a genuine empathy with the other that eradicates any kind of superiority. We need to "see" every person as someone we can truly love and with whom we can form a friendship. We are to love every person as our neighbor, no matter their capacities or capabilities: "Loving another with integrity means you cannot do, say or think things that would damage or diminish the other and still claim to truly love."[8] In Western cultures particularly, we need to be reminded that love is not just an emotion, but it involves attitudes, intentions, and actions.

4. The whole passage is from Luke 6:27–36 (NIV).
5. Green, *Gospel of Luke*, 266–68.
6. Green, *Gospel of Luke*, 270.
7. John 13:34–35 (NIV).
8. McEwan, *Life of God in the Soul*, 4.

In this brief paper, I want to reflect on the challenge the people of God face when relating to people who live with moderate to severe intellectual impairment. For the Christian, even the initial gift of divine love in our hearts by the Spirit does not automatically result in a hospitable embrace of every person we meet. In many Western Protestant congregations there is a tendency to link the quality of a person's faith with their ability to rationally process and understand doctrine. James Torrance explains that for the past 1500 years Western theology has been enamored with a concept of the person as a "substance possessing three faculties, reason, will, and emotion, with primacy given to reason."[9] This has resulted in many Christians believing that an individual must possess and demonstrate certain intellectual capacities to be recognized as a "person."[10]

Such an understanding is problematic for people living with intellectual impairment, as it inevitably marginalizes them. They are then relegated to a second-tier class of Christianity or, even worse, regarded as incapable of being a Christian because they cannot cognitively affirm doctrinal content.[11] For people living with this form of impairment, it is vital that personhood is no longer seen as a quality that is either awarded to, or recognized in, an individual by virtue of their capacity to think or act in certain ways. A church that fails to allow its theological doctrines to be "interrogated by disability"[12] is doomed to perpetuate the inhospitable, ostracizing, and dehumanizing approach that appears so prevalent in our society.

Human beings tend to survive and thrive better in groups than in isolation, and it requires not merely a general connection with those around you now, but a range of intimate and supportive relationships throughout life.[13] It has been pointed out that the critical element in many poor health and well-being outcomes is not simply the lack of social connection, but the quality of those connections. The flourishing of a society is closely related to the flourishing of the persons in the society and vice versa; you cannot have a healthy society if the people in it are disconnected from each other. In a recent set of interviews, conducted by my colleague Jim Good, with the parents of children living with moderate to severe intellectual impairment,

---

9. Torrance, "Doctrine of the Trinity in Our Contemporary Situation," 14. See also Grenz, *Social God and the Relational Self*.

10. See, for example, Turner, "Approaching 'Personhood' in the New Testament," 212–13.

11. For some specific examples, see Swinton, "Building a Church for Strangers"; Berg, "Give Me Please!," 181–83.

12. This is a term and an approach used by Amos Yong in his *Theology and Down Syndrome*.

13. McEwan, "Personal and Community Well-Being," 132–53.

two overwhelming desires emerged: that their child would be treated as a person, and that they would know genuine friendships, not just care and support.[14] It is this lack of meaningful friendships that makes life for them and their families so challenging. The work of governments, government agencies, charitable institutions, churches, and many private individuals does make a positive impact on the lives of those living with an impairment, as well as their families, friends, and communities.

However, almost all government and agency support take the form of education, therapies, financial help, material benefits, or the provision of paid carers and support workers. While this has significantly improved the life of the person and their families, what it cannot do, by its very nature, is to foster long-term friendships as a normative outcome.[15] If the person living with the impairment has no genuine friendships, then all the good that is done is always of limited value.[16] Forming a meaningful friendship with people is critically dependent on whether you are ever in their social space and whether you notice them as a person who would be good to know. When a child living with moderate to severe intellectual impairment never receives social invitations from people outside of their immediate family, they are immediately diminished as persons. This all suggests that we need a different model of what it means to be a person than the dominant paradigms we work with in our Western culture.[17]

From a Christian perspective, our understanding of the nature of human beings is foundationally located in God's revelation to us through the Person of Jesus Christ, Scripture, and the great tradition of the church. The definition of personhood commonly centers on the biblical claim that we are made in the "image of God." A Wesleyan theological anthropology stresses that the nature of the "image" is tied to love and relationship rather than a particular trait or function that we might possess: "love is the very image of God: it is the brightness of his glory. By love man is not only made like God, but in some sense one with him."[18] In this understanding, the essence of the "image" is found within a relationship. Furthermore, this is primarily determined by God and not by us. We are loved by God simply because it is his very nature to love, and we experience his love before we return love to him or share it with the neighbor. It is God's creative initiative that is critical

---

14. McEwan and Good, *Sustaining Hope*.

15. Many of these supporters do become genuine friends with those they serve, but in most cases, it is limited by the caseload to be managed, the length of the support package offered and the demands of their own personal and family life.

16. See Pridmore, "Christian Reformed Church as a Model," 94.

17. For a deeper exploration of this, see McEwan and Good, *Sustaining Hope*, 48–65.

18. Wesley, *Sermons*, 4:355–6. See also *Sermons*, 1:184, 581; 2:439.

to defining personhood and removes its essential nature from any substantive or functional trait we possess biologically. Just as parents expecting the birth of their child can love this new person long before there is any viability outside the womb, so God has loved us before we demonstrated any capability of returning it. This strong emphasis on love and relationships "suggests that the image of God is not something we possess, but something we experience; we are in the image of God when we are in authentic relationship with God or with one another. This does not mean the image of God may not require certain qualities to be expressed, however these qualities in and of themselves are not enough to constitute the image."[19] The relationship is grounded in God and his love, not our experience of that love or ability to express it. Because of the generosity of the divine love expressed through Christ and then through every Spirit-filled Christian, no one will ever cease to be a person because of God's involvement; "God gives all his children a significant identity by knowing them, regardless of the limitations they might bear."[20]

There is nothing automatic about establishing and maintaining relationships with those who would otherwise be overlooked and neglected. If we are to be part of the answer to the loneliness of those living with moderate to severe intellectual impairment, we are the ones who need to change and actively provide for their physical, spiritual, and relational needs. Families and people living with intellectual impairment need real friendships, not just a relationship that occurs at set times when a care program or support ministry is running. Families, with good reason, are often deeply hurt when people make little or no effort whatsoever to form a friendship with their child. Our culture tends to locate the "fault" for the lack of friendships in the person living with the impairment, rather than locate the responsibility for the development of the requisite social skills with people who are developing typically. And this is one of the key tests of the true state of our hearts—if divine love fills the heart, then this love must be shared with all, not just with those with whom we have a natural affinity. To establish and then maintain any friendship presents challenges, and we are being less than honest if we do not admit that from the beginning. Every human relationship has times of struggle, and it is not just an issue when engaging with people who live with moderate to severe physical or intellectual impairment.

It is important to remember that sometimes people met with Jesus where he was, but at other times he intentionally sought them out and entered their space because it was unlikely that they would take the initiative to

19. Herzfeld, "*Imago Dei/Imago Hominis*," 48.
20. Rosner, *Known by God,* 258.

ask him. In Luke 19:1–10, Jesus "invites" himself to the house of Zacchaeus because he knew it was improbable that a Roman tax-collector would invite him in for a meal. Many of the parables that Jesus told, and relationships he initiated, demonstrate that God is a seeking God, who intentionally reaches out to those who are excluded from public areas or private homes because of illness, social status, occupation, gender, or nationality. The whole point of the Incarnation was God coming to be with people where they were and as they were. God "goes to" because he longs to "be with." God comes to us because he loves and values us, desires to be with us, and longs to provide for us. All Christians are called, enabled, and empowered by the Spirit to be this same kind of friend, following God's example. Becoming involved in the lives of people that we would not naturally connect with is not likely to survive the initial encounter unless there is a degree of intentionality involved. Likewise, maintaining the relationship in the face of the inevitable difficulties that will arise takes a firm commitment because it is very easy to walk away when it becomes more than we are initially prepared to handle.

Wesley was very conscious of this type of difficulty and admitted "Indeed it is hard for any to persevere in so unpleasing a work unless [God's] *love* overpowers both pain and fear."[21] He understood that sometimes you simply must do something because it is the right thing to do before it becomes a pleasure for its own sake. This is where his understanding of the command of Jesus to take up our cross (Matt 10:38; 16:24; Mark 8:34; Luke 9:23) is very helpful. We see a practical illustration of this in Wesley's correspondence with Miss J. C. March, who was a wealthy, educated lady of high social status.[22] She wrote to Wesley to obtain his advice on how to develop her spiritual life so that she would know the fullness of God's love in her heart. Like all Methodists, Miss March was expected to be involved in visiting the poor and sick in her local community. Given her status and lifestyle, the poor were not a part of her regular social circle, nor would she naturally seek to build a friendship with them. She was quite happy to give money to support a ministry amongst the poor, but she did not want personal involvement. Wesley was clear that she would never make real progress in her Christian life, nor would her witness be authentic, without forming real relationships with the poor and sick in their hovels, no matter how distasteful it was to her personally. He encourages her to put off the gentlewoman and "Take up your cross" and follow the example of Jesus.[23]

---

21. Wesley, *Sermons*, 2:314.
22. For a fuller account, see McEwan, *Life of God in the Soul*, 141–52.
23. Wesley, *Letters* (Telford), 6:153.

Being a friend is not a "ministry" that we can take up and then put down or pay someone else to do in our stead. The wisdom Wesley offered in his day is no less pertinent now, and it is applicable to relationships in the family, workplace, and social settings. It is very easy to say you love someone in the abstract but the real test happens when you meet face-to-face, forcing us to deal with our prejudices and dislikes.[24] As Wesley pointed out to Miss March, you cannot fully love another from a distance; the incarnation of Christ is the most profound evidence for that. If we are to get beyond our discomfort, it requires a personal decision to seek out, begin, and maintain the friendship.

In healthy friendships it is normal for people to visit each other's homes, or to meet at a venue that one of them may particularly like. For those living with impairment, questions of accessibility or suitability regularly arise because they cannot always cope with a particular location or environment, and this is a constant challenge. They need the type of friend who intentionally looks to build a bond and is willing to go to the safe spaces favored by the one living with the impairment. This is one of the most significant gifts that can be offered to a person and their family. It is not only the willingness to visit regularly, but it is also the readiness to consistently adjust their own plans to meet the needs of the other. Strong and meaningful friendships in these circumstances can take many years to develop and that is why genuine friendships with parents/carers/families can only really be achieved when we have a long-term commitment.

In the end, each friendship needs to move from interacting with the family because you feel like you must (ministry) to interacting with the family because you want to (friendship).[25] When this happens, a community is formed where everyone is both a giver and a receiver, where people are accepted for who they are, and where people are recognized for their intrinsic value and worth simply by virtue of their very existence. Once this relationship with the family ceases to be a "ministry" and begins instead to emerge out of love and desire, then at that point you become a true friend—one who relates in ways that are individualized, deeply meaningful and genuinely helpful. A family that has been impacted by impairment needs more community rather than less and that is why it is vital that the family be given the opportunity to be welcomed into a larger network of friendships. This will also take being intentional and looking for specific ways to enlarge the circle of friendships.

24. McEwan, *Life of God in the Soul*, 160–61.
25. For more specific steps in forming strong friendships with those living with moderate to severe intellectual impairment, see McEwan and Good, *Sustaining Hope*, 103–27.

It is important for us as Christians that we live out of the reality of God's vast love for his whole creation and every single person within it. Scripture affirms that God only has one friendship circle, and that encompasses every single one of us. This is demonstrated supremely in the life and ministry of Jesus, and we are called and equipped by his Spirit to live that out in our daily life. It is only too easy to stay within the friendship circles drawn naturally by our church fellowships, programs, and ministries. In John 10:1–18, Jesus creates an extended metaphor about the good shepherd, the sheep, and the sheep pen. In a way, we can see how natural it is for Christians to remain within the home sheep pen (local church fellowship) where things are safe and secure. It is Jesus's own depth of love that led him to seek out those in other sheep pens and invite them into the one great community of God. If we are truly "to love and serve the Lord," then we cannot be any less committed to building bridges of genuine friendship with those that our society marginalizes and overlooks so frequently.

WORKS CITED

Berg, Bob. "Give Me Please!" *Journal of Religion, Disability and Health* 13 (2009) 181–83.

Green, Joel B. *The Gospel of Luke*. Grand Rapids: Eerdmans, 1997.

Grenz, Stanley. *The Social God and the Relational Self: A Trinitarian Theology of the Imago Dei*. Louisville, KY: Westminster John Knox, 1998.

Herzfeld, Noreen LuAnn. "*Imago Dei/Imago Hominis*: Interacting Images of God and Humanity in Theology and in Artificial Intelligence." PhD diss., Graduate Theological Union, Berkeley, CA, 1999.

Lennon, John, and Paul McCartney. "All You Need Is Love." London: Olympic Sound and EMI, 1967.

McEwan, David B. *The Life of God in the Soul: The Integration of Love, Holiness and Happiness in the Thought of John Wesley*. Milton Keynes, UK: Paternoster, 2015.

———. "Personal and Community Well-Being: A Wesleyan Theological Framework for Overcoming Prejudice." In *Wellbeing, Personal Wholeness and the Social Fabric: An Interdisciplinary Approach*, edited by Doru Costache et al., 132–53. Newcastle: Cambridge Scholars, 2017.

Mackay, Hugh. *The Kindness Revolution: How We Can Restore Hope, Rebuild Trust and Inspire Optimism*. Allen & Unwin. Kindle Edition.

Pridmore, Eric. "The Christian Reformed Church as a Model for the Inclusion of People with Disabilities." *Journal of Religion, Disability and Health* 10 (2006) 93–107.

Rosner, Brian S. *Known by God: A Biblical Theology of Personal Identity*. Grand Rapids: Zondervan, 2017.

Swinton, John. *Building a Church for Strangers*. Edinburgh: Contact Pastoral Trust, 1999.

Torrance, James. "The Doctrine of the Trinity in Our Contemporary Situation." In *The Forgotten Trinity: A Selection of Papers Presented to the BCC Study Commission on*

Trinitarian Doctrine Today, edited by Alasdair I. C. Heron, 3–17. London: BCC/CCBI Inter-Church House, 1991.

Turner, Max. "Approaching 'Personhood' in the New Testament, with Special Reference to Ephesians." *Evangelical Quarterly* 77 (2005) 212–13.

Wesley, John. *Sermons*. 4 vols. Edited by Albert C. Outler. Nashville: Abingdon, 1984–1987.

———. *The Letters of the Rev. John Wesley*. 8 vols. Edited by John Telford. London: Epworth, 1931.

Yong, Amos. *Theology and Down Syndrome: Reimagining Disability in Late Modernity*. Waco, TX: Baylor University Press, 2007.

Embracing the Ongoing Challenges of Intersectional Identities and Identifying

A Re-reading of Acts 16:16–18

MiJa Wi

INTRODUCTION

"What do you think happens to the slave woman in Philippi in Acts 16?" To this out-of-nowhere question, Dr. Kent Brower said to me something like: "I've never thought about her much, to be honest. But I think I will, from now on." Since then, we have had many stimulating conversations about her, the unnamed female slave in Acts 16:16–18, other biblical characters like her, her place at the church, and the holy people of God. He has always been gracious to my challenging, at times confronting, questions over a wide range of issues, particularly issues around ethnicity, gender, and class. His listening ears have encouraged me to speak up with my voice even when I feel intimidated by my own ethnic and gender minority presence among others. Hence, this essay which rereads Acts 16:16–18 in light of the intersectional identities of the female slave is dedicated to Dr. Kent Brower with whom I shared numerous conversations about her and about what it means to be a holy people of God with her in our midst.

The unnamed female slave in Acts 16:16–18 is a radical outsider and a multiply marginalized figure in terms of her status, gender, and religion. Despite many epithets due to her complex intersectional identities of being a slave woman, having a spirit of Python, and generating great profit by fortune-telling, this enslaved woman remains nameless. Rather, "the spirit is named," Python.¹ She is owned and exploited by her masters for their business. Functionally, she serves as a medium of fortune-telling and of profit-making.² Narratively, she serves as a bridge to connect the two household conversion accounts in Philippi, that of Lydia and of the jailor.³ Theologically, she serves as a figure to highlight Paul as a successful exorcist alongside Jesus and Peter.⁴ She disappears when the spirit is gone and the hope of the profit-making is gone (Acts 16:18–19).⁵

Ironically, she is perhaps the only female slave, for that matter, the only woman, who prophesies,⁶ albeit with a spirit of Python, in the Book of Acts. Regardless of the content and the nature of her message which need further discussion, her abrupt disappearance is unsettling. The text offers no further explanation, but remains silent. Indeed, she is not the only person who disappears after being healed or exorcized in Luke-Acts.⁷ Nevertheless, the silence speaks loudly in this particular case due to her complex intersectional realities—an enslaved woman exploited by multiple owners for business purposes. What happens to the female slave makes us ask whether Paul and his companions' call to proclaim the good news (Acts 16:10) takes her into account?

On the one hand, Ivoni Richter Reimer has already offered a positive resolution to this challenge, based on "a historical possibility,"⁸ suggesting the female slave's acceptance into, and manumission by, Lydia's community.⁹ This would be the most welcomed ending of her story. On the other hand, I wonder whether the disturbing silence of the text on her fate should remain unresolved so that it might continue to challenge the readers to hear the marginalized, minoritized, and silenced voices. Hence the primary aim of this paper is not on finding answers from the text, but on encountering upsetting challenges both in the text and in present reality.¹⁰

For this purpose, I will first discuss an alternative way of reading the text, using intersectionality as "a hermeneutical prism" to highlight the

---

1. Seim, *Double Message*, 172.
2. Smith, *Literary Construction*, 44.
3. Parsons, *Acts*, 227; Smith, *Literary Construction*, 39.
4. Gaventa, *Acts*, 238. See also Klutz, *Exorcism*, 13.
5. Note the use of *exerchomai* (gone) in Acts 16:18, 19. Pervo, *Acts*, 406; Tannehill, *Narrative Unity*, 198; Johnson, *Acts*, 295.
6. Keener, *Acts*, 2422; Klutz, *Exorcism*, 217.
7. See Luke 7:1–10; 14:1–6; Acts 3:1–10.
8. Reimer, *Women*, 180.
9. Reimer, *Women*, 180–83.
10. Kartzow, *Destabilizing*, 5.

intersectional identities of the female slave.[11] Next, I will examine her intersectional realities within three domains of power, namely the structural, interpersonal, and spiritual. Finally, I will revisit the challenge: What happens to the female slave who encounters Paul and his companions on the way to a place of prayer, persistently reminding them of God's call to proclaim the good news?

INTERSECTIONAL REALITIES OF IDENTITY AND IDENTIFYING

"With whom can I identify in scripture? Which characters does the narrator cast as 'others'"?[12] These questions, posed by Lai Ling Elizabeth Ngan in her reading of Hagar, have led me to the unnamed female slave in Acts 16. While there is hardly any distinguishable connection between a first century female slave, fortune-telling in Philippi, and a twenty first century East Asian female immigrant, teaching the NT in the UK, this woman is the one with whom I identify as I read Acts 16, not Paul or Silas or Lydia or the jailor. I am not trying to draw any direct parallels between this woman and myself as many minority readings have successfully done. What I am trying to do, instead, by making my own identities visible as a reader of this particular text is to acknowledge that I am an "alive, active, and interested" reader, not a "neutral and disinterested one"[13] and to note how a different reader brings a different reading as she may see or hear different things from the text and may be interested in or even identify herself with a different character in the text.[14]

My own complex identities, though not directly linked to the slave woman in Philippi, interact with the text as a reader. In this regard, Yee's point is helpful here.

> As a method of interpretation, intersectionality presumes that our own unique social locations, our own distinctive fusions of gender, race, class, et cetera, influence our readings of texts and our interpretations of them. It encourages us to think beyond familiar boundaries of biblical studies to expose the diverse power relations of inequality in the text and uncover subjugated voices that were previously invisible or unheard.[15]

11. Yee, "Thinking Intersectionally," 8.
12. Ngan, "Boundary and Identity," 71.
13. Dube, "Current Issues," 45.
14. Liew, "Colorful Readings," 178.
15. Yee, "Thinking Intersectionally," 7.

Intersectionality was originally coined by Kimberlé Crenshaw in 1989 to show how intersectional identities, particularly of race and gender, collide and compound discriminations against multiply marginalized or minoritized people.[16] It requires an "intersectional way of thinking" about the issues of marginalization and their relation to power.[17] With its fitting recognition in race and gender studies,[18] it has been used as an interpretive framework to explore gender, race, and class issues in early Christian studies particularly among feminists and scholars of color.[19] For instance, Kartzow has employed "intersectionality" and "memory theory" to bring the marginalized figures in early Christian texts to the fore to challenge historical constructions of identity and thereby power relations.[20] Similarly, Yee has applied "intersectionality" in exploring widows of ancient Israel in 2 Kgs 4:1–7 particularly within "interpersonal" and "structural domains of power."[21]

The female slave in Philippi indeed lives in intersectional realities within diverse dynamics of power. But what do we do with the text where little is being said? After all, she is a marginal figure both in social-historical and literary contexts. Here my reading is in line with those who intentionally highlight silenced voices and the margin over the center.[22] For instance, Charles and Cobb focus on enslaved bodies, silenced voices, and the invisible. Their intentional reading strategies of "reading against the grain" and hearing other voices reveal not only the buried truth in the text, but also the underlying power relations.[23] When the texts are read from perspectives of the marginalized and the minoritized, it allows the reader to hear silenced voices and to see the invisible.

INTERSECTIONAL REALITIES WITHIN DYNAMICS OF POWER: A RE-READING OF ACTS 16:16–18

The complex intersectional identities of gender, class, religion, et cetera are crucial to hear the voice of the female slave in the text. But more critical is how the intersection of multiple identities implicates within power

---

16. Crenshaw, "Demarginalizing," 139–67.
17. Cho, Crenshaw, and McCall, "Intersectionality Studies," 795.
18. Nash, "Re-thinking Intersectionality," 3.
19. See Nasrallah and Fiorenza, *Prejudice and Christian Beginnings*; Yee, *Hebrew Bible*; Kartzow, *Destabilizing*.
20. Kartzow, *Destabilizing*, 21–23 (22).
21. Yee, "Thinking Intersectionally," 16–25.
22. Cobb, *Slavery*, 1–35, 163–203; Charles, *Silencing*, 1–25, 132–65.
23. Charles, *Silencing*, 1; Cobb, *Slavery*, 4–5.

relations,[24] both in social-historical contexts and in the narrative. In this re-reading of Acts 16:16–18, I will frame the discussion 1) by positioning the female slave as presented in Acts 16:16 which locates her multiple identities within structural domains of power; 2) by following and hearing her and her words as she encounters "Paul and us" in Acts 16:17–18a within interpersonal domains of power; 3) by asking which spirit is active within spiritual domains of power in the exorcism account in Acts 16:18b. This alternative reading of the text will shed light on challenges and dilemmas of the female slave, impacted by multiple forces, and of the reader who hears her afresh.

Her Intersectional Identities within Structural Domains of Power (Acts 16:16)

What does it mean to be a female slave in first century Philippi? While the presence of slaves is ubiquitous in the Roman Empire, hearing their voices is a huge challenge. They are spoken of, written about, and acted upon in almost all the sources available.[25] The conditions and possibilities of life in slavery are diverse, ranging from highly esteemed and freed slaves with privileges to those who lived and died as chattels.[26] Despite the complexity in understanding ancient slavery, Glancy notes that slaves are first and foremost defined as "bodies" in "corporeal terms" since they are considered as properties, not as "persons."[27] Hence slaves can be inherited, sold, rented, offered as a gift or shared by multiple owners.[28] Their productivity, either by physical labor or by childbearing, matters to masters while their enslaved realities incorporate physical vulnerability to any forms of abuse, torture, and sexual advances by masters.[29] They are enslaved, profitable, saleable, (sexually) available bodies to their masters.

The term, *paidiskē*, may refer to a young girl, a female slave of any age,[30] or a prostitute.[31] Perhaps the female slave in Philippi may have had a similar route to Abaskantis, a ten-year-old slave girl, sold at the marketplace

---

24. Crenshaw, "Mapping the Margins," 93–94.
25. Bradley, *Slavery*, 7; Glancy, *Slavery*, 4–7.
26. See Bradley, *Slavery*, 1–4.
27. Glancy, *Slavery*, 7, 38.
28. Glancy, *Slavery*, 9–12.
29. Glancy, *Slavery*, 10–12; Knapp, *Invisible*, 133–38, 161–63.
30. Cobb, *Slavery*, 1, 8.
31. Flemming, "Sexual Economy," 40–42; Glancy, *Slavery*, 27–28.

in Asia Minor far away from her home in 142 CE.[32] It is also possible for the female slave to work as a prostitute.[33] Unlike other female slaves in Luke-Acts, she is found on the street, economically exploited for profit.[34] In any case, her relationship with her masters should not be so different from that of slave prostitutes with their masters in terms of how most, if not all, of the earnings are channeled to the masters.[35] In sum, "though the labour is hers the profits are not."[36] Her state as an enslaved female body, owned and exploited by multiple masters for business, entails that she is "bound by socio-economic forces" both of her masters and of the society which institutionalizes slavery.[37] She is a subordinate body within social-economic structural domains of power.

Nonetheless, the fact that she has a special gift of fortune-telling makes her a valuable asset to her masters since this gift generates great profit for them.[38] Although not all slaves were involved in profit-making works—for example, those maintained as domestic slaves—it is attested that slaves who benefit their masters financially may enjoy some privileges.[39] Perhaps this is where she subverts structural dynamics of power which subordinate her in every aspect. While the content and nature of her fortune-telling by a spirit of Python will be explored later, what is intriguing here is a discrepancy between the favor of her fortune-telling in relation to profits and the disfavor of any relations with spirit and money in Acts where the narrative makes it clear that spirit and profits are incompatible.[40] Hence her gift of fortune-telling is an ambiguous factor which may subvert her status within structural domains of power, but subordinates her within the narrative. Her intersectional identities of gender and status place her at the margins within social-economic dynamics of power relations.

32. Bradley, *Slavery*, 2.

33. Barrett, *Acts 15–28*, 784; Keener, *Acts: 3*, 2465–66. Despite their caution, both Barrett and Keener do not eliminate the possibility.

34. See McGinn, *Prostitution*, 292–96.

35. Knapp, *Invisible*, 259–60.

36. Flemming, "Sexual Economy," 42.

37. Charles, *Silencing*, 147.

38. Reimer, *Women*, 153–54.

39. Bradley, *Slavery*, 34–35; Reimer, *Women*, 165; Valentine, "Reading," 365.

40. See Acts 5:1–11; 8:18–24; 19:11–20.

Her Encounter with "Paul and Us" within Interpersonal Domains of Power (Acts 16:17–18a)

What are her relations to those whom she meets on the street, particularly "Paul and us"? Paul and Silas, though immigrants, are free males, Roman citizens, and undoubtedly central figures in Acts 16. What is striking, however, is that she is the one who takes active roles and speaks while the two free males remain passive.[41] She finds them in her proximity, identifying them as slaves and as proclaimers. In her interaction with Paul and his companions, she meets and follows them, cries out, and speaks about them, not only in their hearing but also in the hearing of the passers-by. She does so for many days. Her action is visible and her voice is loud. Even the content of her speech, which reveals the identity and mission of Paul and his companions, seems to be on the mark.

But her every action and word has been under scrutiny by scholars. This is not surprising in that she subverts interpersonal domains of power by acting justifiably and speaking truth. First, it has been noted that the two verbs, "meeting" and "crying out," which depict her action and voice are frequently used in the context of exorcism.[42] She stands with the demon-possessed.[43] However, "crying out" is as frequently, if not more, used by those who ask for Jesus's mercy as by the demonic voices in the Gospels and is used for the voices of the apostles, including Paul in Acts.[44] Hence it appears unnecessary to make her demon-possessed, as nowhere in the text suggests so.

Second, it has been argued that the problem lies not so much with the messenger but the message, which is taken at best as "ambiguous."[45] Kauppi is certain that the female slave speaks by a non-demonic prophesying spirit. But it is the ambiguity of Greek oracles in general, and that of the Most High God, in a polytheistic setting in particular, which contrasts with

---

41. Smith, *Literary Construction*, 45. See also Klutz, *Exorcism*, 219–20.

42. Reimer, *Women*, 157–59; Keener, *Acts*, 3:2426; Pervo, *Acts*, 405. Both verbs are used in the Synoptic accounts of the Gerasene demoniac except that Luke uses "speaking" (*légō*) instead of "crying out" (Matt 8:28, 29; Mark 5:2, 5, 7; Luke 8:27, cf. 8:28).

43. Twelftree, *Name*, 146; Barrett, *Acts 15–28*, 786; Klutz, *Exorcism*, 245–46.

44. Note "crying out" in the context of asking mercy in Matt 9:27; 14:30; 15:22; 20:30; Mark 9:24; 10:47; Luke 18:39 and "crying out" by demonic voices in Matt 8:29; Mark 3:11; 5:5, 7; 9:26; Luke 9:39. Note also Acts 7:60 (Stephen); 14:14 (Paul and Barnabas); 19:28, 32, 34 (the crowd in Ephesus); 21:28 (the Jews); 21:36; 23:6 (Paul). See Cobb, *Slavery*, 188–89.

45. Kauppi, *Foreign*, 33.

the unambiguity of Paul's message.⁴⁶ Trebilco avers that the identity of the Most High God, used in a gentile setting, is "misleading" and "confusing."⁴⁷ Thus, her message is false and syncretic.⁴⁸ But the Jewish backgrounds of this term, the Most High God, are strongly evidenced in the LXX and Luke-Acts.⁴⁹ Both Levinskaya and Reimer demonstrate its prevailing uses in Jewish epigraphic and literary contexts.⁵⁰ Furthermore, this is Luke's favored expression, occurring exclusively in Luke-Acts in the New Testament, two of which (Luke 8:28; Acts 16:17) are spoken in gentile settings.⁵¹ For the latter, the awareness of Paul and Silas's Jewishness by her owners (later with the crowd) suggests that the passers-by in Philippi may have understood "the Most High God" as a Jewish God (Acts 16:20).

The absence of a definite article in "(a) way of salvation" has troubled some scholars, noting that the anarthrous use of way (*hodos*) is "exceptional" and this opens possibilities of one among many paths to salvation.⁵² Hence her message leads to "a syncretistic misunderstanding."⁵³ However, Luke uses "way" both with an article and without. Perhaps more importantly, it is often used in plural with or without an article.⁵⁴ Luke seems more fluid in his use of a way of salvation, meaning both "religious/ethical sense" and the way to achieve salvation.⁵⁵ It is rather questionable to what extent the interpreters impose on her to speak their own orthodox Christian message.

Finally, her persistent actions, noting the use of imperfect verbs, "crying out" and "doing," are taken as a "nuisance" which eventually arouses Paul's "righteous indignation."⁵⁶ Hence what is problematic is her "incessant" annoying activity of speaking and acting.⁵⁷ One may wonder here whether her voices and actions are unduly suppressed. In fact, the narrative lets her take active roles in her interactions with Paul and his companions.

46. Kauppi, *Foreign*, 32–39 (36).

47. Trebilco, "Paul and Silas," 59–64 (95).

48. Trebilco, "Paul and Silas," 62; Klauck, *Magic*, 68.

49. Note that all occurrences of the Most High in the LXX clearly refer to the Jewish God except in Num 24:16.

50. Levinskaya, *Diaspora Setting*, 98–100; Reimer, *Women*, 161–65. See also Spencer, "Out of Mind," 148.

51. Luke 1:32, 35, 76; 6:35; 8:28; Acts 7:38; 16:17.

52. Twelftree, *Name*, 147. Also see Trebilco, "Paul and Silas," 64–65; Klauck, *Magic*, 68.

53. Klauck, *Magic*, 68.

54. See Luke's anarthrous use of way: Luke 1:76, 79; Acts 2:28 and ways in plural: Luke 1:76; Acts 2:28; 13:10.

55. Barrett, *Acts 15–28*, 787.

56. Klutz, *Exorcism*, 222.

57. Parsons, *Acts*, 231.

She may find them in close proximity in terms of their relationship to the gods and to their social location as they encounter her on the outskirts in Philippi.[58] More importantly, the following account proves her words to be true, that Paul and Silas are "slaves of the Most High God" and proclaiming a way of salvation, although she is not benefited by it (Acts 16:19–34).[59] But her subversion of the interpersonal dynamics of power relations are short-lived and soon to be overturned within spiritual domains of power.

Which Spirit is Active within Spiritual Domains of Power (Acts 16:18b)

Unmistakably, the Book of Acts in general and Acts 16 in particular invite the readers to a world full of spirits. Paul and his companions' journey is forbidden by the Holy Spirit and by the Spirit of Jesus (Acts 16:6, 7). The vision leads them to Philippi and they are met by a slave woman with a spirit of Python (Acts 16:9–10, 16). Paul speaks to the spirit in the name of Jesus Christ. In one level, the encounter is between a spirit, functioning in Philippi, and the Holy Spirit, directing Paul and his companions. While boundaries between spirits remain vague in antiquity, the distinction between the Holy Spirit and other spirits is made by their association with financial gains particularly in Acts.[60] Then, how does the female slave with a spirit of Python function within spiritual domains of power?

First, what is a spirit of Python which enables her to speak oracles? It has been widely noted that this spirit relates to the oracles in Delphi due to its specific reference to Python which, the legend says, was killed by Apollo.[61] The Delphic oracles, delivered by the Pythia, are well known both in the Roman World[62] and to Diaspora Jews living there. Keener remarks: "Educated Diaspora Jews would have had no trouble understanding Luke's association; they were also aware of Apollo's association with prophecy and his oracle in Delphi."[63] Thus, the female slave with a spirit of Python may have her religious allegiance to Apollo.[64] Her prophetic activity in relation to a spirit of Python seems to strengthen the case (Acts 16:16). Although the negative connotation of "fortune-telling" is clear in the LXX in contrast to

58. Charles, *Silencing*, 146.
59. Cobb, *Slavery*, 202–3.
60. Seim, *Double Message*, 173–74.
61. Keener, *Acts*, 2422–28.
62. Cobb, *Slavery*, 180–81.
63. Keener, *Acts*, 2423.
64. Matthews, "Elite Women," 129.

"prophesying,"⁶⁵ the distinction is not so clear in the context of the Delphic oracles. Maurizo notes that both Apollo and the Pythia are called "*mantis* and *prophetes*" despite their etymological differences.⁶⁶ She may be a "Pythia" who issues oracles of Apollo⁶⁷ or may be one among many who utter oracles and offer fortune-telling.⁶⁸

Second, how, then, does one make sense of Paul's exorcism in this particular account? The text simply notes Paul's word to the spirit: Paul, being annoyed,⁶⁹ commands the spirit to come out of her in the name of Jesus. It does so that very hour (Acts 16:18b). In one level, the narrative makes it crystal clear that it is the Holy Spirit who takes the highest authority over all other spirits.⁷⁰ In the name of Jesus, a lesser spirit, a spirit of Python, should be subordinated and silenced. So is the female slave. Smith's remark is telling here: "It is Paul's evaluative words combined with the successful exorcism that discursively and theologically seal her fate as subordinated, triply marginalized other."⁷¹

On the other level, the questions are raised from two different directions: 1) The necessity of exorcism from her perspective; 2) The motive of Paul's exorcism from his perspective. Those who are sympathetic to her gift of prophecy wonder whether she is deprived of her very gift due to Paul's exorcism, caused by his annoyance.⁷² Others defend Paul's exorcism as necessary not only to demonstrate the power of the Holy Spirit but also to liberate her from the spirit and to challenge the exploitative system, working under this spirit.⁷³ No matter which question one may raise here, the disturbing issue remains: So, what happens to her after all?

CONCLUSION

Scholars, in line with Reimer, posit the possibility of her incorporation into the early Christian community in Philippi, as noted already.⁷⁴ This offers

65. Keener, *Acts*, 2422; Klutz, *Exorcism*, 217.
66. Maurizo, "Pythia's Role," 70.
67. Reimer, *Women*, 156.
68. Kauppi, *Foreign*, 32–33.
69. Cf. Acts 4:2
70. Matthews, "Elite Women," 129.
71. Smith, *Literary Construction*, 46.
72. Charles, *Silencing*, 142; Kartzow, *Destabilising*, 131.
73. Klutz, *Exorcism*, 222; Twelftree, *Name*, 147–48; Klauck, *Magic*, 69.
74. Reimer, *Women*, 180–84; Klutz, *Exorcism*, 247–51; Keener, *Acts*, 2465–67; Klauck, *Magic*, 72–73.

a resolution to the unsettling silence of the text. Instead, my intentional choice of reading is to embrace this disturbing silence so that it may continue to challenge and raise further questions for the readers. Let us hear the disturbing silence on her fate. She is not helped or included in the Macedonian man's "us" as he pleads with Paul: Come over to Macedonia and help "us" (Acts 16:9). Her persistent following and crying out seem to end in vain. She benefited neither from the missionaries nor their mission, namely proclaiming the good news to "them" (Acts 16:10). Thus, she is not included in "them" to whom good news is proclaimed although she most explicitly demonstrates her recognition of their identity and call to preach good news. She still stands in a liminal place, not belonging to "us" or "them," just as her intersectional identities disqualify her from all her possible pairings.

She exists as a challenge for those who identify with her and speaks as a reminder of "our" failure in living out our identity and call. Hence, I see "complexity in identifying" in the text, observing that the "complexity and fluidity" of my intersectional identities play out in locations of the margins and of the center and of the oppressed and of the oppressor.[75]

WORKS CITED

Bradley, Keith. *Slavery and Society at Rome.* Cambridge: Cambridge University Press, 1994.

Barrett, C. K. *Acts 15–28.* International Critical Commentary. London: T. & T. Clark, 1998.

Charles, Ronald. *The Silencing of Slaves in Early Jewish and Christian Texts.* London: Routledge, 2020.

Cho, Sumi, et al. "Toward a Field of Intersectionality Studies: Theory, Applications, and Praxis." *Intersectionality: Theorizing Power, Empowering Theory* 38 (2013) 785–810.

Cobb, Christy. *Slavery, Gender, Truth, and Power in Luke-Acts and Other Ancient Narratives.* Cham, Switzerland: Palgrave MacMillan, 2019.

Crenshaw, Kimberlé. "Demarginalizing the Intersection of Race and Sex: A Black Feminist Critique of Antidiscrimination Doctrine, Feminist Theory and Antiracist Politics." *University of Chicago Legal Forum* 1 (1989) 139–67.

———. "Mapping the Margins: Intersectionality, Identity Politics, and Violence Against Women of Color." In *The Public Nature of Private Violence,* edited by Martha Albertson Fineman and Rixanne Mykitiuk, 93–118. New York: Routledge, 1994.

Dube, Musa W. "Current Issues in Biblical Interpretation." In *Theological Education in Contemporary Africa,* edited by Grant LeMarquand and Joseph Galgalo, 39–62. Eldoret, Kenya: Zapf Chancery, 2004.

Flemming, Rebecca. "Quae Corpore Quaestum Facit: The Sexual Economy of Female Prostitution in the Roman Empire." *Journal of Roman Studies* 89 (1999) 38–61.

---

75. Dube, "Current Issues," 44.

Gaventa, Beverly R. *The Acts of the Apostles*. Abingdon New Testament Commentary. Nashville: Abingdon, 2003.
Glancy, Jennifer. *Slavery in Early Christianity*. Oxford: Oxford University Press, 2002.
Johnson, Luke T. *The Acts of the Apostles*. Sacra Pagina. Collegeville, MN: Liturgical, 1992.
Kartzow, Marianne Bjelland. *Destabilizing the Margins: An Intersectional Approach to Early Christian Memory*. Eugene, OR: Pickwick, 2012.
Kauppi, Lynn Allan. *Foreign But Familiar Gods: Greco-Romans Read Religion in Acts*. London: T. &. T. Clark, 2006.
Keener, Craig S. *Acts: An Exegetical Commentary*. Grand Rapids: Baker, 2014.
Klauck, Hans-Josef. *Magic and Paganism in Early Christianity: The World of the Acts of the Apostles*. Edinburgh: T. & T. Clark, 2000.
Klutz, Todd. *The Exorcism Stories in Luke-Acts: A Sociostylistic Reading*. Cambridge: Cambridge University, 2004.
Levinskaya, Irina. *The Book of Acts in its First Century Setting. Volume 5: Diaspora Setting*. Grand Rapids: Eerdmans, 1996.
Liew, Tat-siong Benny. "Colorful Readings Racial/Ethnic Minority Readings of the New Testament in the United States." In *Soundings in Cultural Criticism: Perspectives and Methods in Culture, Power and Identity in the New Testament*, edited by Francisco Lozada and Greg Carey, 177–90. Minneapolis: Fortress, 2013.
Matthews, Shelly. "Elite Women, Public Religion, and Christian Propaganda in Acts 16." In *A Feminist Companion to the Acts of the Apostles*, edited by Jill Levine, 111–33. London: T. & T. Clark, 2004.
Maurizo, L. "Anthropology and Spirit Possession: A Reconsideration of the Pythia's Role at Delphi." *Journal of Hellenic Studies* 115 (1995) 69–86.
McGinn, Thomas A. J. *Prostitution, Sexuality, and the Law in Ancient Rome*. Oxford: Oxford University, 2003.
Nash, Jennifer C. "Re-thinking Intersectionality." *Feminist Review* 89 (2008) 1–15.
Ngan, Lai Ling Elizabeth. "Neither Here nor There: Boundary and Identity in the Hagar Story." In *Ways of Being, Ways of Reading: Asian-American Biblical Interpretation*, edited by Mary F. Foskett and Jeffrey K. Kuan, 70–83. St. Louis: Chalice, 2006.
Parsons, Mikeal C. *Acts*. Paideia. Grand Rapids: Baker, 2008.
Pervo, Richard. *Acts: A Commentary*. Hermeneia. Minneapolis: Fortress, 2009.
Reimer, Ivoni Ritchter. *Women in the Acts of the Apostles: A Feminist Liberation Perspective*. Minneapolis: Fortress, 1995.
Seim, Turid Karlsen. *The Double Message: Patterns of Gender in Luke-Acts*. London: T. &. T. Clark, 2004.
Smith, Mitzi. *The Literary Construction of the Other in the Acts of the Apostles: Charismatic, the Jews, and Women*. Eugene, OR: Pickwick, 2011.
Spencer, F. Scott. "Out of Mind, Out of Voice: Slave-Girls and Prophetic Daughters in Luke-Acts." *BibInt* 7 (1999) 133–55.
Tannehill, Robert. *The Narrative Unity of Luke-Acts: A Literary Interpretation*. Volume 2. Minneapolis: Fortress, 1986.
Trebilco, Paul R. "Paul and Silas—'Servants of the Most High God' (Acts 16.16–18)." *Journal for the Study of the New Testament* 36 (1989) 51–73.
Twelftree, Graham H. *In the Name of Jesus: Exorcisms among Early Christians*. Grand Rapids: Baker, 2007.

Valentaine, Katy E. "Reading the Slave Girl of Acts 16:16–18 in Light of Enslavement and Disability." *BibInt* 26 (2018) 352–68.

Yee, Gale A. *The Hebrew Bible: Feminist and Intersectional Perspectives*. Minneapolis: Fortress, 2018.

———. "Thinking Intersectionally: Gender, Race, Class, and the Etceteras of Our Discipline." *Journal of Biblical Literature* 139 (2020) 7–26.

Wisdom for Marginalization (Acts 6:1–7)

Ezekiel Shibemba

INTRODUCTION

Recent trends and events reported by conventional and social media have highlighted marginalization and justice in public life. The growing influence of Critical Race Theory (CRT), especially in America, with both positive and negative Christian responses, is one.[1] The other is the persistent death of black men and women at police hands.[2] The subsequent anti-racism protests that swept the globe were perhaps evidence of a shocked society awakened by the realization racism may be alive and well in the twenty-first century. The COVID-19 pandemic is another news item which, according to the UN, revealed the extent of marginalization. This was observed in the inordinate impact of the virus on poorer societies and countries. More recently, the invasion of Ukraine by Russia has raised questions regarding international justice and national sovereignty. The relevance of biblical studies is that while seeking to understand how the text was understood by early readers, the Bible speaks to modern readers too. What then might be the relevance of Acts 6:1–7 to today's questions?

Acts 6:1–7 has been studied for a variety of subjects. Scholars often discuss the text's possible insight into early ecclesiastical organization and leadership.[3] Typically, questions asked surround whether Luke's use of the word deacon (*diakoneō*) established the office of deacons. A second is the

---

1. BNC News, "Debate Over Critical Race Theory."
2. BBC News, "George Floyd."
3. Malina and Pilch, *Acts*, 106; Lüdemann, *Acts*, 93; Pelikan, *Acts*, 91–96.

distinction between Hellenistic and Hebraic widows.[4] Did Luke include only linguistic differences, or were ideological distinctions in view? Did the Hellenists hold a "liberal view" of being Jewish while the Hebraic a conservative one,[5] since the Greeks spread both language and culture?[6]

Another subject discussed is the perceived abruptness of the narrative.[7] In contrast to Luke's earlier portrait of the early church as benevolent and altruistic, it seems surprising to find grumbling (*gongusmos*) in the community.[8] Furthermore, but to a lesser extent, some scholars have associated the text with discrimination in the early church.[9] Thus, although some attention is given to the text's concern for inequality, instructive lessons for dealing with race relations, treatment of the poor, and national and international economic inequality remain unappropriated.

This article argues that Luke's use of "overlooking" (*paratheōreō*) in Acts 6:1 yields insight and wisdom that impacts both religious and secular discussions of CRT, marginalization, and international justice. Beginning with the context of Acts 6:1–7, the distinction of Hellenistic and Hebraic widows, and the perceived abruptness, the article considers "overlooking" (*paratheōreō*) and the solution to the complaint (*gongusmos*). It then identifies lessons for dealing with marginalization by suggesting touch points between overlooking and modern discussions of marginalization. The conclusion signposts some specific issues.

THE CONTEXT

While Luke's use of "In those days" in 6:1 can suggest a new section of the book,[10] the phrase may function to place the pericope within the description of the early church.[11] The prior story of Ananias and Sapphira (Acts 5:1–11) narrates a mishandling of the presence of the Spirit in the community. Acts 6:1–7 narrates a mishandling of table fellowship. Hitherto, the early church shared all in common. In Acts 2:44, the believers had everything in common with gladness and sincerity of heart. In Acts 4:34, the phrase

---

4. Dunn, *Acts*, 80.
5. Pao, "Waiters," 138.
6. Keener, *Acts*, 1258; Dunn, *Acts*, 82.
7. Dunn, *Acts*, 79.
8. Pao, "Waiters," 127–44.
9. Fitzmyer, *Acts,* 348; Witherington, *Acts*, 248–49; Johnson, *Acts*, 105. He has linked the text to discrimination.
10. Bruce, *Acts*, 153.
11. Holladay, *Acts*, viii.

"that there was no needy person among them" (*oude gar endeēs tis en autois*) further reinforces the portrait of Acts 2:44–45. The phrase "there was not a needy person among them" is an allusion to Deut 15:4, "there will be no one in need among you" (NETS). This suggests Luke portrays the community as fulfilling OT expectations of the people of God thus making the episode fit into Luke's description of the early community of Jesus.

Two subsequent chapters (Acts 7 and 8) narrate stories of Stephen and Philip. Stephen is described as full of grace and power, performing great wonders and signs among the people (Acts 6:8). His ministry caused a sharp response from Jewish authorities culminating in his death. Acts 7 is seen as an indictment against the temple or/and temple authorities; a relativizing of the temple.[12] Acts 8 details the ministry of a second character[13] in the chosen seven. Philip took the gospel to Samaria, fulfilling an aspect of Acts 1:8. Thus, the two function in two decisive ways: a relativizing of the temple and providing the first martyr, and fulfilling the agenda of Acts 1:8.

In summary, Acts 6:1–7 fits into Luke's description of the early community. It is not abrupt[14] but a continuation of Luke's narration of the community's early days within Jerusalem. This should allow Acts 6:1–7 to be seen as narrating a second and complimentary challenge in the community to that of mishandling the presence in Acts 5:1–11. Here the problem is the mishandling of table fellowship. In the description of the two, the episode transitions to the ministry to the end of the earth[15] by highlighting two of Luke's important themes: treatment of the marginalized and the universal mission.

THE PROBLEM

Luke identifies a problem that reflects disunity in the community.[16] Lüdemann sees the problem as unlikely since the Jewish Christian community would have been still part of the temple care system.[17] Witherington, however, sees verse one as indicating the problem.[18] The key issues are the identity of Hebraic and Hellenistic Jews, and "overlooking" (*paratheōreō*) expressed through a complaint (Acts 6:1).

12. Dunn, *Acts*, 90.
13. Lüdemann, *Acts*, 92; Malina and Pilch, *Acts*, 56.
14. Dunn, *Acts*, 80.
15. Pao, "Waiters," 142.
16. Holladay, *Acts*, 150.
17. Lüdemann, *Acts*, 93.
18. Witherington, *Acts*, 249.

Hebraic and Hellenistic Widows

First, the identification of the two groups is a Lukan distinctive.[19] Luke is the only NT writer who uses Hellenistic (Acts 6:1; 9:29; 11:20).[20] Scholars propose several meanings. One is that Luke distinguishes the two groups linguistically. This is possible since Hellenization was abundant, as evident in many Jewish documents that employ Greek interpretive methods.[21] This could mean Hellenists were Greek-speaking Jewish Christians. This is Witherington's preference in view of 9:29 and 11:20.[22] This possibility is enhanced by Luke's account of Pentecost Jews from every nation as present in Acts 2:1–5.[23] The second is that the distinction included culture and ideology. If the Hellenists were Greek-speaking Jewish Christians who had deep ideological differences with their Hebrew/Aramaic-speaking Christian counterparts, then two sharply contested theological outlooks were present in the church at this early stage.[24]

A third possibility is that the Hellenistic Christians were non-Jewish. If this is so, the origins of gentiles in the community, largely associated with Paul, should be traced to this early period of the community.[25] This, however, is unlikely as Luke highlights Cornelius as the first gentile convert to Christianity (Acts 11:18; 15:7).[26] Dunn has suggested a further possibility that those who spoke only Greek may have met separately from Aramaic speakers (2:26; 5:42). However, he cautions, as does Holladay, that the extent of the separation between the members of the church is difficult to determine.[27] Thus, their identity remains unclear.[28]

Whatever the distinction, the key issue was "overlooking" (*paratheōreō*). The summaries of Acts 4:35 and 5:1–3 place the responsibility of the community's resource distribution "at the apostles' feet." The apostles' proposition, not to wait on tables, is further evidence they were involved,[29] or were avoid-

19. Malina and Pilch, *Acts*, 56.
20. Holladay, *Acts*, 152.
21. Keener, *Acts*, 1258.
22. Bruce, *Acts*, 153; Witherington, *Acts*, 99.
23. Keener, *Acts*, 1258. Keener has postulated many diaspora Jews would come to Jerusalem in their old age to die there. This may account for the number of Hellenistic widows.
24. Holladay, *Acts*, 152.
25. Holladay, *Acts*, 152.
26. Witherington, *Acts*, 243, 364. See Acts 11:18.
27. Dunn, *Acts*, 83. Holladay, *Acts*, 150. Witherington, *Acts*, 242.
28. Holladay, *Acts*, 150. Witherington, *Acts*, 242.
29. Witherington, *Acts*, 248. Holladay, *Acts*, 152.

ing being too involved leading to the neglect of prayer and the word. This is the only time Luke uses the "twelve" to refer to the apostles in Acts. This seems to recall the promise of Jesus in Luke 22:28–30 in which the apostles were to reign over Israel. If this is so, the apostles were the hegemony. Thus, the episode reveals diversity, in language and/or possibly culture, and theology in the early church. It seems there was never a time when the church did not know the tensions which come from diversity of language and culture.[30] It is this that makes this episode both comforting and instructive.

Overlooking (*paratheōreō*)

The preceding discussion leads to the key issue. The treatments of Acts 6:1 by Witherington and Keener do not discuss Luke's use of the term in relation to discrimination and marginalization today.[31] Pelikan's brief commentary begins at Acts 6:2 and provides no translation nor a discussion of Acts 6:1.[32] Discussing the solution without sufficiently appreciating the problem means the text's wisdom for marginalization today is not appropriate.

The term "overlooking" (*paratheōreō*) is *hapax legomena* in the Greek New Testament and the LXX. Riensfield defines *para* on its own as placing something "by the side of"[33] while *paratheōreō* has to do with gazing or contemplating.[34] Those who were responsible for food distribution were setting aside, neglecting, and overlooking Hellenistic widows. Barrett's brief treatment of *paratheōreō* is helpful as he notes the indicative should be understood as Luke's attempt at showing the complaint was true.[35] The Hellenistic widows were being disadvantaged,[36] but exactly how is unclear.[37]

Luke uses complaint (*gongusmos*) to describe the concern. Both the OT and Greco-Roman backgrounds are suggestive. Keener notes Luke's audience might have winced at the complaints.[38] The appropriate response to any gift in the Greco-Roman world was gratitude; complaining was utterly inappropriate.[39] The OT background suggests an allusion to the wilderness

---

30. Dunn, *Acts*, 84.
31. Witherington, *Acts*, 240–51; Keener, *Acts*, 1260–68.
32. Pelikan, *Acts*, 91–96.
33. Silva, *NIDNTTE*, 2:425; Riensefield, "παρά," *TDNT*, 5:727–36.
34. Michaelis, "ὁράω," *TDNT*, 5:315.
35. Barrett, *Acts*, 309.
36. Roloff, *Apostelgeschichte*, 107.
37. Roloff, *Apostelgeschichte*, 107; Keener, *Acts*, 1253.
38. Keener, *Acts*, 1262.
39. Keener, *Acts*, 1262.

complaints in Num 11:1–5 and 14:26–28. In both texts, the complaints were to do with food. Since this is so, the complainants risked disapproval from the community and God's judgment. However, the opposite transpires.

At this point it is worth noting how Luke's use of "overlooking" (*paratheōreō*) resonates with aspects of modern discussions of marginalization; an exhaustive treatment is impossible in the brief scope of the paper. The first note of resonance is exclusion. The UN defines marginalization as "discrimination, exclusion and sometimes including physical violence."[40] Vasas sees marginalization as difficult to define, but key concepts deal with inclusion and exclusion, are applied to various people, locations, and events, and convey a vague sense of disadvantage and injustice.[41] The core feature of exclusion is the inability to fully participate in socio-economic life.[42] In Acts 6:1–7, discrimination and exclusion were present in the treatment of Hellenistic widows, since the food distribution (4:35) was "not always carried out with" equality.[43] The specific location was Jerusalem. A second consonant feature is the function of hierarchical power.[44] Vasas relates marginalization to the function of hierarchical power structures, dovetailing with Acts 6:1–7,[45] where the apostles were either at the center or responsible for distribution of resources.

Third, if marginalization is viewed as a process—an aspect that also facilitates change[46]—Luke's use of "in those days" suggests a period of the marginalization of Hellenistic widows. The phrase functions as a transition device and evokes earlier narratives,[47] suggesting an indefinite time to the marginalization prior to Acts 6:1–7. Fourth, modern discussions of marginalization see it as multiform and so it may not be apparent to the observer or even the individual concerned.[48] There is also the recognition of the lived experience of the individual.[49] In Acts 6:1–7, those who were marginalized recognized the practice against them. This raises an important question: "If an individual does not recognize their life as marginalized by

---

40. United Nations, "Marginalised Minorities."
41. Vasas, "Margins," 194–202; Leimgruber, *Globalization, Marginalization*, 3–11.
42. Spyrka-Chlipała, "Shaping Civic Attitudes," 107–113.
43. Fitzmyer, *Acts*, 348.
44. Vasas, "Margins," 194–202.
45. Vasas, "Margins," 194–202.
46. Vasas, "Margins," 194–202.
47. Keener, *Acts*, 1253; Lüdemann, *Acts*, 92.
48. Mowat, "Marginalisation," 454–76.
49. Mowat, "Marginalisation," 454–76.

Wisdom for Marginalization (Acts 6:1–7)

what legitimacy can they be considered by others to be marginalized?"[50] Those who were marginalized in Acts 6:1–7 were aware of the treatment towards them.[51]

Fifth, marginalization is seen as affecting groups.[52] Razer defines social exclusion as a state in which individuals or groups lack effective participation in key activities or benefits of the society in which they live.[53] Similarly, Obeng-Odoom observes marginalization in how research from "the whole of Africa" continues to experience "peripheralization and systemic neglect."[54] In the text, marginalization affected the Hellenists as a group.[55] These resonances between modern definitions of marginalization and Acts 6:1–7 mean marginalization of individuals, groups, or nations and the unequal distribution of resources, is a long-standing issue.[56] The claim, however, is not that the text provides wholesale authentication of every concept and organization addressing marginalization today.

THE SOLUTION: CHOOSE AMONG YOURSELVES

The solution begins with the apostolic reaction. Although not clearly stated, the apostles listened to the complaint (*gongusmos*) without question. Their response to this complaint would be considered extraordinarily charitable.[57] Second, the solution involved the whole community (Acts 6:3) choosing from among themselves those who would wait on tables. In response, the seven were chosen.[58] Third, and although it is difficult to prove, the seven chosen were likely from the marginalized. Based on the Greek names of all seven, it is likely all the seven were Hellenists.[59] Perhaps this is why Wither-

---

50. Mowat, "Marginalisation," 454–76.

51. Keener, *Acts*, 1255.

52. Mowat, "Marginalisation," 454–76; Messiou, "Collaborating with Children," 1311–22.

53. Razer et al., "Schools as Agents," 1152–70.

54. Obeng-Odoom, "Marginalisation of Africa," 211–34; Keener, *Acts*, 1255–56.

55. Baucham, "Biblical Justice vs. Social Justice." Baucham's argument is critical of social justice because of its emphasis on justice for groups.

56. Spyrka-Chlipała, "Shaping Civic Attitudes," 107–13.

57. Keener, *Acts*, 1255–56.

58. Pao, "Waiters," 127–44.

59. Dunn, *Acts*, 83; Lüdemann, *Acts*, 93; Roloff, *Apostelgeschichte*, 107; Holladay, *Acts*, 154; Bruce, *Acts*, 153.

ington sees this as the first instance of "affirmative action" where those with political power handed over the whole system to the offended minority.[60]

Fourth, although Koet sees the seven as invited to the ministry of the word,[61] this is not explicit in the text. What is true is that Luke uses the choosing of the seven to set the stage for highlighting the evangelistic activity of Stephen and Philip.[62] Being chosen to attend to material needs opened the way for Hellenists to be included in preaching and performing miracles. Thus, with Pao, the role of the seven in continuing the ministry of Jesus is confirmed in subsequent activities.[63]

SUMMARY AND LESSONS

It might be worthwhile highlighting salient aspects of this discussion at this point. The first is the importance of creating a safe environment in which "overlooking" and marginalization can be addressed. One wonders what would have happened if the complaint was never raised or the apostles had passed it off as negativity. In contrast to the Greco-Roman and OT background, a safe environment without recrimination was provided. A second is that growth of the church, and presence of Spirit-filled preaching, does not automatically preclude discrimination.[64] Inclusion seems the strongest way to address marginalization as it provides remedial action in resolving discrimination. Third, the study in no way suggests a wholesale approval of CRT, Black Lives Matter or other pressure groups seeking to address marginalization. What it suggests, however, especially to the church, is that complaints should be heard, rather than be dismissed wholesale. This should be so even when modern discussions of marginalization come loaded with ideas that could be biblically challenged.

Fourth, what is ironic is that those chosen to wait on tables function as preachers of the word with miracles, signs, and wonders, just as the apostles did.[65] The implication of this domino effect is limitless. There is no way to predict the positive outcomes of resolving an instance of marginalization. This may be the single most important contribution of this text to dealing

60. Witherington, *Acts*, 248; Lightfoot, *Acts*, 106.
61. Koet, "Diakonia," 184–5.
62. Holladay, *Acts,* 149.
63. Pao, "Waiters," 139.
64. Contra Baucham, "Biblical Justice vs. Social Justice." The challenge to Christianity's involvement in marginalization is neither new nor a preserve of CRT protagonists, but is part of adherence to the gospel.
65. Dunn, *Acts*, 83.

with marginalization. Luke depicts the whole community as pleased by the appointment of the seven. This avoided any further appearance of favoritism,[66] and further propagated the community's ideals (Acts 1:8).

CONCLUSION

For such a broad and widely discussed topic, one can only provide signposts to some areas of application. First, at the international level, there should be inclusion of other countries in settings of global trade, security, and relations. Many organizations that regulate international relations were founded during the period of colonialism. For example, although the WTO was formed in 1995, its own website admits its existence goes back to 1948.[67] The UN was formed in 1945 and is still headquartered in America.[68] The WHO was formed in 1948. NATO was formed in 1949 with the chief concern of dealing with the now defunct Soviet Union.[69] The predecessor to the EU, the EEC, was formed in 1957.[70] Although other member countries have joined in various capacities, power remains with hegemonic countries so that formulation and approach to fulfillment of goals still serves the interest of influential countries. One example is France's relationship with its former colonies. Fifty percent of those countries' income is banked in the French treasury and only fifteen percent is accessible to them per year. If they require more, it is regarded as a loan.[71]

Second, in dismantling racism, this reading of Acts 6:1–7 agrees with much of the suggestions by Derald Wing Sue.[72] There must be an understanding of one's racial identity, acknowledgement of the issues, validation and facilitation of discussions, control of the process (not the content of discussion) and validation and encouragement. Additionally, the marginalized must be heard and given space to verbalize their felt experiences. This means other races must have equal voice and access to facilities and resources. Perhaps CRT and Black Lives Matter could be heard as a cry for

---

66. Witherington, *Acts*, 250.
67. World Trade Organization, "About WTO."
68. United Nations, "History of the United Nations."
69. NATO, "Key Events."
70. Gabel, "European Community."
71. Sylla, "CFA Franc as a Vivid Symbol of Colonial Continuities in Francophone Africa."
72. Sue, "Race Discussions."

help. In one case, the Southern Baptists took a negative stance towards CRT. This was without consultation with black leadership of the convention.[73]

The wisdom of Acts 6:1–7 suggests that there ought to be genuine inclusion in policy and decision making at all levels allowing those marginalized to shape international relations today. This might, for example, reverse the historical relationships between Africa and the West in which western domination and marginalization continue today.[74] Could the Russia/Ukraine situation benefit from inclusivity? Could other nations outside NATO and Russia provide a voice of peace? Just as in Acts 6:1–7, where the inclusion of the marginalized released a forward movement in the ideals of the community, inclusion in international and ecclesiastical arrangements of the marginalized will open possibilities of an equitable world.

There is a better world available and attainable for all: a world where everyone is provided for and fulfilled, a world in which injustice and inequitable distribution of wealth is relegated to the past. There are, however, difficult decisions to make to get there. Acts 6:1–7 provides the required wisdom.

WORKS CITED

Barrett, C. K. *A Critical and Exegetical Commentary on The Acts of the Apostles 1–14*. International Critical Commentary 1. London: T. &. T. Clark, 1994.

Baucham, Voddie. "Biblical Justice vs. Social Justice." Friendship Baptist Church of Girard Ohio, March 3, 2021. https://www.youtube.com/watch?v=jhmONchRuC8.

BBC News. "George Floyd: Timeline of Black Deaths and Protests." April 22, 2021. https://www.bbc.co.uk/news/world-us-canada-52905408.

BNC News. "Debate Over Critical Race Theory Impacting Southern Baptist Convention, Churches." June 11, 2021. https://www.youtube.com/watch?v=JWDsyk9wqGw.

Bruce, F. F. *The Acts of the Apostles, The Greek Text with Introduction and Commentary*. London: Tyndale, 1962.

Dunn, James D. G. *The Acts of the Apostles*. Grand Rapids: Eerdmans, 1996.

Fitzmyer, Joseph. *The Acts of the Apostles: A New Translation with Introduction and Commentary*. New Haven, CT: Yale University Press, 1998.

Friedrich, Gerhard, and Geoffrey W. Bromiley, eds. *Theological Dictionary of the New Testament*. 10 vols. Stuttgart: W. Kolhammer Verlag, 1970.

Gabel, Matthew. "European Community." *Britannica*. https://www.britannica.com/topic/European-Community-European-economic-association.

Holladay, Carl R. *Acts*. The New Testament Library. Louisville, KY: Westminster John Knox, 2016.

Keener, Craig S. *Acts of the Apostles, 3:1–14:28 An Exegetical Commentary*. Grand Rapids: Baker Academic, 2013.

73. BNC News, "Debate Over Critical Race Theory."
74. Mlambo, "Domination and Marginalisation," 161–79.

Koet, Bart J. "Luke 10, 38–42 and Acts 6, 1–7: a Lucan diptych on Diakonia." In *Studies in the Greek Bible*, edited by J. Corley and V. Skemp, 163–85. CBQ Monograph Series 44. Washington, DC: Catholic Biblical Association of America. 2008.

Lightfoot, J. B. *The Acts of the Apostles*. Volume 1. Downers Grove, IL: InterVarsity, 2014.

Lüdemann, Gerd. *The Acts of the Apostles*. New York: Prometheus, 2005.

Malina, Bruce J. and John Pilch. *Book of Acts: Social-Science Commentary*. Minneapolis: Fortress, 2008.

Messiou, K. "Collaborating with Children in Exploring Marginalisation: An Approach to Inclusive Education." *IJIE* 16 (2012) 1311–22.

Mlambo, Alois S. "Western Social Sciences and Africa: The Domination and Marginalisation of a Continent." *American Sociological Review* 10 (2006) 161–79. http://www.jstor.org/stable/afrisocirevi.10.1.161.

NATO. "Key Events." https://www.nato.int/nato-welcome/index.html.

Pao, David W. "Waiters or Preachers: Acts 6:1–7 and the Lukan Table Fellowship Motif." *Journal of Biblical Literature* 130 (2011) 127–44.

Pelikan, Jaroslav. *Acts*. Grand Rapids: Brazos, 2005.

Razer, M. V. J. Friedman, and B. Warshofsky. "Schools as Agents of Social Exclusion and Inclusion." *International Journal of Inclusive Education* 17 (2013) 1152–70.

Roloff, Jürgen. Die Apostelgeschichte, Das Neue Testament Deutsch. Göttingen: Vanderhoeck & Ruprecht, 2010.

Silva, Moisés, ed. *New International Dictionary of New Testament Theology and Exegesis*. 5 vols. Grand Rapids: Zondervan, 2014.

Spyrka-Chlipała, Renata. "Shaping Civic Attitudes as a Means of Preventing Social Marginalization." *Acta Et Commentationes Sciences of Education* 15 (2019) 107–13.

Sylla, Ndongo Samba. "The CFA Franc as a vivid symbol of colonial continuities in Francophone Africa." March 22, 2021. https://taxjustice.net/2021/03/22/the-cfa-franc-as-a-vivid-symbol-of-colonial-continuities-in-francophone-africa/.

United Nations, "History of the United Nations." https://www.un.org/en/about-us/history-of-the-un.

———. "Marginalised Minorities in Development of Programming: A UNDP Resource Guide and Toolkit." 2010. https://www.ohchr.org/documents/issues/minorities/undpmarginalisedminorities.pdf.

Vasas, E. "Examining the Margins." *Advances in Nursing Science* 28 (2005) 194–202.

World Trade Organization. "About WTO." https://www.wto.org/english/thewto_e/history_e/history_e.htm.

Witherington, Ben, III. *The Acts of the Apostles: Socio-Rhetorical Commentary*. Grand Rapids: Eerdmans, 1998.

Holiness in the Margins

The Ethiopian Eunuch as an Example of the Spirit Being Poured out "on All Flesh" (Acts 2:17), in Fulfillment of Joel's Prophecy (Joel 2:28), and the Relevance to Gender Non-conforming Christians

Kate Bowen-Evans

PURPOSE OF THE ESSAY

The baptism of the Ethiopian eunuch in Acts 8:26–40 is a boundary shattering example of the fulfillment of the prophecy of Joel 2:28–9 that God's spirit will be poured out on all flesh (Acts 2:17). This is an invitation to reconsider how radically disruptive it was and is to the holy people of God today. This is most relevant to those who identify as gender-non binary, meaning those who are transgender, intersex, gender different, or gender queer[1] and those who exclude them. Believers with non-conforming gender identity have not been permitted to find themselves in the biblical narrative let alone provide interpretation of that narrative for the benefit of the whole church. My aim is to include the experience of those outside the hetero-, gender-normative bodily experience, whose bodies are regarded as "false, unreal or unintelligible,"[2] to expand the possibilities of interpretation.[3]

    1. Apostolacus, "Bible and the Transgender Christian," 19.

    2. Moxnes, "Jesus in Gender Trouble," 31–46.

    3. As a white, English speaking, cis-gendered, heterosexual and able-bodied woman, I am acceptable to the Biblical studies community that has been privileged to interpret

Holiness in the Margins 149

As a God-fearing gentile of ambiguous gender-identity, and irrevocably blemished flesh, the Ethiopian eunuch is converted and blessed with the Holy Spirit after baptism and deemed faithful in heart and cleansed by faith. Although he remains of liminal gender-identity and there is no alteration of his bodily form, he is made holy and belongs among the people of God based on his turning to God and his receipt of the Holy Spirit in baptism. The people of God are no longer only Jews, male or female, but gentiles and those of non-conforming gender-identities who seek and turn to God and are faithful to God.

METHODOLOGY

The narrative forms of Luke-Acts, linked by a common, anonymous author,[4] share a common popular history form of narrative, constructed with the intention of imparting a theological understanding of the events therein.[5] It has been suggested that the Ethiopian eunuch pericope exhibits Lukan theology in a nutshell.[6] Our concern is with *what* the text says but also *why* and *how*.[7] This is done by looking at sequencing, characterization, use of themes, and scenes throughout the book and the intertextual connections prompted by them.[8] Luke uses one-to-one encounters between characters to illuminate a particular point that has also been made programmatically.[9] The pericope of Philip and the Ethiopian eunuch is one such example. It is therefore valid to assume that its contents are of some importance to the point Luke is trying to make.

WHAT MAKES US HOLY?

To start, we must understand what it means to be holy and how individuals are made into the holy people of God. Genesis 17 recounts the first instance of the covenant between God and a faithful people by the mark

---

the Bible for millennia. The only aspect of my identity that puts me away from the center of power is my female gender. My position of privilege requires that I hold open the space for those whose voices, interpretations, lives, and faiths have not been heard in the hermeneutical community or in holiness discourse.

4. Thompson, *Acts*, 42, 47. See also Wi, *Path to Salvation*, 19.
5. Thompson, *Acts*, 42, 47. See also Wi, *Path to Salvation*, 19.
6. Pervo, *Lukan Theology in a Nutshell*, quoted in Solevåg, "No Nuts?," 81–99.
7. Thompson, *Acts*, 49.
8. Green, *Methods for Luke*, 93–95.
9. Scott-Spencer, "Philip the Evangelist," 154.

of circumcision: "[s]o shall my covenant be in your flesh an everlasting covenant" (17:13). This was added to by the Levitical holiness codes from whence the understanding of blemished flesh comes: "no one who has a blemish shall draw near" (Lev 21:18–20). This includes what we would now call acquired or congenital disabilities, such as blindness, paralysis, disfigurement or dwarfism as well as the crushed testicles of those who have been castrated and made eunuch. These regulations remained in place throughout the Old Testament (OT) and into the Second Temple Period (STP) in which the New Testament (NT) was authored.

The modern day holiness movement continues to be occupied by understanding holiness and what it means for the people of God today. Brower's succinct answer to the question: how can we live holy lives today, is "through the ongoing presence of the Spirit."[10] Holiness is always a derived holiness which cannot be divorced from relationship with the Holy One.[11]

SPACE FOR THE MARGINALIZED IN HOLINESS THEOLOGY

Few holiness writers explicitly address those marginalized by the holiness agenda, based on their gender or sexual identities. However, Brower's writings leave space for testing the understanding of holiness in the lives of believers and the body of Christ, the church.[12] As we put the baptism of the Ethiopian eunuch at the center of our interpretation, Brower's words on Gen 1:27 and the creation of humankind resonate:

> "So God created humankind in his image, in the image of God he created them; male and female he created them" (Gen 1:27). At first reading, this seems to indicate that God must somehow be related to gender. But to read the text this way is to reverse "image" and "source." We cannot read gender back into deity on the basis of this (or any other text). The image of God is a plurality because God exists in plural form.[13]

The dualist and gender binary interpretation of God's creation of humanity in their own image has led to millennia of grotesque alienation of humans who do not fit this interpretation.[14] Butler describes these binary gender

10. Brower, *Holiness*, 43.
11. Brower, *Holiness, 43*
12. See Brower, *Holiness*; *Living As God's Holy People.*
13. Brower, *Holiness,* 70.

14. This includes the perpetual use of only male gender pronouns for all forms of God in bible translations.

roles exerting control and performing violence on those of non-conforming gender identities. Transgender Jewish Torah scholar Joy Ladin's work reminds us that the "Torah/Hebrew Bible is a powerful guide that God created human beings without gender, without specific expectations based on their sex," suggesting that it "is human beings who have been complicating things ever since."[15] Ladin does not search for literal gender non-conforming people in biblical text as such a pursuit would be anachronistic, but listens to text that speaks to their experience.[16] Philip's encounter with the Ethiopian eunuch is one such text.

THE ETHIOPIAN EUNUCH, NON-CONFORMING GENDER IDENTITY AND LIMINAL GENDER IDENTITY

The Ethiopian eunuch is undoubtedly an individual who does not conform to binary gender norms. The eunuch has an ambiguous set of gender identity markers, and yet, using (arguably insufficient) male pronouns, Acts describes his faith, turning towards God, baptism, and reception of the Holy Spirit to join the new holy people of God. The one-to-one encounter with, and the repeated designation of the character in Acts as the eunuch, suggests the importance of the designation to what Luke is communicating and its significance to interpretation.[17]

Eunuchs in Greek and Roman texts were "gender-liminal" figures who upset the male/female gender binary and had access to the realms of both men and women.[18] Transgender theologians Kearns and Hartke affirm that the eunuchs of the ancient world inhabited the same in-between space that transgender people experience today; in between genders, in a liminal space, consistently on the outside of biblical narrative, expelled from the gathering whilst longing to be in community.[19] It is my proposition that as Acts narrates the progression of the gospel and the Holy Spirit of God across ethnic and status lines, from Jerusalem, to all Judea and Samaria, and to the ends of the earth (Acts 1:8), it also does so across gender lines. From a promise for the Israelites to a pouring out of God's Spirit on all flesh (2:17) and everyone who God calls (2:39), the eunuch is positioned as a convert

---

15. Crasnow, "Soul of the Stranger," 908–11.
16. Crasnow, "Soul of the Stranger," 908.
17. Wilson, *Eunuch*, 405.
18. Wilson, "Neither Male nor Female," 406–7.
19. Kearns, "Transgender Christian," 20; Hartke, *Transforming*, 94.

who falls between all of these categories.[20] The pericope of the eunuch's baptism is itself at a pivotal point in the narrative at the intersection of the acceptance of the gospel by Jews (Acts 2:1—8:25) and gentiles (10:1—11:18) and the rejection of circumcision as a requirement for admittance into the way (15:1—35).[21]

THE BLEMISHED FLESH OF THE ETHIOPIAN EUNUCH IN RELATION TO OLD TESTAMENT TEXT

Brower and Solevåg agree that the castration of the eunuch is a key identifying trait in the narrative, based on its relevance to the understanding of circumcision as a boundary marker for holiness amongst the people of God.[22] Given the practice of interpreting OT texts in the NT to provide theological insight, texts from both Isaiah and Joel are seen in a new light, following the baptism of the eunuch.

Isaiah Citation Reconsidered

There are three points to consider in the Isaiah citation (Isa 53:7-8) from Acts 8:32-33. First, the Ethiopian eunuch is blemished and excluded. The OT is clear that "[n]o one whose testicles are crushed or whose penis is cut off shall be admitted to the assembly of the Lord" (Deut 23:1, cf. Lev 21:16-20). Thus, castration left eunuchs physically blemished and in a permanent state of ritual impurity,[23] barred from access to the Temple courts. Second, the suffering servant and the Ethiopian eunuch share afflictions. The visceral connection between being cut off from the land of the living in the Isaiah text and the cutting off in castration implicit in the eunuch of Acts links the afflictions of these two characters. A eunuch's life suggests an experience of oppression and affliction, carried out against their will and placing them in a contentious and marginalized position. The Ethiopian's curiosity about the suffering servant in Isaiah is understandable as their afflictions are shared. Third, castration left eunuchs unable to reproduce, and therefore unable to have a future in their own name through descendants. Implicit is the compounded exclusion of those unable to reproduce from the promise that God made to Abraham in Gen 12:1-3. Gender non-conforming

---

20. Wilson, *Eunuch*, 421.
21. Wilson, *Eunuch*, 422.
22. Solevåg, "No Nuts?," 81-99; Brower, "Post-Christian."
23. Scott-Spencer, *Philip*, 188.

theologians associate themselves with the experiences of being oppressed, afflicted, refused justice, cut-off from fullness of life and from reproduction based on their gender identity, and therefore find themselves "squarely in the eunuch's shoes."[24]

How then is the Isaiah citation reconsidered by the baptism of the eunuch? For those listening to texts that speak to gender non-conformity, what the ongoing text of Isaiah 56 says about eunuchs is startling. Both Brower and Solevåg note the further text of Isa 56:1–5, without knowing if the eunuch went on to read it or not:[25]

> [T]hus says the Lord . . . soon my salvation will come, and my deliverance be revealed . . . Do not let the foreigner joined to the Lord say, "The Lord will surely separate me from his people"; and do not let the eunuch say, "I am just a dry tree." For thus says the Lord: To the eunuchs who keep my Sabbaths, who choose the things that please me and hold fast my covenant, I will give, in my house and within my walls, a monument and a name better than sons and daughters; I will give them an everlasting name that shall not be cut off (Isa 56:1, 3–5).

First, the foreign/gentile Ethiopian eunuch, blemished and permanently excluded, is saved by God's deliverance. By a turning to God (Acts 15:19), his heart is cleansed by faith (Acts 15:9) and baptism, circumcision of the flesh which he cannot perform is no longer required for him to access the people of God. Second, this afflicted character is affirmed as obedient and faithful. "He went on his way rejoicing" (Acts 8:39) like David whose "heart was glad" and whose "tongue rejoiced," whose flesh can live in hope (Acts 2:26; cf. Ps 16:8–11). Third, having been left unable to produce a family of his own due to his affliction, the eunuch, like the suffering servant, is promised a house within God's walls and "a monument and a name better than sons and daughters" (Isa 56:5). Viewed with this text in mind, it is possible to re-read the Isaiah 53 citation from Acts 8:33 with a new perspective: "Who can describe his generation? For his life is taken away from the earth" (Acts 8:33). Through his baptism and cleansing by the Holy Spirit his bodily condition is altered from its earthly limitations and he is transformed into part of Christ's body, the church, and one of the people of God. Just as Jesus's life was taken away from the earth in ascension, so the flesh of the eunuch has been reborn spiritually. Acts 8:33 can no longer be seen as a lament

---

24. Hartke, *Transforming*, 95.
25. Brower, "Post-Christian," 14; Solevåg, "No Nuts?," 93.

of his inability to procreate, but an exaltation of the multitude of spiritual descendants he will bear,[26] just as Abraham and Jesus did.

In sum, the prophecy of the suffering servant (Isa 53) is extended to "all who obey" (Isa 56) and includes an eschatological promise to eunuchs in the community of worship, inviting them into the congregation of God's people, to receive a name in the house of the Lord.[27] For the barren Abraham and Sarah, the unmarried Jesus, and the castrated Ethiopian, the Spirit of God is the originator of their children, their co-heirs[28] and spiritual descendants. The limitations of body and flesh are overcome by the transformation of the Holy Spirit of God on their flesh. This reconsideration of the Isaiah citation adds to our study that the pouring out of the spirit on all flesh, including the eunuchs in Isaiah and Acts, dismantles any belief that the nature of the body can limit the work of the Holy Spirit in making anyone holy.

Joel Citation Reconsidered

Joel prophesied that in the end times God's spirit would be poured out on all flesh without distinction. In Acts, Joel's prophecy was cited again at Pentecost (Acts 2), suggesting the author considered the "last days" of Joel's prophecy to have begun. The conclusion of this citation from Joel states "everyone who calls on the name of the Lord shall be saved" (Acts 2:21). It is a matter of the heart before God, not the nature of the body that brings someone into relationship with the Holy Spirit and therefore holy.

THE PRESENCE OF THE HOLY SPIRIT WITH THE GENDER NON-CONFORMING ETHIOPIAN

In order to reach our conclusion, we must confirm that the Ethiopian was truly baptized in the spirit as this is disputed by some. Scott-Spencer believes the pericope shows the "marked emphasis on the leadership of the Spirit," but that the eunuch's rejoicing was "no automatic guarantee of the Spirit's presence."[29] He bases his belief on Acts 8:8 where the Samaritans experienced "great joy," but the text indicates that even after believing and being baptized in the name of Jesus Christ (Acts 8:12), the Holy Spirit had not come upon any of them (Acts 8:16). From this, he concludes that the

---

26. Scott-Spencer, *Philip*, 199.
27. Solevåg, "No Nuts?," 93.
28. Rom 8:12–17.
29. Scott-Spencer, *Philip*, 171–72.

Holy Spirit had not come upon the eunuch at his baptism just as it had not come upon the Samaritans until the blessing of Peter and John.

By contrast, I conclude with Gaventa that the rejoicing of the Ethiopian eunuch "bristles with significance, since it later becomes the hallmark of the response of Gentiles to the gospel." (Acts 13:48; 15:31)[30] When reading Luke-Acts with an eye to the Spirit's work, though explicitly referenced in many places, in others it is evident only by reading-between-the-lines. Jesus himself is described as rejoicing in the Holy Spirit in Luke 10:21. Peter's reinterpretation of Ps 16:8–11, addressing the crowd at Pentecost, helps us see the Holy Spirit with the Ethiopian eunuch as well, by making it explicit that the joy of David is directly related to the presence of God (Acts 2:25–26; cf. Ps 16:11). These examples affirm a suggested reading that the Holy Spirit was indeed with the eunuch at or after baptism.

BAPTISM WITH THE SPIRIT NOT CIRCUMCISION OF THE FLESH

The castrated Ethiopian's baptism causes a boundary shattering re-evaluation of the markers of holiness for the people of God. Peter affirms that "God, who knows the human heart" testifies to them (the outsiders, gentiles, unclean, and those of liminal gender) by "giving them the Holy Spirit" and that "cleansing their hearts by faith he has made no distinction between them and us" (Acts 15:8–9). It is the pouring out of the spirit on the flesh that is the new boundary marker for holiness. Brower summarizes: "God through the Spirit creates the people of God by purifying their hearts; it is the world of the Spirit without reference to any of the usual criteria."[31] Without explicitly addressing the liminal gender of the Ethiopian eunuch, the inclusion of this character's baptism must be addressed. The inclusion of the Ethiopian eunuch suggests God's knowledge of the heart, and subsequent pouring out of the Spirit is what makes a person holy, not their adherence to bodily purity rituals or the state of their flesh or their compliance with binary gender norms.

The Ethiopian's bodily experience can never be erased or healed sufficiently for him to be able to perform circumcision as the marker of ritual purity to access the holy people of God. Despite the state of his flesh, his heart is turned to God. The state of his heart is sufficient to lead him to baptism without further ritual compliance: "What is to prevent me from being baptized?" (Acts 8:37). His baptism is the fulfillment of Joel's prophecy: the Spirit is poured out on all flesh, unhindered by the nature or state

30. Gaventa, *Acts*, 145.
31. Brower, "Post-Christian," 15.

of the body or bodily experience of the person. Bodily circumcision has become irrelevant as far as holiness and salvation are concerned. The heart must be turned to God, believe in order to be saved, receive the Holy Spirit, and be made holy.[32] The Ethiopian eunuch is pivotal to understanding the fulfillment of Joel's prophecy. The eunuch is both the castrated and the truly circumcised. The eunuch is made holy and acceptable not by the nature or modification of the body but by the relationship of the heart to God, the source of holiness and the ongoing presence of the Holy Spirit.

Baptismal identity trumps all others and relativizes all other relationships.[33] Elizabeth Stuart argues that all other identities, "including sex and gender," are placed under "eschatological erasure" by baptism.[34] What she means is that the identifying biological or gender markers of an individual, be they male, female or non-conforming, are irrelevant in light of the eschatological priorities of the kingdom of God.

THE SPIRITUALIZATION OF THE TEMPLE IN THE BODY OF THE BELIEVER

There is one final move needed to confirm our understanding of the fulfillment of Joel's prophecy in the Ethiopian eunuch. It relates to the spiritualization of the temple and Jesus's replacement of the temple. Beale argues that Acts 2 narrates the establishment of the church, the people of God as the Body of Christ, as the latter-day temple in replacement and escalated continuation of the true temple of God.[35] At the beginning of the Joel 2:28 citation, Peter substitutes the phrase "in the latter days" in place of Joel's "after these things." The substitution comes from Isa 2:2. This is the only place in the LXX where this precise phrase occurs. Beale suggests that Peter is interpreting the Spirit coming in fulfillment of Joel's prophecy as also the beginning of the fulfillment of Isaiah's prophecy of the eschatological temple.[36]

At Pentecost the Spirit's gifting (Acts 2) which was previously imparted at the tabernacle and limited to leaders helping Moses is now universalized to all flesh; God's people of every race, age, and gender.[37] Both Bauckham and Marshall agree that the spiritualization of the temple has begun in Acts, based on Stephen's speech (Acts 7:45b–50), and the Amos citation in

32. Marshall, *Acts*, 249–50.
33. Thiselton, *Corinthians*, 49.
34. Ford, *Transgender Bodies*, 89.
35. Beale, "Descent," 73.
36. Beale, "Descent," 93–94.
37. Beale, "Descent," 93–94.

Acts 15.[38] Beale believes that Jesus's repeated claim that forgiveness came through him and not the temple systems suggests that he was taking over the function of the temple.[39] The relevance to our discussion is this: the baptized Ethiopian eunuch received the Holy Spirit. He was made holy by the presence of the Spirit with him and his body became part of the holy Temple of God. His derived holiness required no bodily alteration or restoration, no confirmation of his gender-identity before this could occur. It was a matter of heart, not flesh. This is not meant to be an argument for those of non-conforming gender to remain the way they are. Whether the body is changed or unchanged is not what matters but what matters is the heart before God, and the relationship to the Holy Spirit is what makes us holy.

CONCLUSIONS

It is my contention that an understanding of this event which included the baptism of an Ethiopian eunuch has yet to be fully understood today. The church continues to act as if it holds the authority to define the holy people of God. This has meant the exclusion of women, people of color, those labeled disabled, and those identifying as LGBTQIA+. What the church has failed to fully perceive is how radically disruptive the baptism of the Ethiopian eunuch was to the parameters of holiness and membership among the holy people of God. As a God-fearing gentile of ambiguous gender-identity, and irrevocably blemished flesh, the Ethiopian eunuch is converted and blessed with the Holy Spirit after baptism and deemed faithful in heart and cleansed by faith. There is no alteration of the character's liminal gender-identity, nor alteration of his bodily form before he is made holy and welcomed among the people of God. His belonging is based on his turning to God and receipt of the Holy Spirit in baptism. The eunuch is made holy and acceptable, not by the nature or modification of the body but by the relationship of the heart to God, the source of holiness and the ongoing presence of the Holy Spirit. Any limitations of body or flesh are overcome by the transformation of the Holy Spirit on all flesh which dismantles any belief that the nature of the body can limit the work of the Holy Spirit in making anyone Holy.

The people of God are no longer only Jews, male or female, but gentiles and those of non-conforming gender-identities who seek and turn to God and are faithful to God. The priorities of the kingdom of God can be worked out in "all flesh." The faith of those of non-conforming gender makes them part of the Temple of God, the place where God dwells.

38. Beale, "Descent," 84–85.
39. Beale and Kim, *God Dwells Among Us*, 20.

WORKS CITED

Apostolacus, Katherine. "The Bible and The Transgender Christian: Mapping Transgender Hermeneutics in the 21st Century." *J. Bible Recept* 5 (2018) 1–29.

Bauckham, R., ed. *The Book of Acts in Its First Century Setting. Volume 4: Palestinian Setting.* Grand Rapids: Eerdmans, 1995.

Beale, G. K. "The Descent of the Eschatalogical Temple in the Form of the Spirit at Pentecost: Part 1: The Clearest Evidence." *TynBul* 56 (2005) 73–102.

Beale, G. K., and D. A. Carson, eds. *Commentary on the New Testament use of the Old Testament.* Grand Rapids: Baker Academic, 2007.

Beale, G. K., and Mitchell Kim. *God Dwells Among Us: A Biblical Theology of the Temple. Essential Studies in Biblical Theology.* Downers Grove, IL: Intervarsity, 2015.

Brower, Kent. "Holiness and Purity In A Post-Christian Age." *Journal of Wesleyan Thought* 1 (2018) 45–63.

———. *Holiness in the Gospels.* Kansas City: Beacon Hill, 2005.

———. *Living As God's Holy People: Holiness and Community in Paul.* Milton Keynes, UK: Paternoster, 2010.

Crasnow, S. J. "Review of The Soul of the Stranger: Reading God and Torah from a Transgender Perspective." *Journal of the American Academy of Religion* 87 (2019) 908–11.

Dunn, James D. G. *The Theology of Paul the Apostle.* Grand Rapids: Eerdmans, 1998.

Ford, C. A. "Transgender Bodies, Catholic Schools and a Queer Natural Law Theology." *The Journal of Moral Theology* 7 (2018) 70–98.

Gaventa, Beverely. *The Acts of the Apostles.* Nashville: Abingdon, 2003.

Green, Joel B., ed. *Methods for Luke.* New York: Cambridge University Press, 2010.

Hartke, Austen. *Transforming: The Bible and The Levies of Transgender Christians.* Louisville, KY: Westminster John Knox, 2018.

Marshall, I. Howard. *Acts: An Introduction and Commentary.* Tyndale New Testament Commentaries. Grand Rapids: Eerdmans, 1980.

Moxnes, Halvor. "Jesus in Gender Trouble." *Cross Currents* 54 (2004) 31–46.

Pervo, Richard I. *Acts: A Commentary.* Minneapolis: Fortress, 2009.

Powell, Samuel M. "The Theological Significance of the Holiness Movement." *Quarterly Review—Nashville United Methodist Publishing House* 25 (2005) 125–39.

Robinson, Geoffrey D. "Paul Ricoeur and the Hermeneutics of Suspicion: A brief overview and critique." *Presbyterian* 23 (1997) 43–55.

Scott-Spencer, F. "Philip the Evangelist in Lucan Perspective." PhD diss., University of Durham, 1989.

Solevåg, Anna Rebecca. "No Nuts? No Problem! Disability, Stigma, and the Baptised Eunuch in Acts 8:26–40." *Biblical Interpretation* 24 (2016) 81–99.

Thisleton, Anthony. *The First Epistle to the Corinthians: A Commentary on the Greek Text.* Grand Rapids: Eerdmans, 2006.

Thompson, Richard. *Acts: A Commentary in the Wesleyan Tradition.* Kansas City: Beacon Hill, 2015.

Westerman, Claus. *Isaiah 40–66: A Commentary.* London: SCM, 1969.

Wi, Mi Ja. *The Path to Salvation in Luke's Gospel: What Must We Do?* LNTS 607. London: T. &. T. Clark, 2019.

Wilson, Brittany. "'Neither Male nor Female': The Ethiopian Eunuch in Acts 8:26–40." *NTS* 60 (2014) 403–22.

PART IV

Confronting Social Injustice

Justification, Sanctification, and Systemic Racism

Reflections on Romans

Andy Johnson

OVER THE LAST FEW years, the continuing effects of racial biases embedded in societal structures in the US—and in the very neural networks of many individuals within it—have been clearly displayed right before our eyes in the agonized faces and situations of George Floyd, Ahmaud Arbery, Breonna Taylor, Trayvon Martin, and numerous others.[1] Far too often, White Americans—and White evangelicals[2] in particular—have simply looked away, rushed to uncover something in the victims' backgrounds that could have justified what they just viewed or heard, or simply insisted that each situation had to be interpreted as an isolated incident rather than as a clear example of a continuing pattern of racial biases and injustice.[3]

Many White Christians in the US—not just self-identified evangelicals—habitually respond in similar ways to other clear patterns of racial

---

1. While this essay focuses on racial injustice in the US, the phenomenon of whiteness orders systems of dominance around the world that foster racism and White supremacy (see Jennings, "Can White People Be Saved?"). Hence, *mutatis mutandis*, the following reflections on Romans may also be relevant in other places outside the US.

2. In the US, the term "evangelicals" might include what has increasingly simply become a conservative voting block with little commitment to belonging to a local church community. However, it also includes those who hold to more typical evangelical religious beliefs (e.g., a high view of Scripture, the importance of a personal relationship with Jesus, a belief in the divinity of Jesus, etc.) and continue attending church regularly. In this essay, I have the latter group mostly in mind.

3 In a 2021 survey by the nonpartisan Public Religion Research Institute (PRRI), at least 70 percent of White evangelicals say that recent police killings of Black Americans are isolated incidents rather than part of a broader pattern of how police treat Blacks.

biases/injustices. We[4] look at the mostly segregated neighborhoods we live in and imagine such segregation happened by accident—by *de facto* forces—rather than recognizing it as the continuing present impact of past intentional—*de jure*—actions supported by federal, state, and local laws.[5] Before our very eyes, we see the red-line maps and yet fail to admit the obvious connections between the intentional injustice *legally* inflicted on red-lined communities in the past and the continuing issues that plague them and other African Americans in the present (e.g., higher unemployment rates, lower household net worth and education level, more chronic health issues with shorter life expectancy, higher incarceration rates). Few Black Christians have any problem recognizing such racialized patterns at work in their lives.[6] But, like crowds of White church members during the lynching era gazing up at a charred lynched victim—crowds sometimes let out early from their Sunday service to get there on time!—many White evangelicals are able to look directly at racial injustice today, but never perceive it as such.

Indeed, like those outside Jesus's circle of discipleship, we look, but don't perceive; we hear but don't understand (Mark 4:12). Like the lawyer of Luke 10:25–29 who attempts to put boundaries around whom he must consider to be his "neighbor," we have a long history of "wanting to justify ourselves" (Luke 10:29). So we deploy our "cultural toolkit"[7] to insist that

---

4. I use the first-person plural here and other places in this essay to signal that I am a part of a denomination (Nazarene) whose US members are overwhelmingly White, with many of them exhibiting the mindset of what I am describing as typical White evangelicalism. However, I also use it because I recognize that I am only now, after almost thirty-two years of teaching Bible and theology, beginning to deal with the racialized history that has shaped me and my own continuing implicit biases.

5. See Rothstein, *Color of Law*.

6. For example, in the same PRRI survey referred to above, 80 percent of Black evangelicals say that recent police killings of Black Americans are part of broader pattern of how police treat Blacks rather than simply isolated incidents.

7. This is language from the now classic 2000 analysis of Emerson and Smith, *Divided by Faith*. By "cultural toolkit," they mean the set of "ideas, habits, skills, and styles" with which White evangelicals tend to organize their experiences and evaluate their world (75–76). The three main tools in this kit are accountable freewill individualism, relationalism, and antistructuralism. These tools are interrelated with each other and arise from theological convictions refracted through the "American way of life." Accountable freewill individualism is the view that "individuals exist independent of structures and institutions, have freewill, and are individually accountable for their own actions" (76). Relationalism emphasizes the importance of interpersonal relationships between accountable individuals and tends to explain any social problem (including race problems) as the result of broken personal relationships between individuals. Because these relationships were broken by individual acts of sin, they can only be fixed at the individual level (77–78). Antistructuralism insists that to argue that broken

what we're seeing is all the result of poor individual choices and broken personal relationships, refusing to recognize that these clear inequities and "poor relationships might be shaped by social structures, such as laws, the ways institutions operate, or forms of segregation."[8] Or to put it in more theological terms, we refuse to recognize the way Sin functions as a power to sculpt social structures such as laws and institutions—including churches—in racialized ways. And perhaps more insidiously, our insistence on understanding sin primarily as intentional individual actions blinds us to the way that our own minds remain shot through with unconscious racialized assumptions that subtly work against our eager desire for "racial reconciliation." In refusing to come to terms with Sin as a sculpting, cosmic power—and this is the best face to put on it—the White evangelical church continues to repeat its history of silent compliance in the face of injustice.[9] Or—and this is the more realistic face to put on it—it continues to repeat its history of not just being complicit in racial injustice, but an *unacknowledged* "conductor" and catalyst of White supremacy.[10]

All of this is melded closely together with the primary way in which most White evangelicals articulate what it means to be a Christian, namely, "having a personal relationship with Jesus." Robert Jones enlarges on this point:

> [T]hese cultural tools—freewill individualism, relationalism, and antistructuralism—coalesce powerfully in White evangelical Christology, which centers on having a personal relationship with Jesus. The personal Jesus paradigm represents, in compressed form, the entire conceptual model for White evangelicals' individualist cultural tool kit . . . In the personal Jesus paradigm, Jesus did not die for a cause or for humankind writ large but for each individual person. Responding positively to this invitation, entering into this relationship, is an intimate decision that must be made freely by each person as an accountable act of the will. In popular language, this act of human agency is articulated as answering a "knock at the door,"

---

social systems or structures contribute to racial problems shifts "guilt away from its root source—the accountable individual" (79).

8. Emerson and Smith, *Divided by Faith*, 78.

9. Tisby chronicles both the past and present complicity of the White church in racial discrimination and racial injustice in *Color of Compromise*.

10. Jones, *White Too Long*, 5, and see also the extensive documentation for this in Marshall, *Christianity Corrupted*. White evangelical churches currently mobilizing to fight "critical race theory" at the very time when patterns of racial injustice are blatantly clear all around them is just the latest example of such churches functioning as conductors (Jones's language) of White supremacy.

"letting Jesus come into your heart," and as reciprocating a gift, such as "giving your life to Jesus." Because the most fundamental religious act is one that takes place in the interiority of an individual's emotional, psychological, and spiritual life, it naturally fuels an antistructuralist mind-set. There's nothing in this conceptual model to provide a toehold for thinking about the way institutions or culture shape, promote, or limit human decisions or well-being.[11]

Ironically, a great deal of the scaffolding of this mutually supporting theological framework and cultural toolkit is challenged in what many White evangelicals would identify as a primary source undergirding their views, namely, Paul's letter to the Romans. This is especially true regarding the way they imagine Paul depicting the nature of justification,[12] the theological term many evangelicals would use to identify the experience—"asking Jesus into their heart"—that initiated their "personal relationship with Jesus."[13] In this essay, I engage in a brief tour of the first few chapters of Romans to show how Paul challenges this mutually supporting theological framework and cultural toolkit, arguing that Paul sews justification and sanctification together with the embodiment of justice in the face of Sin as an enslaving cosmic power. I begin the tour by making some observations about justice in the OT and calling attention to some of the aspects of Paul's argument in Romans 1–5, with a brief side glance at a feature of chapter 7. I then focus on the way Paul connects justice and justification in Romans 6 and give brief attention to how he sews both together with sanctification. I conclude with some reflections on what this—admittedly brief, partial, and no doubt contested[14]—reading of Romans suggests about the current state of much of the White evangelical church in the US.

---

11 Jones, *White Too Long*, 100.

12 For a description of the typical way that most White evangelicals understand the meaning of justification, see my summary of "The Traditional Protestant View of Justification" in "Navigating Justification."

13 To be clear, I affirm the intensely personal aspect of following Jesus. I also affirm the importance of making personal moral choices (e.g., being maritally faithful, refusing to gossip) that are in line with God's will, regardless of whether such choices have a direct connection with issues of public justice. But my focus in this essay is on the vital importance for those "in Christ" of embodying justice publicly.

14. While I will offer exegetical warrants in some places for the following reflections on Romans, to substantiate them more fully would take more space than I have.

SOME OBSERVATIONS ABOUT JUSTICE AND ROMANS 1–5

There is little doubt that the theme of justice permeates Paul's letter to the Romans.[15] But what such justice means is, like much in the interpretation of Romans, disputed. Before moving into the letter, then, it will be helpful to set out my understanding of the nature of God's covenantal justice in Scripture, especially as it is associated with the Greek word *dikaiosynē*. In the Septuagint (LXX) in general, like the usual corresponding Hebrew words in the Masoretic Text (*tsedhaqah* and *mishpat*), *dikaiosynē* and *krisis* are often used in synonymous parallelism referring to the covenantal justice God enacts and expects his people to enact (e.g., Isa 5:7; 32:16–18; Ps 71:1 LXX). Enacting *dikaiosynē* is simply part and parcel of what it means for God to be the God who rightly rules the world (e.g., Ps 82; 146).[16] The type of justice that characterizes God and God's rule of the world is not simply an act that pronounces someone guilty or innocent. Rather, it is more often God (or his representatives) acting to benefit the poor, needy, oppressed, and victims of injustice by breaking the power of oppressors who rob others of justice, thereby restoring the conditions for shalom.[17] Hence, God's *dikaiosynē* is primarily a salvific activity that *delivers* those deprived of justice and shalom and *transforms* their situations by making things right. Given that this is the sort of salvific justice that God characteristically exercises, it is that which God also expects those who reign as God's vice regents to enact as channels of God's justice (e.g., Ps 71 LXX).[18] Since God's enacting *dikaiosynē* is characteristic of God's own nature, we should not be surprised to hear Isaiah say that "the Holy God displays himself as holy by [his and

---

15. For recent examples of readings of Romans that make the theme of justice central to their interpretive agenda, see Gorman, *Romans*; Harink, *Resurrecting Justice*; Keesmaat and Walsh, *Romans Disarmed*.

16. For a more detailed discussion of Ps 82 (81 LXX) along these lines, see Yoder, *Shalom*, 27–28.

17. Note for example the language of Ps 81:3–4 LXX: "Give justice (*krinate*) to the orphan and poor; enact saving justice (*dikaiōsate*) for the lowly and needy. Deliver the needy and poor; rescue them from the hand of a sinner." (Unless otherwise noted, all Scripture translations in this essay are my own.) In addition, Isa 32:16–18 makes the connection between justice and shalom very clear: "Then justice/judgment (*krima*) will rest in the wilderness and saving justice (*dikaiosynē*) will dwell in Carmel. And the effects of saving justice (*dikaiosynē*) will be shalom/peace (*eirēnē*)" (Isa 32:16–17a LXX). The rest of this latter passage (vv. 17b–20) details the overall conditions of well-being (shalom) that results from *dikaiosynē* being enacted. Cf. Yoder, *Shalom*, 10–23.

18. Note the way that Ps 71 LXX (Ps 72) begins: "O God, give the king your justice (*krima*), and your saving justice (*dikaiosynē*) to the king's son."

his people's] *tsedhaqah/dikaiosynē*" (Isa 5:16b).[19] That is God's salvifically enacting justice—whether directly or channeled through his faithful representatives—simultaneously displays God's own holiness.

With these observations in mind, we turn to Rom 1:16-17. When informed by Rom 1:1-7, these verses contain what many would argue is the thesis of Romans:

> For I am not ashamed of the good news because it is the power of God leading to salvation for everyone exercising faith, to the Jew first and to the Greek. For God's *dikaiosynē* is being revealed in it from faith/faithfulness leading to faith/faithfulness, just as it stands written, "The just/righteous one (*ho dikaios*) will live from faith/faithfulness."

The comments above make it unlikely that God's *dikaiosynē* that is being revealed in the good news is something God "imputes" or even "imparts." Rather, what is being revealed in the good news concerning God's Son is God's liberating, justice-restoring activity, in covenantal faithfulness to Israel and the entire created order. In this salvific activity embodying covenantal faithfulness, God reclaims and reveals his rule over a world enslaved by the powers of Sin and Death in order to make right what is wrong with individuals, societies and the cosmos itself, leading to the shalom that God intends for his creation.[20] As shorthand for this broader understanding of *dikaiosynē*, I will use the language of "saving justice."[21]

This saving justice is God's response to the bad news that follows in Rom 1:18—3:20. In that section, *from his perspective of life in Christ*, Paul offers an extended description of life "in Adam," a death-bound sphere of Adamic existence/old humanity ruled over by the power of Sin.[22] In this

---

19. This portion of the verse is translated from the Masoretic Text (MT). It is slightly different in the LXX where it reads: "and the holy God *is glorified* by *dikaiosynē*). However, given that "glory" is the visible form of God's holiness (as Isa 6:3 and other passages suggest), any difference in meaning between the MT and the LXX is more apparent than real.

20. I do not mean to say that God acting in judgment should be excluded from this saving activity (cf. the comments of Brower, *Living*, 8–10).

21. Cf. the more detailed comments of Gorman, *Romans*, 68–71.

22. The only place Paul explicitly uses the language "in Adam" to describe a death-bound sphere is 1 Cor 15:22 ("in Adam all die"). But it fits the way he describes the human condition in Rom 1:18—3:20. Since 1:18-32 clearly echoes typical Jewish critiques of gentiles, it might indeed be understood as a (somewhat caricatured) Jewish portrayal of the gentile world. However, the allusion to the golden calf incident (1:23; cf. Ps 106:19-20) and Paul's following argument in 2:1—3:20 suggest that 1:18 is the beginning of his argument that all, both Jews and Greeks are "under [the power of] Sin" (3:9). Hence, there is little question that we are to imagine this enslaving power

sphere, humans are presently experiencing a foretaste of God's future wrath which God is revealing against "all the idolatry/impiety and injustice/wrongdoing (*adikia*) of those who suppress the truth with injustice/wrongdoing (*adikia*)" (1:18). This experience of present wrath involves God "giving up" humans to the consequences of their own destructive, idolatrous choices. The ultimate consequence of these destructive choices is a debased mind that is no longer able to discern God's will (1:28), leading them to practice every kind of injustice/wrongdoing (*adikia*) embodied in a variety of actions/vices (1:29–31). In their first-century context, such actions/vices may indeed refer to acts of individual sinfulness in general. But most of them also describe actions characteristic of the systemic economic injustice of Rome's predatory economy.[23]

Whoever we take to be Paul's hypocritical imaginary interlocutor in the diatribe beginning in 2:1 (a non-Christian gentile, gentile Christian, a Jew?), by 2:17 Paul adopts a common prophetic trope of turning the focus from God's judgment of the nations to pronouncing God's judgment on an imaginary self-described "Jew." This interlocutor, although relying on the Law and claiming to know God's will because he/she has been instructed by the Law, nevertheless falls under God's judgment because he/she does not keep it (vv. 17–29). While this section is not an empirical description of first-century Judaism,[24] it allows Paul to make the point that even when people understand themselves to be "entrusted with the oracles of God" (3:2), faithfulness to God and God's purposes does not necessarily follow.

This raises questions about the status and efficacy of God's good Law (*nomos*) a few verses later (3:27–31) that Paul comes back to address in more detail in 7:7–25.[25] This latter passage makes it clear that one of the reasons why "no one will be justified (*dikaiōthēsetai*) by doing works of the Law/Torah" (3:20)[26] is that "Torah itself can be taken over by Sin's cosmic

---

that issues in death for all after Adam (Rom 5:12) as working precisely in the human situation as he has described it beginning in 1:18 (cf. Keck, *Romans*, 95). Therefore, one might indeed say that 1:18—3:20 is an extended description of life in the death-bound sphere of Adam *from the perspective of life "in Christ."*

23. Keesmaat and Walsh, *Romans Disarmed*, 217–29.

24. Note, for example, that 2:21–24 in particular is part of Israel's own prophetic self-critique modeled on language from passages like Ezek 36:20, Isa 52:5, Jer 3:8–9, 7:9, and possibly Mal 3:8–9.

25. For a good brief overview of some of the interpretive difficulties of Rom 7:7–25 that ultimately arrives in a similar place as I do, see Brower, *Living*, 17–21.

26. I take the disputed phrase "works of [the] Law" as referring to practices that fulfill Torah's requirements, especially those practices in the first century that would have publicly marked one out as faithful to God's covenant, e.g., sabbath observance, food laws, and circumcision.

power and used as an instrument that ultimately brings death when it was intended to lead to life (Rom 7:4–12)."[27] In fact, Paul's own experience as Saul the persecutor is a classic example of someone desiring to be radically faithful to God and Torah by violently opposing God's enemies.[28] Like Phinehas, his predecessor, whose violent actions (Num 25:1–5) were said to be "reckoned to him for *dikaiosynē*" (Ps 106:31; cf. Gen 15:6; Rom 4:3), Paul too had been zealously (and violently!) "seeking to establish his own *dikaiosynē*" (i.e., his own loyalty to God's covenantal justice, cf. Rom 10:3). And, at least from the perspective of his understanding of Torah prior to his encounter with the risen Christ, he'd done a good job of it (Phil 3:6)! It wasn't until after that revelatory encounter with the one who embodied it that his whole understanding of God's *dikaiosynē* was transformed. Paul began to realize that even actions committed with the full intention of keeping Torah may be sins against the God who gave it.

If indeed Torah—and by extension, Christian Scripture—can be co-opted by Sin's cosmic power and used to justify coercive death-dealing actions, those "in Adam" who *consciously* imagine themselves to be aligned with God's saving justice may *unconsciously* be a "weapon of injustice" in Sin's hands (Rom 6:13a). It is undeniable that this has been the case when White church members, consciously imagining themselves to be acting for God, have used Christian Scripture to justify White supremacy and various actions taken to maintain the "peace" it brings (e.g., lynchings, enforced segregation). Indeed, Sin may not only co-opt Torah/Christian Scripture, but it may also dwell within the very bodies (i.e., their neural networks, shaping their thought, habits, and responses [7:17, 19]) of those using Torah/Christian Scripture to justify coercive, death-dealing actions at odds with God's *dikaiosynē*.[29] Human intentionality, then, cannot be the primary arbiter as to what constitutes a sinful action,[30] nor does a fervent appeal to Scripture or faithfulness to any "law and order" agenda necessarily result in what God has revealed as God's own justice. Sin, then, cannot be narrowed down to *simply* a personal problem, almost exclusively concerned with inner purity

---

27. Johnson, "'But I Never Intended . . . ,'" 135.

28. I understand Rom 7:7–25 as Paul's speech in character *from the perspective of his life in Christ* where the "I" corporately represents those who are "in Adam." Hence, while Paul is not speaking autobiographically about his *present* situation, his own past experience as a persecutor operating in the Adamic sphere may be consciously or unconsciously informing his conceptuality in this section. I presume that something like this is what Kent means in saying, "Paul's corporate language here is clearly personal as well, perhaps even autobiographical" (Brower, *Living*, 18).

29 Croasmun, *Emergence of Sin*, 128–33.

30 On this point, see my "'But I Never Intended . . . .'"

and *avoiding intentional* moralistic acts deemed sinful.[31] Indeed, if it is true that God's good Torah can be co-opted by Sin as a power, how much more can Sin co-opt the law/legal systems of the nations, whether that of imperial Rome, Nazi Germany, or the US.[32] All this is part of the bad news that Paul speaks about in Romans, namely, that Sin can co-opt not just personal relationships but structures like legal systems claiming to produce "justice" that inevitably shape how those personal relationships are lived out.

With this bad news in the background, it is precisely in the good news concerning his Son (1:3) that God's saving justice is revealed *and clarified* in both its human and divine embodiment. That is, *in opposition to other so-called forms of "justice"* used to establish "peace," God did not bring about his saving justice with coercive force involving the destruction of those who refuse to submit to it.[33] Rather God brought it about through Jesus's cruciform faithfulness (3:22) to the point of death, the one true human's obedient "act of saving justice (*dikaiōma*, 5:18)"[34] that simultaneously enacted love for sinful enemies of God and his way of doing justice (5:7–10). Jesus's faithful and loving act was the singular human embodiment of God's *dikaiosynē*, his saving justice (3:21–22). He was first God's primary *human* instrument through which divine shalom-restoring, covenantal justice was channeled to others, after which his own resurrection was a paradigmatic enactment of *divine* saving justice (*dikaiosynē*) on his behalf.[35] Jesus's resurrection, then, was the paradigmatic divine act of *justification* for a human being, what

---

31 Again, to be clear, I am *not* saying that inner purity and avoiding intentional individual sinful actions are unimportant.

32 Cf. Harink, *Resurrecting Justice*, 97–111, esp. 98.

33. Using coercive, dehumanizing force to bring about "justice" and establish "peace" among peoples they depicted as ethnically or culturally inferior and sought to control/"pacify" was the modus operandi of Rome's imperial machinery (see Strait, "Alternative Global Imaginary," 190–97, cf. Brower's comments about the nature of God's peace [*Living*, 22]). The way Romans embodied their "superior" humanity in "beastly" ways closely parallels the way many Whites in America have collectively embodied White humanity, often depicting whiteness as being intrinsic to the highest or truest form of humanity (see my "Resurrection and Ascension," 249–50).

34. Paul characterizes the grace/gift that comes through the one man in 5:17 as (or as consisting of) *the* saving justice (*tēs dikaiosynēs*). I understand this to be *the* same saving justice that has been Paul's focus in Romans all along, viz., God's saving justice. Since God's saving justice is revealed precisely in Christ's faithfulness (3:22), when Paul refers to the *dikaiōma* of the one man in 5:18, it makes sense to take it as an obedient act through which God's saving justice comes. Cf. Keck who argues along similar lines (*Romans*, 153–54).

35. In Second Temple Judaism, "[r]esurrection and divine justice came to be so intimately interconnected that they offered mutual, even inseparable, corroboration" (Elledge, *Resurrection*, 82).

Peter Leithart calls a "deliverdict."[36] It was an execution of God's saving justice that not only declared Jesus to be in the right by *vindicating* his faithful "obedience unto death" (cf. 1 Tim 3:16); it also delivered him from Death's dominion, *transforming* his crucified, dishonored body into a glorified human body (Phil 3:21; by implication 1 Cor 15:43).[37]

One might, then, extend and paraphrase Rom 4:25 as follows: "[Christ] was handed over because of our trespasses *in a cruciform act of faithfulness that was the human embodiment of divine saving justice for others*. He was raised, *thereby himself experiencing divine saving justice*, with a view to (*dia*)[38] our justification (*dikaiōsin*), i.e., *our experiencing God's saving justice so that, in Christ, by the transforming power of the Spirit who raised him, we might then become its human embodiment*. Christ has indeed become the one in whom both human and divine *dikaiosynē* come to their fullest expression (1 Cor 1:30). As such, on the logic of Isa 5:16b referred to above, he is also the one in whom both human and divine holiness (*hagiasmos*) come to their fullest expression (1 Cor 1:30).

Before moving on to Romans 6, a few words about its narrower literary context are in order. Romans 5–8 has often been understood as outlining a temporal sequence of steps in an individual's Christian life where Paul focuses on justification in chapter 5, leaves it behind to focus on sanctification in chapters 6–7, and then discusses glorification in chapter 8. Recent scholarship on Paul, however, suggests that the whole section is better understood as an exposition from numerous angles of the newly liberated and transformed life in Christ of those who are justified by faith/faithfulness.[39] Aspects of that transformed, justified life that Paul discusses before chapter 6 include:

---

36. Leithart clarifies the language of "deliverdict" as follows: "[T]he key point is that for Paul the paradigmatic justification, the justification of Jesus, is not a 'mere verdict,' a mere verbal/judicial declaration that Jesus is righteous. Had the Father pronounced Jesus to be in the right but left Him in the grave, the Father's promise would have been falsified. Jesus's justification takes the form of a resurrection, a transforming event that is also His deliverance from the realm of death. Justification for sinners is precisely the same, an 'enacted verdict' that both declares us in the right and delivers us from the dominion of sin and death" ("Justification," 67).

37. Johnson, "Past, Present, and Future," 210–11. Cf. Wright, *Resurrection*, 248, 270–71.

38. Although his focus is more on the forensic aspect of justification than is mine, Michael Bird offers a good defense of this prospective translation of *dia* ("Justified by Christ's Resurrection," 83–84). For a defense of the retrospective translation of *dia* ("because of"), see Kirk, *Unlocking Romans*, 77–81.

39. E.g., see Gorman, *Inhabiting*, 73–79; Gorman, *Romans*, 165–67.

- reconciliation with God (Rom 5:1, 10–11), necessarily issuing in concrete reconciliation with others (Rom 12–15);
- a reversal of condemnation/guilt (i.e., forgiveness) for participating in the trespass/disobedience characteristic of life in the Adamic sphere (Rom 5:16).

A traditional Protestant/Evangelical view of justification would also affirm these as aspects of justification—although perhaps with less (or no!) emphasis on justification as *necessarily* issuing in concrete reconciliation with others. Both these aspects of justification are crucial. But Rom 6 moves further in its exposition of justification as transformative, insisting that justification includes a moving out of the death-bound Adamic sphere of our old, distorted humanity controlled by the cosmic powers of Sin and Death into the life-bound sphere of Christ, the truly human "last Adam."[40] We now turn to that exposition.

ROMANS 6: JUSTIFIED/SANCTIFIED WEAPONS OF JUSTICE

In Rom 6:1–11 Paul insists that when one dies and is buried with Christ in baptism, we are transferred "into Christ Jesus" (v. 3), i.e., into the corporate body/sphere of the last Adam in which our old Adamic humanity (*ho palaios hēmōn anthrōpos*), that form of humanity characterized by idolatry and injustice/exploitation of others, has been co-crucified with Christ (6:6a).[41] By participating in Christ's death "the body under the control of the cosmic power of Sin (*to sōma tēs hamartias*) is done away with so that we might no longer be enslaved to Sin" (6:6b). This last Adam's one-time death to Sin's ability as a cosmic power to subject him to injustice (6:10)[42] kills the *inevitability* of our being enslaved to that cosmic power (cf. 6:2). Hence, this one man's obedient act of saving justice (*dikaiōma*, 5:18) releases/justifies (*dedikaiōtai*) those who participate in his death from Sin's cosmic, enslaving

---

40. Although Paul uses the language of "last Adam" only in 1 Cor 15:45, the juxtaposition of the actions of Adam and Christ in 5:12–21 suggests that the language is appropriate when describing aspects of his argument from 5:12 on in Romans.

41. In this section, I am drawing on and slightly modifying material from my "Past, Present, and Future," 215–19.

42. Christ was never under Sin's power in that he was a weapon of injustice in its hand. But, as God's paradigmatic weapon of saving justice, he experienced the injustice enacted by those under Sin's power. Hence, his death to Sin was a death to Sin's power to subject him to injustice. His death to Sin, then, is not strictly analogous to ours, but rather its obverse. Cf. Jewett, *Romans*, 407.

power (6:7).⁴³ The language of 6:7 (*dedikaiōtai*), then, makes it clear that this being released from slavery to Sin's cosmic power that makes one a weapon of injustice (*adikias*) in its hand (6:13, 18–19) is constitutive of "having been and remaining justified (*dedikaiōtai*)."⁴⁴

But the event of baptism, like the event of being justified, entails not only participating in Christ's death and burial, but in his resurrection as well,⁴⁵ so that "we might (currently) walk in the newness that is engendered by his risen life" (to slightly paraphrase 6:4c). This comes out clearly in the parallel pattern shared by Christ and those in Christ in 6:10–11, verses which might be paraphrased as follows:

> For the death that Jesus died was a one-time *death to Sin*, and the *risen life* he is currently living (as he is reigning in power until all things are placed under his feet) *is for God*. So also, you all consider yourselves as *dead to Sin* but *alive for God* in the cruciform, corporate body of the now risen and reigning Christ.

In 6:12–14a, Paul enlarges on what it means to be justified when one is *dead to Sin* but *alive for God* (with my interpretive comments in brackets):

> Therefore [since Christ's death has broken Sin's enslaving power], don't continue allowing Sin to rule in/by means of your mortal bodies resulting in your obeying your body's desires. Nor go on presenting the members [of your body] to Sin as [its] weapons of injustice (*hopla adikias*). But present yourselves *to God* as *alive from the dead* and [present] the members of your body as weapons of saving justice (*hopla dikaiosynēs*) to God. For Sin is no longer ruling over you all.

While Paul's prohibitions in these verses assume that Christ's death has broken Sin's power to enslave those in Christ so that they are *dead to Sin*, his positive commands assume that Christ's resurrection has engendered the gift of life-giving power/agency (i.e., the "making-alive Spirit) enabling

---

43. Whether 6:7 is read christologically or as referring generically to everyone "in Christ" makes little difference here since the entire context is about participating in the one man's death/crucifixion.

44. My somewhat wooden translation seeks to convey the effect of the perfect tense of this verb.

45. Although some continue to argue that Paul only speaks of sharing in Christ's resurrection in the future, others have offered compelling arguments that Paul believes those who are "in Christ" participate even now in his resurrected life. For recent examples, see Tappenden, *Resurrection in Paul*, 135–227; Gorman, *Inhabiting*, 73–75; Wright, *Resurrection*, 248–54; Kirk, *Unlocking Romans*, 107–17; Gaffin, "Redemption and Resurrection," 26–27.

Justification, Sanctification, and Systemic Racism

those in him to "present [themselves] *to God as alive from the dead* and the members of their body as weapons of saving justice (*hopla dikaiosynēs*) to God" for use in his continuing saving mission.[46] Since Jesus's resurrection was itself an *act of saving justice/justification*, it engenders the power for freed humans to now present themselves to God as *justified cruciform*[47] weapons of God's saving justice. This *Spirit-enabled* presenting of our bodies/members as channels through whom God—in the face of suffering and opposition—continues the rescue mission of reversing the chaos and injustice of life "in Adam" *completes God's act of justifying us in the present.*[48] Our earlier paraphrase of 4:25, then, rings true. In his resurrection, Christ *experienced God's saving justice* with a view to (or to bring about) our justification (*dikaiōsin*), one aspect of which is our transfer out of the Adamic sphere of Sin and Death into the sphere/body of Christ, a just community whose members practice justice as channels of God's saving justice. The last Adam/truly Human One *first* became God's paradigmatic human instrument of divine saving justice in his cruciform, shalom-engendering life and faithful obedience unto death out of love for others. Only *then* did he experience resurrection as an act of God's saving justice. For those who are *currently* in his corporate body, the order is reversed. They *first* experience being raised to walk in the newness his risen life engenders as God's transformative act of saving justice in order to *then* become the reconciled, forgiven, and cruciform human instruments of that saving justice. As Michael J. Gorman articulates the upshot of this, "Paul understands justification as participatory transformation in the justice of God in Christ that creates a just people."[49]

What is more, this cruciform pattern of life of enslavement to God/saving justice (6:16–17) is constitutive of the nature of holiness/sanctification (*hagiosmos*).[50] Romans 6:18–19 (with my interpretive comments in brackets) makes this clear:

46. Cf. the similar language of Greathouse, *Romans 1–8*, 185.

47. Our present sharing in Christ's resurrected life is best described as being "resurrection suffused but cruciform in shape" rather than as "resurrectiform" in shape (on which, see Gorman, *Participating*, 53–76). Hence, being a "weapon" through whom God continues his saving justice means precisely the opposite of exercising coercive and exploitative power over others to force them into conformity with one's agenda, even—or especially!—when one imagines that agenda as "Christian."

48. In what follows, when I use the language of justification being incomplete, I am referring to the present effects of God's justifying action as described by Paul. I am *not* referring to our *final* justification that is completed only in our future resurrection at Christ's *parousia*.

49. Gorman, *Becoming the Gospel*, 228.

50. I develop this theme more widely in Scripture in *Holiness and the Missio Dei*.

> Now having been freed from Sin [by sharing in the death of the truly Human One], you all have been enslaved to [God's] saving justice (*tē dikaiosynē*) [by sharing in the risen life of the truly Human One] . . . For just as you all presented your members as slaves to impurity resulting in lawlessness leading to more lawlessness, so now [by the enabling life-giving power of the Spirit that emanates from the Last Adam's resurrection] present yourselves as slaves to [God's] saving justice (*tē dikaiosynē*) leading to holiness/sanctification (*eis hagiasmon*).

Being empowered by the Holy Spirit who sets them apart "in Christ Jesus," those who have been and remain justified/released" (*dedikaiōtai*, 6:7) from Sin's enslaving rule are able to freely present themselves as slaves to God's gracious rule by acting as the cruciform channels of God's saving justice (*dikaiosynē*). Because "the Holy God displays himself as holy by his [and his people's] *tsedhaqah/dikaiosynē*" (Isa 5:16b),[51] acting as cruciform weapons of God's saving justice simultaneously displays God's holiness. In this way, those participating in God's rescue mission as transformed, cruciform weapons of God's saving justice (i.e., those who are justified), are set apart and are being reshaped into God's own image, both personally and corporately. As such, they are *being* sanctified.[52] Hence, Paul sews justification and sanctification together, with the practice of God's saving justice being constitutive of both.

CONCLUDING REFLECTIONS: "WHAT THEN SHALL WE SAY?"

What indeed shall White evangelical churches in the US say in light of our brief tour through Romans? Will we continue in the sphere of Sin's power that shapes society, the church, and our very bodies and neural networks in justice-denying, death-dealing, racist ways? Who will rescue us from these bodies of death? Who indeed will rescue us from these corporate and individual bodies that deal out death—even if unknowingly and unintentionally—to those we refuse to listen to, all the while being dragged down to death ourselves? Paul's answer, of course, should also be ours. Only God, working by means of the Spirit, to locate us in the sphere of Christ can rescue us. But doubling down on the claim to already have "a personal relationship with Jesus" that conveniently fits into, and undergirds, our cultural tool kit

---

51. On the words in brackets and the implications of this reading, see Moberly, "Whose Justice?," 63.

52. Cf. the comments of Greathouse, *Romans 1–8*, 193.

that blinds us to injustice and our own unacknowledged and unintentional participation in it will only hinder our rescue.

What then is needed based on our short tour through Romans? Simply stated, much of White evangelicalism needs to have its justification completed with (1) the acknowledgement and co-crucifixion of our old Adamic "White" humanity and (2) the presentation of our bodies as *cruciform* weapons of God's saving justice in situations permeated with racial injustice. Let me expand further on each of these in turn.

White evangelicalism often professes its longing for reconciliation with its African American brothers and sisters in Christ, primarily by forging personal relationships with them. But, before genuine and lasting reconciliation can take place, White evangelicals will first have to become aware of the sort of humanity we have collectively embodied in the past and continue to embody in the present. Quite simply, we first need to get to know ourselves before trying harder to have relationships with our Black brothers and sisters. There are now plentiful resources available that the Spirit may use to unveil with utter clarity America's racialized history[53] and the role played in it by the White (especially evangelical) church.[54] But unless we cooperate with the Spirit and avail ourselves of these resources, we will continue to bear the scars that Sin has inflicted on our whole being rather than having our minds transformed.[55] We will continue to be ignorant about the way that White Americans constructed "true humanity" as intrinsically White and depicted Black males in particular as "beasts" who threatened the purity and superiority of the White race.[56] We will remain unaware as to how such depictions frequently led to false accusations of rape against Black men, with their humiliated, and sometimes physically emasculated bodies, hung on thousands of trees in the lynching era.[57] We will continue to find ways of blaming African Americans for the ongoing injustice produced by such racialized history because we will remain blind to the way that we have collectively embodied a form of Adamic humanity that can only be called "beastly." And we will remain blind to the way that we continue to do so when we not only tolerate, but enthusiastically support Sin-saturated "law and order" agendas that have disproportionate and decimating effects on

---

53. E.g., Kendi, *Stamped from the Beginning*.

54. E.g., Tisby, *Color of Compromise*; Jones, *White Too Long*; Marshall, *Christianity Corrupted*.

55. Cf. the reflections of Brower, *Living*, 39–40.

56. For a brief sketch of this phenomenon, see my "Resurrection and Ascension," 249–50, and the literature cited there.

57. On the clear analogies between Jesus being "hung on a tree" (Acts 5:30; 10:39) and the lynchings of African Americans, see Cone, *Cross and the Lynching Tree*.

predominantly African American communities.[58] We might claim that we are no longer under condemnation/guilt, "reconciled to God," and long for reconciliation with our African American brothers and sisters in Christ. But until our justification is complete with the acknowledgement and co-crucifixion of our old Adamic "White" humanity, our corporate and individual bodies will remain under Sin's powerful control and will be used as weapons of injustice in its hands.

But for our justification to be complete, we not only need the "beastly" form of humanity we have collectively embodied to die; by the power of the Spirit generated by Christ's resurrection, we need to present our bodies as *cruciform* weapons of God's saving justice in situations permeated with racial injustice. In a recent blog post decrying the often-sentimental evangelical preoccupation with "asking Jesus into my heart" with little thought "of what claims he has made on our bodies," Tim Gombis enlarges on this point as follows:

> But what is needed is not emotion, nor feeling, nor sentiment, nor even our thoughts. What is needed in this moment, as ever, is white bodies joined together with black and brown bodies as a body—bodies and body committed to God's public justice.[59]

What is needed to complete our justification, then, is not simply to present our individual bodies as weapons of God's saving justice, but to do so as a part of the *singular/corporate* "living sacrifice" that is indeed "holy and acceptable to God" (Rom 12:1). Our black, brown, and white bodies joined together in one ecclesial body in witness to God's saving justice—thereby publicly displaying God's own character/holiness—would be a powerful public demonstration of God's reconciling power in our contentious US context. Without becoming a part of such a just people whose life together becomes a channel of God's saving justice, our justification—and sanctification as well—remains presently incomplete. We remain conformed to the world as constructed by "whiteness" rather than having our minds renewed. We remain trapped in the sphere of Adamic humanity, unable to discern what is the will of God (Rom 12:2; cf. 1:28), looking but never perceiving, hearing but never understanding. Lord, have mercy. Christ, have mercy.[60]

---

58. On which, see Michelle Alexander, *New Jim Crow*.

59. Gombis, "Anemic Individualism." Emphasis original.

60. With appreciation and gratitude, I dedicate this essay to my friend and colleague, Kent Brower. For the last twenty or so years, his friendship and scholarship have enriched my life in numerous ways.

WORKS CITED

Alexander, Michelle. *The New Jim Crow: Mass Incarceration in the Age of Colorblindness.* New York: New Press, 2012.

Bird, Michael. "Justified by Christ's Resurrection: A Neglected Aspect of Paul's Doctrine of Justification." *SBET* 22 (2004) 72–91.

Brower, Kent. *Living as God's Holy People: Holiness and Community in Paul.* Milton Keynes: Paternoster, 2010.

Cone, James H. *The Cross and the Lynching Tree.* Maryknoll, NY: Orbis, 2011.

Croasmun, Matthew. *The Emergence of Sin: The Cosmic Tyrant in Romans.* Oxford: Oxford University Press, 2017.

Elledge, C. D. *Resurrection of the Dead in Early Judaism 200 BCE–CE 200.* Oxford: Oxford University Press, 2017.

Emerson, Michael O., and Christian Smith. *Divided by Faith: Evangelical Religion and the Problem of Race in America.* Oxford: Oxford University Press, 2000.

Gaffin, Richard B. "Redemption and Resurrection: An Exercise in Biblical-Systematic Theology." *Themelios* 27 (2002) 16–31.

Gombis, Tim. "The Anemic Individualism of White Evangelicalism." https://timgombis.com/2020/06/10/the-anemic-individualism-of-white-evangelicalism/.

Gorman, Michael J. *Becoming the Gospel: Paul, Participation, and Mission.* Grand Rapids: Eerdmans, 2015.

———. *Inhabiting the Cruciform God: Kenosis, Justification, and Theosis in Paul's Narrative Soteriology.* Grand Rapids: Eerdmans, 2009.

———. *Participating in Christ: Explorations in Paul's Theology and Spirituality.* Grand Rapids: Baker Academic, 2019.

———. *Romans: A Theological and Pastoral Commentary.* Grand Rapids: Eerdmans, 2022.

Greathouse, William M., with George Lyons. *Romans 1–8: A Commentary in the Wesleyan Tradition.* NBBC. Kansas City: Beacon Hill Press, 2008.

Harink, Douglas. *Resurrecting Justice: Reading Romans for the Life of the World.* Downers Grove, IL: IVP Academic, 2020.

Jennings, Willie James. "Can White People Be Saved?" Reflections on the Relationship of Missions and Whiteness." In *Can "White" People Be Saved? Triangulating Race, Theology, and Mission*, edited by Love L. Sechrest et al., 27–43. Downers Grove, IL: IVP Academic, 2018.

Jewett, Robert. *Romans.* Hermeneia. Minneapolis: Fortress, 2007.

Johnson, Andy. "'But I Never Intended . . .': Implicit Hamartiology in the Thessalonian Correspondence." In *Sin and Its Remedy in Paul*, edited by John K. Goodrich and Nijay Gupta, 130–46. Eugene, OR: Catalyst, 2020.

———. *Holiness and the Missio Dei.* Eugene, OR: Cascade, 2016.

———. "Navigating Justification: Conversing with Paul." *Catalyst* 37 (2010) 1–4.

———. "The Past, Present, and Future of Bodily Resurrection as Salvation: Christ, Church, and Cosmos." In *Cruciform Scripture: Cross, Participation, and Mission*, edited by Christopher W. Skinner et al., 207–24. Grand Rapids: Eerdmans, 2021.

———. "The Resurrection and Ascension of True Humanity in Luke-Acts." *Journal of Theological Interpretation* 15 (2021) 247–261.

Jones, Robert P. *White Too Long: The Legacy of White Supremacy in American Christianity.* New York: Simon & Schuster, 2020.

Keck, Leander E. *Romans*. Abingdon New Testament Commentaries. Nashville: Abingdon, 2005.

Keesmaat, Sylvia C., and Brian J. Walsh. *Romans Disarmed: Resisting Empire/Demanding Justice*. Grand Rapids: Brazos, 2019.

Kendi, Ibram X. *Stamped from the Beginning: The Definitive History of Racist Ideas in America*. New York: Nation, 2016.

Kirk, J. R. Daniel. *Unlocking Romans: Resurrection and the Justification of God*. Grand Rapids: Eerdmans, 2008.

Leithart, Peter. "Justification as Verdict and Deliverance: A Biblical Perspective." *ProEccl* 16 (2007) 56–72.

Marshall, Jermaine. *Christianity Corrupted: The Scandal of White Supremacy*. Maryknoll, NY: Orbis, 2021.

Moberly, R. W. L. "Whose Justice? Which Righteousness? The Interpretation of Isaiah V 16." *Vetus Testamentum* 51 (2001) 55–68.

Rothstein, Richard. *The Color of Law: A Forgotten History of How Our Government Segregated America*. New York: Liveright, 2017.

Strait, Drew J. "An Alternative Global Imaginary: Imperial Rome's *Pax Romana* and Luke's 'Counter-Violent' *Missio Dei*." In *Cruciform Scripture: Cross, Participation and Mission*, edited by Christopher W. Skinner et al., 184–206. Grand Rapids: Eerdmans, 2021.

Tappenden, Frederick S. *Resurrection in Paul: Cognition, Metaphor, and Transformation*. Early Christianity and Its Literature 19. Atlanta: SBL, 2016.

Tisby, Jemar. *The Color of Compromise: The Truth about the American Church's Complicity in Racism*. Grand Rapids: Zondervan, 2019.

Wright, N. T. *The Resurrection of the Son of God*. Minneapolis: Fortress, 2003.

Yoder, Perry B. *Shalom: The Bible's Word for Salvation, Justice, and Peace*. Eugene, OR: Wipf & Stock, 2017.

Holiness and a Life Reflecting Justice: Where Do We Go from Here?

Wesley's "Thoughts on Slavery" for the Twenty-First Century

Deirdre Brower Latz

THE COMPLEXITY OF JUSTICE and its interface with faith was introduced to me at a young age. On a long drive across Canadian prairies, in a packed VW Rabbit car, dog, kids and parents all stuffed in, we read books out loud. My life was changed by "Biko," by Donald Woods. Through it my brother and I were introduced to suffering, injustice, crushing oppression of police violence, state-sanctioned policies of terror and systematic racism—undisguised—perpetuated by leaders who claimed obedience to Scripture. The complexity grew because my maternal grandparents were Canadian/American missionaries serving in South Africa at the time. Ideas I didn't have words for rattled around in my teen-aged brain: complicity, complexity, exploitation, death-hermeneutics, corruption, heresy, violation, misappropriation, and intersectionality amongst them. As an adult I've made it my life's pursuit to understand, explore and challenge theological frameworks for injustice and their counterpart: arguments from a Wesleyan-holiness framework to tilt the church towards justice as public and private, institutional, congregation and personal practice. I want to explore an approach to forming a Wesleyan theological framework that might guide the church towards embodying Scriptural Holiness as inherently challenging injustice in all forms.

I recognize the challenges. Wesley does not speak directly into a twenty-first century world in its complexity. Yet within Wesley's theological life there are trajectories that enable us to grapple within our contexts with integrity. I am drawing on contemporary ideas and language to capture Wesley's view: experience and eye-witness accounts (ethnography), dignity, solidarity, structural sin, advocacy, collaboration, agency, and equality are essential parts of justice, empowered by the Spirit.

Wesley was profoundly Anglican, theologically orthodox, shaped by its tradition, the wider European context, his mission, experience, "reason" and Scripture. "[T]heological knowledge gained through the exploration of situations is gained in constant dialogue with scripture."[1] Wesley's unique contribution blended elements (e.g., small groups, education, field preaching and women's preaching) into a systematized approach. He supported his views by nascent ethnography, gathering evidence by visits, observations, correspondence and interviews with those who testified experientially to God's indwelling. People experiencing "vital Christian" life, forgiveness,

and "assurance,"[2] addressed questions: To whom is the life of Jesus given? To what extent can people be changed? What is the nature of Christian obedience and service? How and why should Christians respond to poverty, dehumanization, exploitation and oppression? What bears out "natural law'? What can no right-thinking Christian support? What might make society more holy?

In his day, slavery had been increasingly supported culturally and theologically. The Anglican church set up "Queen Anne's Bounty"[3] in 1704, a fund then designated to support poor clergy, through annuities or farmed land. It invested in the *South Sea Company*, which traded in slaves. In America, in the 1730s Wesley witnessed slavery. His personal encounters with slaves in America and the UK, his reading of material, and correspondence with the Philadelphia anti-slavery campaigner and quaker Anthony Bezenet, and early Anglican abolitionist Granville Sharp shaped him. Wesley's clear sense of humanizing of all people came into sharp focus. His financial circumstances meant that he was distanced from profiteering from the slave trade, but was aware of it.

An essential matter to learn from Wesley, then, is the significance of his first-hand knowledge and research into the problems of the day. From eye-witness accounts, experience recounted in journals and letters, and in personal connection with other leaders, he was compelled to advocate for anti-slavery movements. From the mid-1730s he describes visceral responses to these experiences. His 1755 "Explanatory Notes on the New

---

1. Swinton and Mowat. *Practical Theology*, 16.
2. Baker, "John Wesley and Practical Divinity," 8.
3. The National Archives has the whole formation of the Bounty, but even more recently the Church of England has published a report on the links of the Church to the bounty. See "Church Commissioners' Research."

Testament" emphasized that he had a "perfect detestation" of the slave trade and described the "man-stealers" as "the worst of all thieves."[4] Wesley was convinced slavery was cruel, unjust and incompatible with human life and godliness. As he described unscrupulous and despicable violence and fraud engaged in "procurement" of the Africans, his disdain for slavers, their cruelty and barbarism is clear.

His focus, based on theological anthropology, was equality and direct accountability by those complicit in buying and debasing other humans. His tract is addressed to beneficiaries of slavery: slave owners, those transporting slaves and the profiteering that accompanied slavery in general. He called into question the reasons for slavery, its system of justification and its horror. He did not challenge the scaffolding that propped the system up—either government or monarchy. His critics (there are many[5]) note he does not go far enough. His challenge is to the morality of the slavers, captains of ships, merchants and plantation owners, not to the crown, nor church. This challenge is fair. Wesley was no revolutionary: indeed as a priest, he had sworn an oath to the crown and aligned himself with the establishment. Located in a century not far removed from rebellion and executions for treason, Wesley's family had left non-conformity for Anglicanism but were open to scrutiny—was he loyal to the throne? His penetrating case for change was from amongst and within established religion and the class system of the day.

However frustrating and limited, its publication formed part of the chorus that paved the way for the eventual abolition of slavery.[6] This tract, his pastoral practice, journals and sermons offer trajectories that enable us to wrestle with racism and neo-colonialism today as a matter of holiness.

For Wesley, holiness is rooted in love of God and for the other, expressed as active pursuit of justice. This is a recovery of what he considers to be vital religion and primitive impulses of the church. The starting place of God's love for humankind is the heart of Wesley's expansive holiness, expressed in personal experience, holy-living and sanctification of the whole person, and in public expressions of faithful witness attached to justice and morality. "Methodist" communities were formed ethically; their prioritizing of love for one another shaped them into people willing to work for and alongside one another. Solidarity is an important element for Wesleyans in pursuit of justice. Knowing the Other is essential. The compelling argument

---

4. Wesley, *Notes*, 52.

5. See Robinson Brown, "Why should Christians," for example, or Reddie, "Decolonising."

6. Note that contrary to a UK narrative of it being the first to abolish slavery, slavery was abolished in a range of countries first, either partially or completely, Denmark-Norway being the first to ban transatlantic slavery in 1803.

is for believers to know Others with lived experience of racism or oppression in other forms. He states, for instance:

> One great reason why the rich, in general, have so little sympathy for the poor is because they so seldom visit them. Hence it is that, according to the common observation, one part of the world does not know what the other suffers. Many of them do not know because they do not care to know: they keep out of the way of knowing it -and then plead their voluntary ignorance as an excuse for their hardness of heart. "Indeed, Sir," (said a person of large substance), "I am a very compassionate man. But, to tell you the truth I do not know anybody in the world that is in want." How did this come to pass? Why, he took great care to keep out of their way. And if he fell upon any of them unawares, "he passed over on the other side."[7]

Wesley is also a diagnostician. Sin is at work when there is an inadequate understanding of the image of God in the Other. Understanding all humankind in any way other than God's image bearers—as commodity, product, less-than, Other, enemy—and thus dehumanizing them is sinful, a product of devilish works and a matter of shame. Naming evil was vital for Wesley, though he left his most powerful criticism for those IN the community. Social structures that support racism, voices of extreme nationalism, a culture of violence against women and girls, sexualized cultures, and neo-colonial approaches to world order are violating lives globally. Wesley helps us here: whenever people are debased, challenge must be invoked. His identification that Africans were "Banished from their country, from their friends and relations for ever, from every comfort of life, they are reduced to a state scarce any way preferable to that of beasts of burden . . . Did the Creator intend, that the noblest creatures in the visible world, would live such a life as this! 'Are these thy glorious works, Parent of Good'?"[8] challenged slavery. He excoriates a lack of humankindness, compassion and mercy as incompatible with Christian witness in the world. When faced with people in misery, whether slaves or debtors, a necessary empathetic response in a Christian framework is active engagement. Hearts should be moved to act by the plight of others and naming the sin at work as well as responding to the present need.

Compassion and engagement are matched with advocacy for the least. He exercised his platform in calling for freedom for slaves, release for debtors and restructuring of society for those in most need. His compassion

---

7. Wesley, *Works*, 3:392–93.
8. Wesley, *Thoughts upon Slavery*, 23.

Holiness and a Life Reflecting Justice: Where Do We Go from Here?

revolved around justice and bringing others to understand the sin they engaged in, believing once they saw/understood (were conscientized), transformation would occur. His advocacy took different forms. In "Thoughts upon Slavery," it was directed at those involved actively in slaving. He refused to be silent, but was convinced speaking out was a marker of his loyalty; in this way he is both loyal and oppositional. Where he saw abuse, he named it.

> Who can reconcile this treatment of the negroes, first and last, with either mercy or justice. Where is the justice of inflicting the severest evils, on those who have done us no wrong? Of depriving those that never injured us in word or deed, or every comfort of life? Of tearing them from their native country, and depriving them of liberty itself? . . . where is the justice of taking away the lives of innocent, inoffensive men?[9]

Recovering humanized approaches and emphasizing the image of God in all others was a clear emphasis. His approach to dignity was not limited to Christians but extended to all. For Wesley, that hearts would be moved by the plight of those enslaved was a Christian imperative. He insists that Christians see the Other as Christ's: dehumanizing people treated as chattel or commodity. In the current North Atlantic world, high rates of imprisonment, arrest, criminalized innocents and adultified young people in cycles of poverty are clear to see and are sin and oppression.[10] The analysis of systems and structures of oppression and the church's role as a vehicle and source of anti-oppression as a means to rehumanize and work for the dignity of others is imperative.

Although addressed to the "public" and calling for wholesale change, Wesley's primary call was to "Methodists"—since releasing captives, visiting, relieving and being present with the suffering Other is what Christians do. Because he held to an essential dignity of each human, anything that diminished or obstructed human flourishing was scrutinized: if people suffered, the Christian's role was to understand it, be in solidarity, engage and commit. Wesley was ruthless in expecting that faith would be matched by practice: morally, socially and personally. Methodists were to be immersed in the world for the Gospel's sake. For Wesley, distance or outsourcing to professionals (priests) was anathema: instead, it was imperative that Christians think rightly, see wisely, speak clearly and personally engage to bring about change and transformation. He had a high expectation that Christians would live as they professed.

9. Wesley, *Thoughts upon Slavery*, 34.
10. E.g., Edelman, *Not a Crime to be Poor*.

Wesley's Methodist groups were multi-dimensional. Successful ones incubated personal change and gathered people who worked in solidarity to participate in social change. As avid readers, listeners and discipled people, they were convinced and convicted by some of Wesley's words, which in turn affected actions. The impetus of Wesley's work here meant that in some places subsequent to his death (the UK, Barbados), Methodists were anti-slavery agitators and seeded abolition support in the minds of the Methodist movement. Movements like these, agitating against slavery, racism, violence against women, oppression, exploitation, poverty and inequality, are vital for the church: they are on the side of justice and God's life in us as liberating and transformative. Of course, these are contested views in such a way that they polarize the church and sow division. For Wesley, however, collaborating with others who saw rightly was significant. Wesley aligned himself with others around shared vision for emancipation and dared to do so against strong opposition from within the church. Personal courage to speak, witness and act powerfully and courageously on behalf of the marginalized is a clear Wesleyan imperative. The church's public role, however, and the escalation into public engagement on behalf and alongside the marginalized is essential. This is a logical outcome of Wesley's approach, taking his arguments to the next level of constructive engagement for the sake of those most affected by systems and forms of oppression.

Thoughts upon Slavery did not challenge the primary system of the day, the monarchy or the governing model which gave permission for companies, the church, and individuals—including aristocratic Christians —to profit from slavery. A trajectory to be developed from Wesley is related to finding ways of speaking against systemic injustice—both in the church and wider society. In some areas Wesley was clear about naming and unpicking structural injustices—in relation to food prices, enclosure acts and taxation he drew very clear lines between the structures and oppression. Wesley understood people who lived in poverty or as slaves did so through no fault of their own. He saw the impact of sin and greed on the lives of the poorest around him.

To this end, Wesley's followers should emphasize the dignity and intrinsic worth of humankind and courageously call for freedom and equality. Wesley made his case for dignity by invoking natural law. In *Thoughts upon Slavery*, he says "Liberty is the right of every human creature, as soon as he breathes the vital air. And no human law can deprive him of that right, which he derives from the law of nature."[11] For Wesley, humankind is intrinsically worthy of dignity and to be afforded respect.

---

11. Wesley, *Thoughts upon Slavery*, 34.

Holiness and a Life Reflecting Justice: Where Do We Go from Here?

Drawing on his own experience, Wesley commended others to come to a point and place of compassion and conviction. The magnitude of his vision for the whole person embraced his understanding of Scriptural Holiness as a whole person ethic empowered by the Spirit.

> What Wesley . . . did was to change entirely the grounds of debate over religion . . . He was not interested in interminable debate about religion, nor was he interested simply in manners and morals . . . He was interested in a vital religion, we would say existential, faith which involved the whole [hu]man.[12]

Wesley's call to personal, internal engagement in the life of faith and an assurance of salvation was paired with a commitment to a public testimony and witness to that same encounter with God and from this testimony came witness and action for transformation. In this aspect of Wesley's thought, "freedom of choice" given to the Other is significant. Every person had agency, each one could truly respond and truly receive. For Wesley, the initiator of response and life was always located in Godself, not human will, always a feature of God's love, not of human drive. Nevertheless, the freedom and the need for people to have the freedom to exercise their inherent worth was essential. His pragmatic actions as a priest meant that all people needed to be free. Literally free, from poverty, repression, oppression and slavery. This was a matter of grave importance—without freedom and agency people could not choose God.

For Wesley, voice and "power" then was located in God, first, but then in the whole-life of a person who responded to God. For him, and his followers, the reality of life together was focused in receiving, offering and living out the power of the Spirit. That all people—slaves and free, male and female— were in the scope of God's love was a further element of his thinking. The Spirit's assurance of adoption, enabling true transformation, engagement with the scope of salvation and the fruits of repentance[13]—including a new outward-looking vision of works of mercy and piety—are vital aspects of the Via Salutis and are empowering, bringing about solidarity in God's family.[14]

In my reading of Wesley, the source of empowerment came from the Spirit, of course, but then from his stance of listening, eye-witness and personal engagement, supporting the voices of the oppressed, followed by his insistence that their participation in the movement enabled them to truly

---

12. Best, *Religion*, 186.

13. See Wesley, sermon 8, "The First Fruits of the Spirit," and sermon 4, "Scriptural Christianity," *Works* 1.

14. Brower Latz, *Contextual Reading*, 78.

live. Participation of all-comers in small groups, in formational communities, in reading, learning, speaking, praying, worshiping, feasting, giving and serving in the core practices of faith was one of inclusion and redemption leading to a new faith—not only in God, but also in one another and the possibility of life restored to wholeness, including justice. The impact on values, experiences and relationships was powerful and transformative. Inclusion in community was for all who professed faith—including slaves, free, former slaves, women and children. The aftereffects of the power encountered was a further element of Wesley's "vital religion"—people changed their lives and their communities were reshaped. The reality of "redemption and lift" was a reality for the earliest Methodists—encounters with God enabled a profound change of life. The recovery of a "primitive" faith of worship and love also resulted, however, in the making of what eventually became a powerful and influential social movement. Within Wesley's lifetime some of the advocacy he offered was of harnessing a movement in response to structural sin and for the sake of justice:

> If therefore you have any regard to justice, (to say nothing of mercy, nor of the revealed law of GOD) render unto all their due. Give liberty to whom liberty is due, that is to every child of man, to every partaker of human nature. Let none serve you but by his own act and deed, by his own voluntary choice.—Away with all whips, all chains, all compulsion! Be gentle towards men. And see that you invariably do unto every one, as you would he should do unto you.[15]

WORKS CITED

"Church Commissioners' Research into Historic Links to Transatlantic Chattel Slavery." https://www.churchofengland.org/sites/default/files/202206/Church%20Commissioners%20research%20report%20final.pdf.

Baker, Frank. "John Wesley and Practical Divinity." *WTJ* 22 (1987) 7–15.

Best, Ernest E. *Religion and Society in Transition: The Church and Social Change in England, 1560.* New York: Edwin Mellen, 1982.

Brower Latz, Deirdre. "A Contextual Reading of John Wesley's Theology and the Emergent Church: Critical Reflections on the Emergent Church Movement in Respect to Aspects of Wesley's Theology, Ecclesiology and Urban Poverty." PhD diss., University of Manchester, 2009.

Edelman, Peter. *Not a Crime to be Poor: The Criminalization of Poverty in America.* New York: The New Press, 2017.

---

15. Wesley, *Thoughts upon Slavery*, 56.

Reddie, Anthony. "Decolonising Methodist Mythology: The Search for a Usable Postcolonial Ethic." Oxford Centre for Methodism and Church History. YouTube (May 30, 2023). https://www.youtube.com/watch?v=b_PemFlLPCQ

Robinson Brown, Joel. "Why should Christians care about reparations?: Black Bodies and the Justice of God." St. Mart Magdalene School of Theology: Thinking Faithfully, (November 20, 2020). https://www.theschooloftheology.org/posts/essay/why-should-christians-care-slavery-reparations

Swinton, John, and Harriet Mowat. *Practical Theology and Qualitative Research.* London: SCM, 2016.

Wesley, John. *Explanatory Notes on the New Testament.* London: William Bowyer, 1755. *Early English Books Online Text Creation Partnership, 2011.*

———. *Thoughts upon Slavery.* Repr. with notes. Philadelphia: Joseph Crukshank, 1778. Electronic edition, UNC-CH digitization project, Documenting the American South. http://bibles.wikidot.com/wesley.

———. *The Works of John Wesley Vol. 1–4 Sermons.* Bicentennial Edition. Edited by A. Outler. Nashville, Abingdon, 1984–1987. https://docsouth.unc.edu/church/wesley/wesley.html.

The Interplay of Spiritual and Economic Aspects of *Metadidōmi* in Paul's Writings and the Implications of Economic Justice in Africa

Gift Mtukwa

ECONOMIC JUSTICE[1] IS SOMETHING that is desperately needed in Africa today. The African economies are growing yet many people still find themselves on the fringes of the economic prosperity taking place.[2] Even though Africa is endowed with many natural resources, which include oil, natural gas, precious metals, and wildlife, it still has some of the poorest people on the planet. No wonder scholars like George B. N. Ayittei have noted that Africa is a continent of paradoxes.[3] Many Africans risk their lives crossing the Atlantic oceans on boats in search of jobs which they cannot get at home. Foreign companies (Multi-national Corporations) impoverish Africans since they pay meager wages.[4] Even African leaders exacerbate the situation through rampant corruption.[5] President Uhuru Kenyatta of Kenya has stated that his country loses approximately two billion Kenyan Shillings per day (USD 17,331,022.40) to corruption. Corruption results in some

---

1. Economic justice is here defined as "a set of moral principles for building economic institutions, the ultimate goal of which is to create an opportunity for each person to create a sufficient material foundation upon which to have a dignified, productive, and creative life beyond economics." In Galea, "On Economic Justice," para. 3.

2. Methula, "Black Theology," 103.

3. Ayittey, *Africa in Chaos*, 6.

4. Oyier points out that these MNCs for the most part represent their predecessors the colonial companies whose "core characteristic was the alienation of natural resources." Oyier, "Multinational Corporations," 73.

5. Corruption is here defined as the giving and taking of bribes with the aim of gaining unfair advantage.

The Interplay of Spiritual and Economic Aspects of *Metadidōmi*

Africans having more resources than others. An Oxfam report has noted that "Africa is the most unequal continent in the world, and home to seven of the most unequal countries." This report further states that "[t]he richest 0.0001 percent own 40 percent of the wealth of the entire continent. Africa's three richest billionaire men have more wealth than the bottom 50 percent of the population of Africa, approximately 650 million people."[6] Some of the money that is looted from public coffers ends up in offshore accounts; approximately 75 percent of Africa's wealthy individuals have funds held offshore.[7] It has been noted that "offshore tax havens offering low tax rates and high levels of secrecy to companies and rich individuals are sucking immense amounts of wealth from the continent."[8]

There is a great need to redistribute wealth to benefit the ordinary *wananchi* (citizens), which is the goal of economic justice, and which seems to be at the core of Paul's ministry. He relocates economic resources from where they are to where they are most needed. Instead of taking resources to the empire (Rome) as was common practice, he redistributed resources to the poverty-stricken believers in Jerusalem from the Roman colonies.[9]

In fact, Paul's principle arising from his letters is that sharing among the people of God should be more than just spiritual (distributing of the spiritual gifts or imparting the gospel message). For Paul people of God are to share economic resources (that includes exchange of goods and services)[10] with one another and especially with those who are in need. This paper will consider Rom 1:11, 12:8, Eph 4:28, and 1 Thess 2:8, where Paul uses the word *metadidōmi* urging his audience not to choose one set of sharing against the other. The intention is to use the insights gained in this study to address the problem of economic injustice in Africa.

---

6. Seery et al., "Tale of Two Continents," 38.

7. Seery et al., "Tale of Two Continents," 23.

8. Seery at al., "Tale of Two Continents," 23.

9. Carter, *Roman Empire*, 21.

10. In Greek, the word *oikonomia* referred to "the operation of a household" whereby the economic matters were only one aspect of the household along with other aspects like administration or organization of the home. Economy is "the sum of all actions that are responsible for the provisioning of a society with goods and services." See Stegemann and Stegemann, *Jesus Movement*, 16. The exchange of goods and services was done through a system of redistribution which had its aim to control others, the result of which was the impoverishment of the people on the lower social scale. In the ancient world the "elements of the economy are . . . embedded in non-economic institutions, the economic process itself being instituted through kinship, marriage, age groups, secret societies, totemic associations and public solemnities." See Polanyi, *Primitive*, 81–82, 84. The household is the institution in which economic activities were embedded. Since the house churches functioned like households, economic exchange of goods and services was expected in them.

I will tackle one more issue of why studying Paul is significant to addressing the problem of economic injustice in the African context before turning attention to Paul. John Mbiti rightly asserts that "Africans are notoriously religious."[11] For Mbiti "[r]eligion permeates into all the departments of life so fully that it is not easy or possible to isolate it."[12] Just like in the ancient Mesopotamian and Greco-Roman society, economic and political issues were not separated from religious matters. In most African societies God is seen to be the one who provides. In the African view, God made the world and all that is in it, and he provides for humanity so that life can be sustained and continue to flourish.[13] Consequently, God is involved in all affairs. As Ayittei has noted, "Thus, every human activity on earth, including economic activity, was heavily influenced by religion."[14] The abilities and the material possessions that men and women possess come from God; the word used in Shona is *akaropadzwa na Mwari* (he/she is blessed by God). This connotes the idea of being gifted; to be gifted is to be blessed.

Ownership of the land is another important issue for our purposes. Even though land is owned by members of the family, they know that it is a gift from the ancestors, and they hold it in trust on their behalf. As Michael Bourdillon has noted concerning the Shona of Zimbabwe, "The land forms a close and enduring bond between the living and the dead: through their control of the fertility of the land they once cultivated, the spirits are believed to continue to care for their descendants and the descendants are forced to remember and honor their ancestors."[15] Land ownership is not individual but communal and it should be remembered that the community includes the living as well as the dead.[16] In fact "the real 'owners' of the land are the spirit guardians of the chiefdoms, the spirits of founders or early rulers of the chiefdom and their immediate kin."[17] Here we see the nexus between gift giving and economic activities among Africans.

No activity could be undertaken without divine blessing. It can safely be concluded that in traditional African society there is no separation between spiritual and physical. With this background, let us turn to the Pauline texts that use the word *metadidōmi*.

---

11. Mbiti, *African Religions*, 1.
12. Mbiti, *African Religions*, 1.
13. Mbiti, *African Religions*, 41.
14. Ayittey, *Indigenous African Institutions*, 37.
15. Bourdillon, *Shona Peoples*, 88.
16. Bourdillon, *Shona Peoples*, 88.
17. Bourdillon, *Shona Peoples*, 87.

METADIDŌMI AS SHARING SPIRITUAL GIFTS FOR THE COMMON GOOD

In Rom 1:11 the object of Paul's sharing or imparting is a spiritual gift (*pneumatikos charisma*) which will help the Romans to be established in their Christian walk. Scholars are divided on what the gift is: some suggest that it is a "spiritual gift" (Cranfield and Fitzmyer), while others suggest that it is "an insight" or "ability" (Moo).[18] C. K. Barrett has warned though, "Since elsewhere Paul lays stress on the variety of such gifts it is hardly profitable here to inquire what precise gift he may have had in mind."[19]

The gift is "a truly spiritual gift" or an act of ministry which comes from "both the spirit and a means of grace."[20] The link between the gift and gospel proclamation is undeniable, since, for Paul, ministry is sharing spiritual gifts with the people of God.[21] Imparting the spiritual gift is, for Paul, to strengthen the Roman Christians' faith. Yet, this encouragement is mutual. Paul realizes that the Romans can also be of help to him in his faith.[22] Paul knows that what he has is not his, but a gift from the Spirit, just like in the African traditional worldview where all known things come from the hand of God. So, he gives what he has and expects the Romans to reciprocate with what they have, including sharing their economic fruit with Paul so that he may evangelize further (11:13). In 1:13 Paul talks about his desire to visit the Romans, so that he can have some fruit (*tina karpon*). Fitzmyer makes an important connection between the use of the word "some fruit" with the collection for the poverty-stricken believers in Judea.[23] This interpretation clearly sees fruit in economic terms even if it does not exclude other interpretations. This clearly points to the exchange that Paul expects to take place between him and the Romans. Paul expects this exchange to result in mutual encouragement as a result of his faith and that of the Romans (Rom 1:12).

John Barclay has demonstrated the importance of reciprocity in gift giving in the ancient world in his magnum opus *Paul and the Gift*.[24] Barclay states, "This reciprocity of relations which does not eradicate but continually

---

18. Moo, *Epistle to the Romans*, 59–60.
19. Barrett, *Epistle to the Romans*, 26.
20. Dunn, *Romans 1–8*, 30.
21. Osborne, *Romans*, 37.
22. Mounce, *Romans*, 68.
23. Fitzmyer, *Romans*, 250.
24. Barclay, *Paul and the Gift*, 440.

inverts a hierarchical order, is a hallmark of Pauline social ethics."[25] Paul knows that there is no other way to discharge his apostolic calling; the gospel cannot be shared by itself alone, one has to share self as he says elsewhere in 1 Thess 2:8.[26] The apostle is also aware that what he has is not for oneself alone but rather for the common good.[27] The same is true for the recipients of the gospel. Once they have been given "the spiritual gift" it is also for the common good, and it should result in them sharing their material goods.

METADIDŌMI AS SHARING WEALTH

In Rom 12:8 when speaking of spiritual gifts Paul uses the participial of *metadidōmi* as a subject describing the one who contributes to the needs of others with the gift of giving. Paul obviously has material things in mind, including money that ought to be shared with those in need. Paul's recommendation is that they must give/impart in generosity. Such an individual is to do the giving "straightforwardly and without ulterior motives."[28] There is an echo of the Wisdom of Solomon's instruction for one not to give "grudgingly."[29] For Paul the focus is not so much on the participle itself since it is primarily "concerned with the need of the other person only."[30]

There is no doubt the giving here has to do with "sharing one's private wealth for the needs of others and for the advance of the gospel."[31] Yet, we should not limit it only to the needs of others but it also implies "one who dispenses both spiritual gifts and material goods, a meaning that would find some support in Paul's use of [*metadidōmi*] in Rom 1:11 and in 1 Thess 2:8."[32] John Calvin was of the opinion that Paul had here the deacons in mind, who were tasked with allocation of church property.[33] However, there is nothing in this text that should cause us to limit the giver to a specific

---

25. Barclay, *Paul and the Gift*, 435.
26. Fitzmyer, *Romans*, 248.
27. Dunn, *Romans 1–8*, 30.
28. Moo, *Epistle to the Romans*, 768.
29. In *Wisdom of Solomon* the author speaks of how he prayed, and God gave him understanding and the spirit of wisdom (7:13). He proceeds to compare wisdom to wealth. Yet, wisdom came with "unaccounted wealth" in 7:11. In 7:13 where the word *metadidōmi* appears, the author first declares that he "learned without guile" which has to do with "not having a selfish interest." Lange et al., *Apocrypha*, 248.
30. Morris, *Epistle to the Romans*, 442.
31. Longenecker, *Epistle to the Romans*, 929.
32. Fitzmyer, *Romans*, 648.
33. Calvin, *Commentary*, 463.

The Interplay of Spiritual and Economic Aspects of *Metadidōmi*

category of people. It is our contention, contra Calvin, that the giving must have involved what the individuals owned. Paul only stipulates how the giving is to be done by the giver: they are to give without consideration for the gifts that others possess or how they go about dispensing them.[34] Given that in this context we are speaking of spiritual gifts, the connection between the spiritual and the material is very evident. Even though what is being shared is the material/economic, the motivation for doing so is the Spirit. Let us now turn to the Ephesians.

METADIDŌMI AS SHARING THE PROCEEDS FROM LEGITIMATE WORK

Ephesians 4:28 is part of the exhortation on the old life in contrast to the new life. Paul writes in this passage, "Thieves must give up stealing; rather let them labor and work honestly with their own hands, so as to have something to share (*metadidonai*) with the needy (Eph 4:28 NRSV). The thief is one who seeks his or her own gain by any means. Various options exist that could explain thievery in the church. These range from pilfering of masters' goods by slaves to the use of unfair scales in the marketplace and even price fixing.[35] The slaves would steal from their master as a way to supplement their income primarily because they had no legal protection.[36] Some scholars read Philemon from this perspective; it is assumed that Onesimus was guilty of this crime.[37]

Instead of stealing, the thief is advised to labor honestly with their own hands. Paul himself is an example of one who works with his own hands (1 Thess 4:11; 2 Thess 3:8). Paul recommends that believers work so that they are not dependent on anybody and so that they are not idle or disorderly (1 Thess 4:12; 2 Thess 3:11–12). I have argued elsewhere that Paul's exhortations concerning work are aimed at community formation.[38] Paul's vision is to create a community in which every member contributes meaningfully to its wellbeing. The contrast between a thief and a believer is vivid: whereas the thief takes from others, the believer works for the purpose of sharing with those in need.[39] Ps.-Phocylides 153–54 says, "Work hard so that you can live from your own means; for every idle man lives from what his

34. Moo, "Romans," 1151.
35. Fowl, *Ephesians*, 157.
36. Wiersbe, *Bible Exposition*, 41.
37. Lincoln, *Ephesians*, 303.
38. Mtukwa, "African Reading."
39. Hoehner, "Ephesians," 2637.

hands can steal." In this passage work and stealing are discussed in the same context. However, the motivation for working is different from that given in Ephesians. Sharing/giving cannot happen unless one has something to share. Work then is an important aspect of *metadidōmi*.

Working and sharing are the intended outcomes; the problem that stands in the way is theft. After ensuring that he has dealt with it Paul follows the exhortation with a motivation for working.[40] Since what is shared is acquired through good means, it is also "to be *expended* in a good way, to a good purpose: 'that he may share with him who has need.'"[41] In Eph 4:28 what is to be shared is what one has worked for; it is the result of one's economic pursuits. Clearly, *metadidōmi* here has material or economic use. Yet, the spiritual is not far off, since the motivation for doing so is rooted in the gospel. It is after one has experienced salvation (putting off the old humanity and putting on the new)[42] that they are to stop stealing and start working in order to be able to share. As Goran Agrell has noted, "Theft and indolence cause damage to Christ and his body, whereas work, by enabling the worker to aid the needy, builds up the body of Christ."[43]

Although Eph 4:28 seems to concern material resources as the object of *metadidōmi*, the motivation for working is rooted in the gospel which transforms humanity from the old life to the new life. Working is considered "something good" since it "produces that which becomes the means of sharing."[44]

METADIDŌMI AS SHARING LIFE

In 1 Thess 2:8 Paul addresses his audience with these words: "So deeply do we care for you that we are determined to share *metadidōmi* with you not only the gospel of God but also our own selves, because you have become very dear to us" (NRSV). Sharing in this context is closely related to the idea of caring deeply. The word "deeply" (*himeiromai*) is a *hapax legomena* in the New Testament. It was often found on funerary inscriptions conveying the love parents had for their child who is now no more.[45] Paul and his associates care for the Thessalonians so deeply, that they are determined to share their lives too. This care resonates with what Paul says in 2:7 where he

---

40. Liefeld, *Ephesians*, Eph 4:28.
41. Lenski, *The Interpretation*, 580.
42. Lincoln, *Ephesians*, 304.
43. Agrell, *Work*, 128.
44. Lincoln, *Ephesians*, 304.
45. Green, *Letters to the Thessalonians*, 128.

uses the metaphor of a "nursing mother' (*trophos*), who also deeply cares (*thalpo*) for her child.[46]

The object of *metadidōmi* is the gospel and our own selves.[47] Peter Lange has perceptively noted that "The two objects of μεταδοῦναι [*metadounai*] are joined to one another ascensively by *not only—but also*, so that the second is held up as the one of greater importance for the connection."[48] Clearly, here Paul has both the material and the spiritual aspects of *metadidōmi* in view.[49] The evangelist's lives are to be shared the same way the gospel is shared. As Ernest Best has succinctly observed, "Paul not only gives what he has, the gospel, but what he is, himself."[50] This certainly accentuates "the inseparability of speaking the good news and embodying it."[51]

1 Thessalonians 2:8 is followed immediately by verse 9 in which Paul reveals how he and his co-workers worked while in Thessalonica. The two verses are "joined to what precedes, by γάρ [*gar*] (and), and [are] therefore illustrative of it."[52] Sharing life and work results is sharing the results of work.[53] Paul makes it clear that the results of his work were available to the community. Although his work as an artisan was not financially stable most of the time,[54] Paul is ready to share the works of his labor with the community. Paul shares his life with the Thessalonians as an act of self-giving. Peterman has noted that "The model of selflessness, the willingness to give up one's own status and share another's troubles, is the ultimate sign of true friendship."[55] The giving up of status, which entailed "engaging in such strenuous, low-status activity was intimately connected with their proclamation of the good news of God."[56]

F. F. Bruce has succinctly noted "The meaning is not simply 'we were willing to give (lay down) our lives for you' but 'we were willing to give ourselves to you, to put ourselves at your disposal, without reservation.'"[57] Since the Thessalonians also gave of themselves to the apostles (2 Cor 8:5), the

---

46. Beale, *1–2 Thessalonians*, 73.
47. Malherbe, *Letters to the Thessalonians*, 147.
48. Lange et al., *Commentary*, 31.
49. Constable et al., "1 Thessalonians," 2694–95.
50. Best, *First and Second Epistles to the Thessalonians*, 102.
51. Johnson, *1 and 2 Thessalonians*, 67.
52. Lange et al., *1 and 2 Thessalonians*, 31.
53. Míguez, *Practice of Hope*, 66.
54. Peterman, *Paul's Gift from Philippi*, 7.
55. Peterman, *Paul's Gift from Philippi*, 115.
56. Johnson, *1 and 2 Thessalonians*, 67.
57. Bruce, *1 and 2 Thessalonians*, 32.

result was "mutuality and love that would unite them into a cohesive community, thereby strengthening them to face a hostile environment."[58] The reason for sharing life was that they [the Thessalonians] "had become very dear to us." This clause intensifies how much Paul loves the Thessalonians.

1 Thessalonians 2:8 brings together the two aspects of *metadidōmi* in a unique way. The two objects, "the gospel" and "our very lives," follow each other in the same sentence. Paul makes it clear that the gospel cannot be preached without sharing one's life with one's converts. Such sharing includes working and sharing the results of work. It was Martin Luther who observed that "[a] gospel messenger who stands detached from his audience has not yet been touched by the very gospel he proclaims. The gospel creates a community characterized by love."[59]

SYNTHESIS

This paper sets out to investigate Paul's usage of the word *metadidōmi* to determine ways in which it encompasses both the spiritual and economic usage. The purpose for doing so was to address the issue of economic justice in Africa. We demonstrated that in African traditional society we have a worldview that does not divide religious and economic matters; religion permeates every aspect of life. With that background, we embarked on reading Paul's letters primarily where he uses the word *metadidōmi*. Paul's usage ranges from sharing the gospel, money and other material things that are needed by those who are without. Romans 1:11 encourages sharing the gospel but the economic aspect of sharing can be detected in the background since Paul expects the Romans to reciprocate. In Rom 12:8 and Eph 4:2 it is clearly money and other material things that are to be shared, yet these can only be shared because of the gospel message which demands movement of economic resources from those who have to those who have not. In 1 Thessalonians 2:8 both the gospel and the lives of the missionaries (including their work life) are to be shared. Just like in African traditional society where kinship plays an important role in redistribution of resources,[60] the members of the house church have to share with one another because the gospel is the basis on which sharing takes place. By using *metadidōmi*, Paul brings together the different ways in which the gospel is to be imparted—it encompasses the message and the lives of the messengers. As Best has noted, "The true missionary is not someone specialized in the delivery of

---

58. Wanamaker, *Epistles to the Thessalonians*, 102.
59. Martin, *1, 2 Thessalonians*, 81.
60. Mbiti, *African Religions*, 104.

the message but someone whose whole being, completely committed to a message which demands all, is communicated to his hearers."[61]

This analysis has much to offer to the people of God as they proclaim the gospel: they are to pay attention to the economic aspects of this proclamation. The gospel cannot be proclaimed without the issue of economic justice being considered. Resources must move from where they are to where they are most needed. This is exactly what the apostle Paul did, and what his gospel demanded. Sharing should go beyond the gospel message; it should include goods and services being given to those who need them.[62] Certainly, justice ought to extend to various domains; to be just is to ensure that community resources remain community resources—Africans must avoid corruption (stealing public resources).

WORKS CITED

Agrell, Goran. *Work, Toil and Sustenance: An Examination of the View of Work in the New Testament, Taking into Consideration Views Found in Old Testament, Intertestamental, and Early Rabbinic Writings*. Stockholm: Verbum Lund H. Ohlsson, 1976.

Ayittey, George B. N. *Africa in Chaos*. New York: St Martin's Place, 1999.

———. *Indigenous African Institutions*. Leiden: Brill, 2006.

Barclay, John M. G. *Paul and the Gift*. Grand Rapids: Eerdmans, 2015.

Barrett, C. K. *The Epistle to the Romans*. Black's New Testament Commentary. Rev. ed. London: Continuum, 1991.

Beale, G. K. *1–2 Thessalonians*. Downers Grove, IL: InterVarsity, 2003.

Best, Ernest. *The First and Second Epistles to the Thessalonians*. Peabody, MA: Hendrickson, 2003.

Bourdillon, Michael F. C. *The Shona Peoples*. Gwelo: Mambo, 1976.

Bruce, F. F. *1 and 2 Thessalonians*. Word Biblical Commentary. Waco, TX: Word, 1982.

Bullard, Roger A., and Howard A. Hatton. *A Handbook on the Wisdom of Solomon*. United Bible Societies' Handbooks. New York: United Bible Societies, 2004.

Calvin, John. *Commentary on the Epistle of Paul the Apostle to the Romans*. Translated by John Owen. New York: Logos Bible Software, 2010.

Carter, Warren. *The Roman Empire and the New Testament: An Essential Guide*. Nashville: Abingdon, 2006.

Chambo, Filimao Manuel. "*Metadidonai* as Ethical Principle on Material Possessions According to the Gospel of Luke (3:10–14) and the Book of Acts." PhD diss., University of Johannesburg, 2008.

Cousar, Charles B. *Reading Galatians, Philippians, and 1 Thessalonians: A Literary and Theological Commentary*. Macon, GA: Smyth & Helwys, 2001.

---

61. Best, *First and Second Epistles*, 103.

62. Filimao Chambo has successfully applied the concept of *metadidōmi* in Luke's gospel to the issue of corruption in Mozambique. See Chambo, "Metadidonai as Ethical Principle."

Constable, L. Thomas, et al. "1 Thessalonians." In *The Bible Knowledge Commentary: An Exposition of the Scriptures*, 2:687–711. Wheaton, IL: Victor, 1985.

Dunn, James D. G. *Romans 1–8*. Word Biblical Commentary 38A. Waco, TX: Zondervan, 1988.

Fitzmyer, Joseph A. *Romans: A New Translation with Introduction and Commentary*. Anchor Yale Bible. New Haven, CT: Yale University Press, 2008.

Fowl, Stephen E. *Ephesians: A Commentary*. The New Testament Library. Louisville, KY: John Knox, 2013.

Galea, Sandro. "On Economic Justice." Boston University. https://www.bu.edu/sph/news/articles/2017/on-economic-justice/.

Green, Gene L. *The Letters to the Thessalonians*. The Pillar New Testament Commentary. Grand Rapids: Eerdmans, 2002.

Hoehner, Harold W. "Ephesians." In *The Bible Knowledge Commentary: An Exposition of the Scriptures*, edited by J. F. Walvoord and R. B. Zuck, 2:3–138. Wheaton, IL: Victor, 1985.

Johnson, Andy. *1 and 2 Thessalonians*. The Two Horizons New Testament Commentary. Grand Rapids: Eerdmans, 2016.

Lange, John Peter, et al. *A Commentary on the Holy Scriptures: 1 and 2 Thessalonians*. Edinburgh: T. &. T. Clark, 2008.

———. *A Commentary on the Holy Scriptures: Apocrypha*. Edinburgh: T. &. T. Clark, 2008.

Lenski, R. C. H. *The Interpretation of St. Paul's Epistles to the Galatians, to the Ephesians and to the Philippians*. Columbus: Lutheran Book Concern, 1937.

Liefeld, Walter L. *Ephesians*. The IVP New Testament Commentary Series 10. Downers Grove, IL: IVP Academic, 2010.

Lincoln, Andrew T. *Ephesians*. Word Biblical Commentary 42. Dallas: Word, 2015.

Longenecker, Richard N. *The Epistle to the Romans: A Commentary on the Greek Text*. New International Greek Testament Commentary. Grand Rapids: Eerdmans, 2016.

Malherbe, Abraham J. *The Letters to the Thessalonians: A New Translation with Introduction and Commentary*. New York: Doubleday, 2000.

Martin, D. Michael. *1, 2 Thessalonians*. The New American Commentary. Nashville: Broadman and Holman, 1995.

Mbiti, John S. *African Religions and Philosophy*. Repr. Nairobi: East African Educational, 2015.

Methula, Dumisani Welcome. "Black Theology and the Struggle for Economic Justice in the Democratic South Africa." Master's thesis, University of South Africa, 2015.

Míguez, Néstor Oscar. *The Practice of Hope: Ideology and Intention in First Thessalonians*. Minneapolis: Fortress, 2012.

Moo, Douglas J. *The Epistle to the Romans*. The New International Commentary on the New Testament. Grand Rapids: Eerdmans, 2015.

Morris, Leon. *The Epistle to the Romans*. The Pillar New Testament Commentary. Grand Rapids: Eerdmans, 1988.

Mounce, Robert H. *Romans*. The New American Commentary 27a. Nashville: Broadman & Holman, 2001.

Mtukwa, Gift. "An African Reading of Paul's Work Exhortations in the Thessalonian Correspondence." PhD diss., University of Manchester, 2020.

Osborne, Grant R. *Romans*. The IVP New Testament Commentary Series. Downers Grove, IL: IVP Academic, 2010.
Oyier, Christopher. "Multinational Corporations and Natural Resources Exploitation in Africa: Challenges and Prospects." *Journal of Conflict Management and Sustainable Development* 1 (2017) 69–71.
Peterman, Gerald W. *Paul's Gift from Philippi: Contemporary Conventions of Gift-Exchange and Christian Giving*. New York: Cambridge University Press, 1997.
Philo of Alexandria. *On the Creation*. Translated by F. H. Colson and G. H. Whitaker. Loeb Classical Library Vol. 5. Cambridge, MA: Harvard University Press, 1934.
Sandro Galea. "On Economic Justice." Boston University. https://www.bu.edu/sph/news/articles/2017/on-economic-justice/.
Seery, Emma, et al. "A Tale of Two Continents: Fighting Inequality in Africa" Oxfam Report. https://www.oxfam.org/en/research/tale-two-continents-fighting-inequality-africa.
Wanamaker, Charles A. *The Epistles to the Thessalonians: A Commentary on the Greek text*. New International Greek Testament Commentary. Grand Rapids: Eerdmans, 1990.
Wiersbe, Warren W. *The Bible Exposition Commentary, Volume 2*. Wheaton, IL: Victor, 1996.

"You Are Asked to Witness"[1]

Liturgical Use of Scripture as Mission in S'ólh Temexw

Matthew Francis

THIS IS A PERSONAL narrative in honor of Dr. Kent Brower. In one of my first conversations with Dr. Brower, which took place in a church basement in Calgary, Alberta in the late 1990s, prior to my coming to Manchester to study with him, he asked me about my theological interests. I enthusiastically found myself saying, "ecclesiology." He responded with the encouragement I came to know him for: "there is a real need for good work in that area!" After pouring over the Gospels with "K.E.B.," and being mentored by him both intellectually and spiritually—in the Senior Common Room, in the Church, and in his home—I stepped out into the fields of ecclesiological praxis. By that I mean that I have been assigned to establish a new congregation in our common home-soil of western Canada. I hope Dr. Brower will take a measure of joy in the experience of Holy Scripture lived out in its ecclesiological and missional context.

    As a pastor, one of the central activities of my life is the familiar moment when I stand in the midst of the people of God, the assembly of the faithful, to proclaim the Gospel passage assigned for that day. Speaking and hearing these specific holy words, we communally experience the drawing near of the Kingdom of God. The inbreaking reality of "God with us," takes place, in some mysterious way—in our human speech, and in our human hearing. In the common prayer and worship of the Church, God's life is given to us. Encountering the Word in Scripture calls worshippers into the presence of the Word made flesh, in the bread and wine of His Eucharistic Body and Blood. In Him, we find life. Heaven and earth are bridged in

---

1. Carlson, *You Are Asked to Witness*.

Christ's life, in time, space, and history. The place and the people, transfigured by the luminous presence of the Divine, are sanctified. It is in this context that we practice living in community, as "God's holy people."[2]

Engaging with Scripture is essential to the fabric of all Christian worship, and ecclesial identity. Whether in the Wesleyan-holiness tradition of my upbringing, or in the Eastern Orthodox Church in which I serve in pastoral ministry—or pretty much all traditions in between—the biblical Law, Prophets, Writings, Psalms, Gospels, Epistles and Apocalypse shape our response to God. Christian liturgies have tended to "center" the reading of the sacred texts, though in some contexts this now takes place with less formality or ceremony. In other settings these readings are placed at the center of the liturgical time and space, and in others they form a kind of apex.

Traditionally, Christian liturgies have followed the model laid out in Luke 24. In this passage, Jesus joins two of His disciples on the road to Emmaus, "opens their minds to understand the Scriptures," and shares a meal with them, where they both recognize His presence and become strikingly aware of His absence.[3]

What is often called "the Liturgy of the Word," or the "Liturgy of the Catechumens," reveals the Risen Lord, Jesus Christ, in all of the Scriptures that speak about him. We partake—through speaking and listening—of the Word of God. In Christian worship, a door is then opened, liturgically speaking, into the Kingdom of Heaven, now made present to us, and into which we are beckoned to enter. That door is Jesus Christ Himself. Upon recognizing Him in the breaking of the bread, and having been given His resurrection life, he disappears from our sight. Why? It is because we—the Church—have been called to become the Body of Christ in this world, for the life of this world, and for its salvation. Through participation in the Eucharist, we partake of the Word of God, and vice versa. The Word and the Holy Mystery function as a kind of nourishing, liturgical symbiosis.

In 2015, I was assigned by my Bishop to establish a new parish of the Orthodox Church in America in Chilliwack, British Columbia. This is the city I grew up in, a city of about 100, 000 people, 100 kilometers east of Vancouver. I returned home after twenty years away. We started with a group of thirty-five people, twenty of whom were children under ten years old. As I got to know the people entrusted to my pastoral care, the words of the Creed began to come alive for me in a new way. When we proclaimed, week by week, Jesus's resurrection from the dead, "according to the Scriptures,"

---

2. Brower, *Living as God's Holy People*.

3. See the worthwhile exploration of the Emmaus narrative as a hermeneutical lens provided by Jersak, *More Christlike Word*.

I began to see that the Scriptures reveal Christ in a specific, local reality. Perhaps it should not have surprised me that our Bishop dedicated our mission parish to the Holy Apostles, since the word *apostle* means "sent." In His "Great Commission," Jesus sent out the Apostles to make disciples of all nations, promising His presence would always be with them. He meant even in *this* place, on the westernmost edge of a continent then totally unknown to them. Christ promised to be with his disciples not only to the boundaries of the known and mapped Roman *oikoumene* ("inhabited world"), but to the limits of the cosmos. We believe that includes *this* place. This place is S'ólh Temexw. That's the name given to the traditional territory of the Stó:lō ("River") people. Meaning "our world," or "our land," in the Halq'émeylem language, according to *swxoxwiyam* (oral history), Stó:lō people have lived here since time immemorial.[4] Their civilization prospered, richly interwoven with the cedars that towered overhead, and the abundant salmon flourishing in the River. The Stó:lō traditional territory includes the whole southwestern corner of the Province of British Columbia. What is known as S'ólh Temexw extends from the Village of Yale to the City of Langley, British Columbia, along what is often referred to as the Fraser River.

These are the colonial settler names of these places, ascribed in recent times, since the first European contact and colonial settlement of the region began in the eighteenth century. As we began to learn more about the community we had been called to serve, however, we learned that even today, in the City of Chilliwack, there are fourteen distinct First Nation Reserves. The faithful people that I have been called to serve include the people of this place, including those living both on and off Reserves.

Reserves are places of designated habitation for Indigenous people in Canada, with boundaries defined by nineteenth century Canadian legislation. That racialized legislation is still in force. The Reserve system continues to pervasively influence the ways in which Indigenous people live and especially their rights and access to services provided by the Government of Canada. Established by the Canadian parliament in 1876 as part of the broader project of colonization, the *Indian Act* was created precisely to assimilate Indigenous peoples into mainstream Euro-Canadian society. This law contains policies intended to terminate the cultural, social, economic, and political distinctiveness of Indigenous peoples. Even today, many Reserves do not have basic services such as clean drinking water or minimally adequate healthcare. Those laws are still in effect, governing the lives of Indigenous Peoples, on their own traditional and unceded territories, S'ólh Temexw.

---

4 See Schaepe, *Being Ts'elxwéyeqw*.

With the tragic realities of the *Indian Act* and the Reserve system in mind, I began to prayerfully wonder, how can the Scriptures bear witness to the Kingdom of God in *this* place? How can we, called to be Christ's own Body, live out that life *here*? I sought to find a way to embody a kind of practice that would be able to bear witness to the Good News in a way that could be heard by everyone, including our Stó:lō friends.

Chilliwack today is known for its breathtaking scenic beauty. Our community is showcased as an outdoor enthusiast's paradise—ready for a panoply of recreational adventures. Yet *S'ólh Temexw* is also a place in which things have happened. There is 'baggage.' There is sin. There is trauma and systemic injustice. We believe there is also hope and redemption in Christ, who is the Creator, and the Giver of every good gift. But to encounter that reconciliation, we have to face the truth. As Jesus said, only the truth will set us free.

In the Summer of 2021, thousands of unmarked graves of children began to be discovered at former Church-run (and later Government-run) Indian Residential Schools across Canada. The first 215 of these graves were found at the former Kamloops Indian Residential School, not far from our area. Headlines around the world brought the evidence of this terrible reality into the light. The tragically painful role of Christian missionaries in the cultural and physical genocide of Indigenous Peoples has been uncovered and publicized. An international light has been shone upon this darkness. As a result of this pain, and the outcry of many Indigenous people here in Canada, Pope Francis finally visited Canada in the Summer of 2022, offering a formal apology for the role of the Roman Catholic Church in the Residential Schools abuse. While his apologies were well-received by some—including many Indigenous Catholics—as an important step in the reconciliation journey, many others felt his actions did not go far enough. For instance, he did not publicly renounce the "Doctrine of Discovery."[5] In addition, the Pope did not visit Kamloops, ground zero for the discovery of the unmarked graves. Pope Francis did not set foot in *S'ólh Temexw*. As a result, the message I heard from my Stó:lō friend was that reconciliation has to take place in person, face to face, and upon the soil of the injured party, coming to them with a good spirit of humility.

Oftentimes in considering Indigenous-Settler relationships, or other relationships of historical wrongdoing on a global level, there is a desire to rush toward reconciliation, sometimes without fully knowing the truth. In 2015, the Truth and Reconciliation Commission for Canada issued its Final Report and Calls to Action. The Calls to Action compelled us to learn

---

5. Assembly of First Nations, "Dismantling the Doctrine of Discovery."

and go deeper into our community's history, so that we can know and bear witness to the truth, and in so doing, to hopefully also become ministers of Christ's reconciling love in this world.

When we planted the Holy Apostles parish in 2015, we learned that in 1869, the Methodist missionary Thomas Crosby (1840–1914) was appointed to Chilliwack. Notably, he began by preaching the Christian gospel here using the Halq'émeylem language to evangelize the Stó:lō people. His use of the Indigenous language is somewhat unique for the period, showing a certain missionary diligence. Notable Indigenous converts to the Christian faith during this period include Chief William Sepass (K'HHalserten, 1840–1943),[6] who was particularly impressed by the way in which Scripture was used by the missionaries and functioned in Christian worship. Chief Sepass was an incredibly significant bridge figure, preserving and transmitting the Stó:lō oral history, while also wholeheartedly embracing the Christian Gospel and Scriptures.

As a missionary, Crosby was a product of his time and worldview.[7] He was a British-Canadian Methodist preacher, whose default tendencies were shaped by the revivalist and Camp-meeting ethos well-known in the nineteenth century transatlantic Holiness movement. As a preacher, he was eager to learn the Indigenous languages for the sake of his evangelistic work, and was not opposed to the preservation of traditional languages like Tsimshian and Halq'émeylem. On the other hand, Crosby also followed the 'assimilationist' approach of most colonial-mindset missionaries, insisting that Indigenous people converted through his ministry abandon their traditional spirituality and practices, adapting to Victorian norms for family life, work, and behavior. For instance, he insisted that his Indigenous Methodist converts abandon their multi-family, multigenerational dwellings for single-family homes complete with white picket fences. This encumbered and even severed many of the relationships and traditions of intergenerational knowledge-sharing and learning. Crosby was known for his kindness, and was often well-liked by his Indigenous parishioners. He even occasionally was himself photographed wearing traditional Tsimshian and Stó:lō regalia, though it is unclear why he did so. Crosby insisted upon wanting to not only convert the people spiritually to Christ, but also to transform them culturally, along the colonial Anglo-European pattern. His missionary modality, while typical of the time, is completely foreign to the traditional, apostolic posture of mission, modeled on the West Coast of North America a century earlier than when the Methodists reached *S'ólh Temexw*. In the Valaam

6. K'HHalserten Sepass, *Sepass Poems*.
7. Bolt, *Thomas Crosby and the Tsimshian*.

Mission to Alaska, we can see seeds and a spirit which give us hope for the task set before us in this context today.

While we cannot trace the complex and rich history of Orthodox mission to Alaska here, our efforts in mission in Chilliwack have been informed by several of its unique characteristics.[8] While replete with richly distinct identities, and geographical uniqueness, the cultural character of the Indigenous communities along the West Coast of North America also share many elements in common, including similar worldviews and spiritual traditions such as the *potlatch*. The first Christian mission to bear witness to the Gospel in Alaska,[9] in the late eighteenth century, has numerous characteristics that set it apart from almost all other examples in the history of world missions, and shaped our work in *S'ólh Temexw*.

The Alaskan Mission is the only major missionary movement to North America that began on the West Coast. All others—typically arriving from Western Europe or the population centers along the East Coast—moved West across the continent, accompanying the colonial powers.

The Alaskan Mission, a monastic-led movement, is the longest missionary journey ever accomplished on foot. The missionaries walked approximately 6000 kilometers, from Lake Ladoga (on the far Northwestern borders of Russia and Finland). Starting in 1793, they walked across all Siberia to the Bering Sea, where they finally boarded ships and traveled to the Aleutian archipelago and finally arrived in Kodiak in 1794.

The Alaskan Mission was carried out in "the Orthodox way," which cherishes a principle of using the vernacular languages of the local people in evangelization work and attending to the local spiritual conditions of the people.[10] Similarly, if we observe the example of St. Peter in Acts 10, the apostolic posture of mission begins with listening, as the apostle curiously asked Cornelius about his experience with God, and saw that the Holy Spirit was already present and active. This is the typical missionary ethos of the Orthodox Church, in which prayerful listening most often precedes proclamation and teaching of the faith.

The original group of eight missionaries was sent from Valaam Monastery on Lake Ladoga. Their primary formation for mission work was the ancient rhythms of prayer, which they had learned in the monastery. The missionaries from Valaam were contemporaries and acquainted with St. Seraphim of Sarov, who provided the well-known aphorism of Orthodox

---

8. Best summarized by Oleksa in *Orthodox Alaska*.

9. See Oleksa's "The Good News of the Gospel," in Oxbrow and Grass, *Living the Gospel*, 29–36.

10. See Yannoulatos, *Mission in Christ's Way*.

mission: "Acquire the Holy Spirit, the Spirit of Peace, and a thousand around you will be saved!"[11]

The Alaskan Mission embraced all vocations. There were some ordained priest-monks among the eight missionaries that walked from Valaam to Alaska, including St. Juvenaly, who later became one of the first Orthodox martyrs in North America. Nevertheless, the "Bright Star" of the mission was a lay-monk who served as the group's cook. His name was Herman (1755–1837). When the Russian-American Company, which controlled the fur trade, was horribly exploiting the Indigenous Peoples, it was Father Herman who stood up for them, and became their ardent defender. When all of the other original missionaries either died or returned home, it was Herman who stayed. He nurtured a relationship of respect and love with the Indigenous Aleut people, never ceasing to write letters advocating to the civil authorities on their behalf. In return, they lovingly called him *Apa*, "Grandfather," and asked for his prayers.

From the time of the Valaam mission in 1794, the Orthodox Church in Alaska has been more or less fully Indigenous—among both the faithful and the clergy. One of St. Juvenaly's companions was an Indigenous leader, whose name has been lost to history. Fr. Yacov Netsvetov (1802–1864), the first Aleut priest, was a renowned evangelist and pastor, and was officially recognized as a saint by the Orthodox Church in America in 1994, as the "Enlightener of the Peoples of Alaska." Another more recent example of such holiness is Matushka Olga Michael (1916–1979), of the Village of Kwethluk, Alaska. Married to the local priest, a highly regarded midwife, Matushka Olga's spiritual gifts brought consolation and healing to many, especially to women who have experienced various kinds of abuse. It is thought by many that she will soon be officially glorified as the first Indigenous woman in North America to be recognized as a saint by the Orthodox Church.[12]

To this day, despite the tragic history of the nineteenth and twentieth centuries in Alaska, the Orthodox faithful there are still primarily composed of the Indigenous Peoples of Alaska. On Sunday October 2, 2022, I had the blessing to serve the Divine Liturgy with His Grace, Bishop Alexei and local clergy at St. Innocent's Cathedral in Anchorage. There were twelve

---

11. This popular quotation of St. Seraphim of Sarov (1754–1833) was recorded as part of a personal conversation between St. Seraphim and Nicholas A. Motovilov, in Motovilov's memoirs. This document was discovered in 1902 and published in Moscow the following year. The meaning of this spiritual and evangelical aphorism is described by Fr. Thomas Hopko in his podcast, "A Conversation with St. Seraphim on the Holy Spirit," part of the Ancient Faith Radio series *Speaking the Truth in Love*, originally broadcast January 14, 2010.

12. Clark, "Will Blessed Olga Be The First Female Orthodox Saint Of North America?"

priests serving with him, and nine were Indigenous Yupik priests. This is the norm in Alaska. I had the experience, as I have elsewhere in the world, of experiencing life as a minority. For us as non-Indigenous settlers on these lands, this is a critically important experience, which I will carry with me in my heart. The Divine Liturgy was served largely in the Yupik language, and the traditional Orthodox hymns of the Resurrection were sung with great spiritual fervor in several Indigenous languages. It was awe-inspiring to witness, and to be present. The rich spiritual legacy of Indigenous Christianity in Alaska has shaped our approach to mission work in Chilliwack.

One hundred and forty-six years after Thomas Crosby first began preaching in Chilliwack, in the same year that the *Truth and Reconciliation Commission* issued its Calls to Action, we planted the Holy Apostles Orthodox Mission. The stated goal of this new parish has always been to "reflect the love of the Holy Trinity in the Heart of the Fraser Valley." The question lingered for us, however, in this specific missional context: how can we bear witness to Christ in this environment which is so wounded, and in such great need of truth and reconciliation? Embodying the traditional liturgical praxis of the Orthodox Church, and inspired by the missiological principles of the eighteenth century Valaam mission to Alaska, we have been called to find ways to open the Scriptures and break the bread in such a way that all people can see Jesus Christ for who He truly is. This begs the question: How do we engage the Scriptures in *Sólh Temexw*?

We did not seek to innovate or embrace any kind of novelty. Instead, in the spirit of listening to the teachings of the elders, we allowed our traditional liturgical practices to form our engagement with the Bible. This kind of liturgical engagement with Scripture has been lived out in at least three ways, that we hope are experienced as truly "good news" by both the Indigenous and non-Indigenous people we serve.

First, we realize that our Liturgy is an intertextual immersion into the Scriptures. Each line of the Liturgy of St. John Chrysostom, sung Sunday by Sunday, is steeped in quotations from and allusions to the Law, Prophets, Psalms, Gospels, and Epistles. The Liturgy is story-shaped, in its central *anaphora* recounting the whole sweep of the biblical drama of salvation in Christ.[13] In the words of this anaphora, this includes, "All those things which have come to pass for our salvation: the Cross, the Tomb, the Resurrection from the Dead, the Ascension into Heaven, the Sitting at the Right Hand, and The Second and Glorious Coming."

Secondly, in the pattern derived from the Road to Emmaus, we open the Scriptures—according to our received lectionary—and proclaim the

---

13. See Pentiuc, *Hearing the Word*.

Word publicly for all to hear. This leads us to encounter and receive Christ into the center of our lives. We feast on and are nourished by the Word so that we might become His Body for the life of the world.

Finally, our hymnody, designed for doxology—glorifying God—is story-shaped and narrative focused. When Chief William Sepass (K'HHalserten) was baptized and accepted the Christian faith, he was positively impressed by how the Bible recorded the authoritative stories of the people of God. He longed for the traditional Stó:lō *swxoxwiyam* (oral history) to be written down in a similar fashion, for the well-being of the community. Indeed, the hymnography of the Orthodox Church bears some correspondence and similarities to the *swxoxwiyam*, in that both are explanations of the world from a spiritual point of view. An example of this is the liturgical canon, which employs the biblical odes or canticles as a way of articulating Scriptural salvation history in relation to the experience of salvation in Christ.[14]

While serving the Divine Liturgy some years ago, as I read the Gospel, I looked out at the faithful. There I saw my friend, a Stó:lō Chief, worshiping God, bearing witness to all that the Scriptures reveal about Christ. I see the good news—taking root and bearing fruit—in *S'ólh Temexw*.

WORKS CITED

Assembly of First Nations. "Dismantling the Doctrine of Discovery." https://www.afn.ca/wp-content/uploads/2018/02/18-01-22-Dismantling-the-Doctrine-of-Discovery-EN.pdf.

Bolt, Clarence. *Thomas Crosby and the Tsimshian: Small Shoes for Feet Too Large*. Vancouver, BC: University of British Columbia Press, 1992.

Brower, Kent. *Living as God's Holy People: Holiness and Community in Paul*. Milton Keynes, UK: Paternoster, 2010.

Carlson, Keith Thor. *You are Asked to Witness: The Stó:lō in Canada's Pacific Coast History*. Fraser River Region, BC: Stó:lō Heritage Trust, 1997.

---

14. Knust and Wasserman, "Biblical Odes and the Text of the Christian Bible," 341–65. The origins of the use of the biblical odes as liturgical texts are also described Getcha, *Typikon Decoded*, 76. These biblical odes include: 1) The Canticle of Moses—Exodus 15.1–19; 2) The Canticle of Moses—Deuteronomy 32.1–43; 3) The Prayer of Hannah—1 Samuel 2.1–10; 4) The Prayer of Habakkuk—Habakkuk 3.1–19; 5) The Prayer of Isaiah—Isaiah 26.9–20; 6) The Prayer of Jonah—Jonah 2.3–10; 7) The Prayer of the Three Youths—Daniel 3.26–56; 8) The Canticle of the Three Youths—Daniel 3.57–88; 9) The Magnificat and the Benedictus—Luke 1.46–55 and Luke 1.68–79. While it is speculative, since they are all epitomes of salvation-historical narrative, I cannot help but wonder whether these include some of the texts which Jesus Christ may have discussed with the disciples while they did not yet recognize him, on the road to Emmaus.

Clark, Meagan. "Orthodox Alaska Part 4: Will Blessed Olga Be The First Female Orthodox Saint Of North America?" https://religionunplugged.com/news/2022/7/26/will-blessed-olga-be-the-first-female-orthodox-saint-of-north-america.

Getcha, Job, Archbishop. *The Typikon Decoded*. Yonkers, New York: St. Vladamir's Seminary Press, 2012.

Hopko, Thomas, Fr. "A Conversation with St. Seraphim on the Holy Spirit." https://www.ancientfaith.com/podcasts/hopko/a_conversation_with_st._seraphim_on_the_holy_spirit.

Knust, Jennifer, and Wasserman, Tommy. "The Biblical Odes and the Text of the Christian Bible: A Reconsideration of the Impact of Liturgical Singing on the Transmission of the Gospel of Luke." *Journal of Biblical Literature* 133 (2014) 341–65.

Jersak, Bradley. *A More Christlike Word: Reading Scripture the Emmaus Way*. New Kensington, PA: Whitaker House, 2021.

Oleksa, Michael J., ed. *Alaskan Missionary Spirituality*. Yonkers, New York: St Vladimir's Seminary Press, 2010.

———. *Orthodox Alaska: A Theology of Mission*. Yonkers, New York: St Vladimir's Seminary Press, 1992.

Oxbrow, Mark, and Tim Grass, eds. *Living the Gospel of Jesus Christ: Orthodox and Evangelical Approaches to Discipleship and Christian Formation*. Oxford: Oxford Centre for Mission Studies, 2021.

Pentiuc, Eugen J. *Hearing the Word: Liturgical Exegesis of the Old Testament in Byzantine Orthodox Hymnography*. Oxford: Oxford University Press, 2021.

Schaepe, David M., ed. *Being Ts'elxwéyeqw: First Peoples' Voices and History from the Chilliwack-Fraser Valley, British Columbia*. Madeira Park, BC: Harbour, 2017.

Sepass, William K'HHalserten, Chief. *Sepass Poems: Ancient Songs of Y-Ail-Mihth*. Mission, British Columbia: Longhouse Publishing, 2017.

Yannoulatos, Anastasios, Archbishop. *Mission in Christ's Way: An Orthodox Understanding of Mission*. Geneva: World Council of Churches Publications, 2010.

PART V

Reimagining Theological Education

The Theological Curriculum

Thomas A. Noble

DR. KENT BROWER AND I *have been associated with the Nazarene Theological College, Manchester since the early 1970s. As the very junior member of the Board of Governors of what was then "British Isles Nazarene College," I recall voting for his appointment, little knowing that that would be the beginning of an association of fifty years. When I became Dean in 1976, our discussion and debates on theological education began. As one of the last doctoral students of F. F. Bruce, he represented the view from biblical studies, defending in those days the validity of the historical-critical method. My perspective was informed by T. F. Torrance's view of theology as a science and by my studies in education. Together, these perspectives shaped a genuinely creative tension always within the context of a firm friendship. My recommendation that he succeed me as Dean led to his creative academic development of the college as a partner college of the University of Manchester. This paper on the theological curriculum is substantially one I wrote in 2004 when, as Director of M.Div. Studies at Nazarene Theological Seminary in Kansas City, Missouri, I was leading curriculum revision.*

The theological curriculum may be viewed from various angles. To start with, there is the historical perspective presented by Edward Farley in *Theologia*.[1] Then, each professor and lecturer tends to view the total curriculum from the perspective of his or her own discipline. Differing keys are proposed—"leadership," "formation," the global perspective, pastoral skills, etc. The different authors in the literature (summarized by Robert Banks) each has his or her own angle.[2]

I want to suggest that the key to the unity of the curriculum is to start (as Farley suggests) with the word "theology." In choosing that word, I do

---

1. Farley, *Theologia*.
2. Banks, *Re-envisioning Theological Education*.

not restrict its meaning to the discipline of "*Systematic* Theology," but I am thinking of it rather as the key word in the very title of this institution. "Seminary" is important, implying that we are the "seed-bed" of future growth.[3] "Nazarene" obviously specifies that tradition of the Church catholic which the institution exists primarily to serve. But the key word is surely the word "theological," and since that word is in the title for the whole institution, it clearly does not refer here only to what happens in the *Systematic Theology* classroom. Everything we do here is "theology."

Edward Farley correctly sees the concept of *theologia* as the heart of the matter, and his history of the meaning of the word is illuminating. But where Farley is very disappointing is in his understanding of what theology *is*. It seems as if, when he discusses theology, he is too sophisticated to mention God too much! Perhaps his old Liberal, Schleiermacherian soul is afraid of offending the "cultured despisers" and ruining the theologian's academic respectability.[4] He never succeeds in bringing together the *subjective* dimension—that *theologia* is a *habitus* within the theologian, that it is *sapientia* or (if you like) "spiritual formation," and the *objective* dimension—that *theologia* is an academic, objective *Wissenschaft* or "science." According to the educationalist, Jerome K. Bruner, the nature of an academic discipline—what the core science essentially *is*—should shape and determine the educational method by which it is taught and learned.[5] We do not teach children mathematics or history: rather we teach them to be mathematicians and historians. Correspondingly, our task is not to teach our students theology, but to teach them to be biblical, historical, systematic and practical *theologians*. Where we must begin therefore is with this question of what theology *is*, and that can only be determined (according to Jerome Bruner) when we all think *as theologians* first and as educationalists second.

I want to take as my starting point an understanding of what theology is, which is quite different from the old Liberal view of Farley. It will not surprise you to know that I take my bearings from T. F. Torrance's ground-breaking work on theology and its method, *Theological Science*.[6] It was this understanding of the nature of theology which I presented in my inaugural address at Nazarene Theological Seminary in 1997,[7] and it

---

3. "Seminary" is widely used in the United States, but "College" is similarly significant and widely used in the United Kingdom and elsewhere for theological colleges as "communities" devoted to learning from undergraduate studies to doctoral research.

4. Schleiermacher, *Speeches on Religion to Its Cultured Despisers*.

5. Bruner, *Process of Education*.

6. Torrance, *Theological Science*.

7. Noble, "Knowledge of the Glory of God."

was this understanding which underlay my suggestion of the formula: "To know the Lord, to speak of the Lord, and to walk with the Lord" at our last discussion on the curriculum several years ago. I believe that Torrance's conception of the nature of theology is "evangelical" and "catholic," and *therefore* appropriate for Wesleyans. It brings together the *subjective* and *objective* dimensions (spiritual formation and academic "science"), and I believe that it presents us with a way of understanding the unity and diversity of the theological curriculum.

Torrance defends the realist thesis that theology is *the science of God*. Substantiating the claim that theology is "science" involves him in some pretty advanced investigation into the philosophy of science and general epistemology into which we need not go now. But in the briefest summary, his claim is that, bearing in mind that *scientia* means "knowledge," a "science" is any area of articulated *knowledge*. In the natural sciences we articulate our knowledge of the natural world, in the human or social sciences, our knowledge of humanity and of human society, and in theological science, our knowledge of *God*. Torrance is specifically concerned of course with *Christian* theology, and therefore the God in question is the God and Father of our Lord Jesus Christ. Some of the dimensions of this claim may be summarized in three points.

1. CHRISTIANS CLAIM TO *KNOW* GOD

Since as Christians we claim to know this God, we cannot take refuge in a lesser claim, such that theology is just an examination of the language we use in the church. Examination of our language is part of the business of theology (and there is therefore a place for philosophical theology). But Christians claim more. We do not just claim to use certain language about a postulated God. The Christian church is unavoidably committed to the claim that we do not just know ways of speaking about God. We actually *know God*. A quick perusal of the Johannine literature, never mind Paul, will make it quite clear that we are committed to some form of realism: that this God is actually there and that our claim as Christians is that we *know* him. Theology therefore cannot accept that it is less than *cognitive*. Bloom's "cognitive domain" as well as the "affective domain" is therefore applicable.[8]

---

8. Bloom et al., *Taxonomy of Educational Objectives*.

2. THIS KNOWLEDGE IS NOT MERELY ABSTRACT KNOWLEDGE OF FACTS OR PRINCIPLES OR DOCTRINES OR "TRUTHS." IT IS *PERSONAL KNOWLEDGE OF A PERSONAL GOD*

Here Torrance makes use of the philosophy of science enunciated by the Hungarian chemist who became a professor at the University of Manchester, Michael Polanyi. Polanyi's Gifford Lectures were entitled *Personal Knowledge* and his point was that *all* knowledge, including the knowledge of the natural sciences, was *personal* knowledge.[9] It was personal in the sense that only persons can know and articulate their knowledge of the natural world. The myth that there existed completely detached, neutral knowledge of anything was a total misapprehension of what "objectivity" meant. Rather, *all* knowledge—knowledge of anything whatsoever—was simultaneously *objective* and *subjective*. All knowledge was "bi-polar." It was ineluctably "subjective" because there could be no knowledge without a knowing personal subject who knows. But it was simultaneously "objective" because there had to be a genuine "object"—a genuinely objective *reality* there to be known. And the more the knowing subject detached himself or herself from her subjective presuppositions and saw the "object" as it truly was, the more "objective" was her knowledge. True scientific detachment was not detachment from the object. How can we know anything at all if we are not in relationship to it, in contact with it? True scientific detachment was detachment *from our presuppositions*—allowing our very questions to be questioned—along with the framework of assumptions which gave rise to them—by that objective reality which we seek *experimentally* (= *experientially*) to know.

When Torrance writes of the way this model of scientific epistemology operates in classic Christian theology, he is committed to claiming as a Christian that the One who gives himself in grace to be the genuine Object of our genuine knowledge is none other than the Lord God. Here therefore, unlike the natural sciences, but like the human sciences, not only the subject (the "knower") but also the Object (the One known) is understood as "personal." The bi-polarity here then is one of *personal relationship*, an "I-Thou" and not an "I-It" relationship. Unlike Buber, however, Torrance speaks of the *corporate* subject, the Church, *our* knowledge "together with all the saints" (Eph 3:18).[10] The personal knowledge of God which we each have is within the Church, the believing people of God. And there is another

---

9. Polanyi, *Personal Knowledge*. See also Colin Weightman, *Theology in a Polanyian Universe*.

10. Buber, *I and Thou*; Torrance, *Reality and Scientific Theology*, 117–23.

correction: the Lord God cannot be simply subsumed under the category of the "personal" as if God were simply like a human person but a bit bigger! Here we confront the mystery that God is not a given, a *datum* within the world as human persons are, but is the unique Tri-personal Mystery of Father, Son and Holy Spirit. Since God is not given within the world, there are of course those who would therefore deny the Lord any objective reality, and so deny that theology is an objective science. That is their business. For Christians who have come to know this God, the Triune God cannot be anything other than the most objective Object—the most real Reality—the most true Truth—in fact, the source of the reality and truth of the being of everything-else-that-is. For Christians therefore, theology cannot be other than a genuine science, but it is a unique science.

3. WE KNOW GOD AS HE REVEALS HIMSELF

What makes theology different from all other sciences is this point that the Triune God is not a *datum* within the world. Therefore, we can only know him (and so engage in theological science) *as the Lord gives himself to be known*. The key category here of course is *revelation*, and the uniqueness of the Christian understanding of revelation is that the Triune God gives himself to be known *in his Word* and *by his Spirit*.

To say that the Lord gives himself to be known *in his Word* is to think supremely of the Word made flesh. Here in Jesus Christ, "conceived by the Holy Spirit, born of the virgin Mary," is God's definitive self-revelation, the Word who in the beginning was with God and was God. But of course, in speaking of him we also speak of the gospel which is "the gospel of his Son" (Rom 1: 3–4). It is the preached *kerygma* of the early Church, the apostolic preaching of the gospel, which throughout the book of Acts is "the word of God." And therefore in an extended way it is the word of the apostles *and prophets*, "the word of the Lord" in the Old Testament as well as the word of the gospel in the New Testament, which is "the word of God" in the canon of Holy Scripture, fully inspired by the Holy Spirit ("who spoke by the prophets").

All this is to say that our God is not a dumb God, and that his revelation in the Word by the Spirit is not a game of charades in which God does the acting and we supply the script. God supplies the script. That is to say (as the Church Fathers and the Evangelical traditions of the Reformation insist) that God's revelation has a verbal, linguistic, conceptual dimension from the beginning. Our God is the God who "has *spoken* in many and various ways in times past by the prophets and in these last days by a Son"

(Heb 1:1–2). One does not need to understand that in a fundamentalist way in order to say with Wesley and all the Evangelical traditions that speech from God is an essential part of the revelation. God has not only *acted* to save us in the Word made flesh, but through the whole of the Old and New Testament revelation he has given us the concepts, the words, the models and metaphors without which we could not know or express who he is and what he has done for us. These include lamb, priest, king, debts, exodus, redemption, kingdom, covenant, spirit/breath, temple, bridegroom, judge, "Father," "Son," and "Holy Spirit." Yet if God's revelation were only words (as the fundamentalist distortion seems to think), then revelation would only be the communication of messages from heaven—abstract truths to be believed and disembodied commandments to be obeyed. Fundamentalism thus gives us a rationalist and legalistic understanding of revelation. But for Wesleyans and all the Evangelical traditions as truly understood, revelation is centered in the Word made flesh, the God who has come among us as one of us, taking our fleshly existence and dying our death, so becoming the definitive Word of God's invincible love.

But this Word only comes to us by the Spirit. Even the Word made flesh is only perceived by the Holy Spirit. "No one can say, 'Jesus is Lord,' except by the Holy Spirit" (1 Cor 12:3). Even as Incarnate, the Word is not at our disposal or under our control or accessible to our natural insight and human intelligence. Receiving this Word by the Spirit means being born anew. So in the power of his Holy Spirit, this Word is not only *informative*—telling us of the love of the Father in the narrative of the gospel (indeed the wider narrative of Holy Scripture), and not only *performative*—achieving our justification (our "rectification") on the cross (Rom 3: 23); but it is also *transformative*—renewing our minds, re-creating and re-forming and sanctifying us ("formation" and "sanctification"). This has crucial implications for theological education which Wesleyans want to emphasize. I cannot help thinking of Piaget's coupling of "assimilation" and "accommodation" in the learning process. As the mind *assimilates* new information, Piaget speaks of it *accommodating* the new information by itself growing and changing like a physical organism absorbing energy from its food.[11] This applies *mutatis mutandis* even to knowledge of God. What this clearly pictures for us is that theological education as spiritual and personal *formation* is in fact a *transformation* which takes place as *we focus our lives and our understanding "objectively" on the Word by the Spirit*. That is surely what "spiritual formation" is. It comes about not by our subjective focus on ourselves as subjects,

---

11. Piaget, *Psychology of Intelligence*; see also the lucid presentation of Piaget's "main theoretical ideas" in Butcher, *Human Intelligence*, 182–98.

but on our objective focus on the Word who confronts us as the true Object (*Gegenstand*), so that our transformation takes place only through our relationship to Him (our abiding *in* Him) by the Spirit. True Christian theology can therefore never be a merely academic exercise in abstract theory. It is always a wrestling with the truth of the Word—the truth about God and about ourselves—in the context of a living relationship with Him. Jacob at Peniel is perhaps the best biblical model of the theologian and of theological education.

If this is our understanding of what Christian theology is, what are the implications for the theological curriculum? Briefly, the following theses seem to follow:

1. THEOLOGICAL EDUCATION MUST CENTER IN WORSHIP OF THE TRIUNE GOD

If Christian theology is truly the articulation of our knowledge of *God*, and not just of our abstract theoretical knowledge about God, then our theology of worship, embodied in the way we worship in our chapel services and prayer times, should be at the heart of our curriculum. Since knowledge of God comes to us through Holy Scripture, consecutive reading of the *narrative* of Holy Scripture in a planned lectionary and its accompanying exposition, and responding prayer and praise to God for his word to us should be at the heart of our life as a theological community. What happens in class should arise out of what happens in the chapel.

2. THEOLOGICAL EDUCATION MUST GIVE PRIMACY TO THE STUDY OF HOLY SCRIPTURE

If the church lives out of "every word that proceeds from the mouth of God" (Deut 8:3, Matt 4:4), then the study of Holy Scripture should be thorough and comprehensive. That has "primacy" in the sense that everything else in the curriculum should arise out of *the narrative* of God's mighty acts. Systematic theology then needs to allow itself to be shaped by biblical theology. Spiritual formation and all areas of practical or pastoral theology need to be in continual conversation with biblical scholarship and accountable to biblical scholarship for the appropriateness of the paradigms and models they work with. To look for "thoroughness" and "comprehensiveness" in biblical studies in the curriculum has implications for the number of biblical courses which should be considered a minimum and for at least a preliminary knowledge of biblical languages. But the scholarship is pursued in a theological college or seminary not for its own sake, but so that the word of God might shape and form our thinking and speaking and our practices.

3. THEOLOGICAL EDUCATION MUST ENCOURAGE DEEP AND REFLECTIVE MEDITATION ON CHRISTIAN HISTORY

Like biblical studies, the history of Christianity can be pursued as a purely secular discipline. But within a confessional theological college or seminary, while rigorous scholarship should not be compromised, "the story of the Church" should inform the judgment of the students on theological and ethical issues which are still with us. This study is essential to that "formation" of the student which takes him or her beyond naivety to catholic wisdom. Without that maturity, church "leaders" are the blind leading the blind. Without that *sapientia*, popular influence and popular success ("growth") is a snare.

4. THEOLOGICAL EDUCATION MUST DEEPEN OUR KNOWLEDGE OF GOD AND OF OURSELVES

Christian theology is not "Systematic Theology" in the sense that it is the study of the Christian "system." That would be a study of ideas and theories and doctrines—a merely scholastic, abstract study—"academic" in the worst sense of the word. Christian theology is "the articulation of our knowledge of *God*." And it is only within the context of our relationship with the Triune God—in his Word by his Spirit—that we can come to a true Christian knowledge of ourselves. As we image and reflect his glory, true self-knowledge is a reflection of our knowledge of God. That is why Christian theology must be centered in the God who has revealed Himself definitively in Jesus Christ, so that our knowledge of salvation (soteriology) comes out of our knowledge of *him*, and our knowledge of how we participate in that salvation (justification and sanctification and all the benefits of his atonement) comes out of a knowledge of *him*. In fact, in *him* "are hidden *all* the treasures of wisdom and knowledge" (Col 2:3). That does not mean that we can ignore the knowledge offered to us in the human sciences, for the Word did indeed become flesh, and flesh is that humanity which we are. But once again, these secular social sciences (as with biblical criticism and history) have to be baptized into Christ. That is to say, they have to understand that true knowledge of ourselves is not the knowledge of our sinful selves belonging to this age—*kata sarka*—but that in the paradoxical "already but not yet" structure of New Testament Christian thinking, we must know ourselves in Christ *kata pneuma*. That may be beyond the terms of reference of the secular human sciences, but it must not be beyond the thinking of the Christian social scientist.

5. OUR THEOLOGICAL EDUCATION MUST BE AN INSEPARABLE UNITY OF *THEŌRIA* AND *PRAXIS*

For the Christian Fathers, *theōria* was not the Platonic contemplation of eternal abstract Ideas or Forms or Truths. That would be a static and inert kind of *theōria*. Rather it meant the vision of God—focusing on the *living* God. And therefore, since He is the God who acts and speaks, and not the inert "One" of Plotinus the neo-Platonist, Christian contemplation and meditation and prayer is inseparable from *praxis*. Somehow this inseparability of *theoria* and *praxis* for the Christian must be embodied in theological education. Classes which focus on the knowledge of God through the Scriptures must be integrally related to classes in pastoral, evangelistic, educational and missionary service. Lecturers need to know each others' syllabuses if any integration of the curriculum is to be a reality. What happens in classes where the focus is on *praxis* must be informed by what happens in classes where the focus is on "knowing God" and articulating that knowledge. And practical experience in ministry must be part of the feed-back loop. Within the walls of what is unavoidably (and properly) an academic institution, one can only engage in "practical" or "pastoral" theology to a very limited and artificial degree. But personal *praxis* in ministry experience must shape the way each student expresses his or her knowledge of God.

In short, "knowing the Lord" must inform "speaking of the Lord" and "walking with the Lord." But conversely, only those who walk with the Lord know the Lord, and so may speak of the Lord.

WORKS CITED

Banks, Robert. *Re-envisioning Theological Education: Exploring a Missional Alternative to Current Models*. Grand Rapids: Eerdmans, 1999.

Bloom, Benjamin S., et al. *Taxonomy of Educational Objectives: The Classification of Educational Goals*. New York: David McKay, 1956.

Bruner, Jerome K. *The Process of Education: Revised Edition*. 2nd ed. Cambridge: Harvard University Press, 1960.

Buber, Martin. *I and Thou*. Translated by Ronald Gregor Smith. Edinburgh: T. &. T. Clark, 1937.

Butcher, H. J. *Human Intelligence: Its Nature and Assessment*. London: Methuen, 1968.

Farley, Edward. *Theologia: The Fragmentation and Unity of Theological Education*. Philadelphia: Fortress, 1983.

Noble, Thomas A. "The Knowledge of the Glory of God." *The Tower: The Journal of Nazarene Theological Seminary* 1 (1997) 9–23.

Piaget, Jean. *The Psychology of Intelligence*. London: Routledge and Kegan Paul, 1950.

Polanyi, Michael. *Personal Knowledge: Towards a Post-Critical Philosophy*. London: Routledge & Kegan Paul, 1958.

Schleiermacher, Friedrich D. E. *Speeches on Religion to Its Cultured Despisers*. Translated by Richard Crouter. Cambridge: Cambridge University Press, 1988.

Torrance, Thomas F. *Reality and Scientific Theology*. Edinburgh: Scottish Academic Press, 1985. Reprint, Eugene, OR: Wipf & Stock, 2001.

———. *Theological Science*. London: Oxford University Press, 1969 and 1990.

Weightman, Colin. *Theology in a Polanyian Universe: The Theology of Thomas Torrance*. American University Studies. Series VII: Theology and Religion 174. New York: Lang, 1994.

Mapping the Landscape of Theological Education in the UK

Peter Rae

W HEN DR. KENT BROWER *first moved to the UK in 1973, the theological college where he was employed was some thirty years old, but had little foothold in British Higher Education. It was neither validated nor accredited, since neither of these options were available in the sector. His arrival coincided with the College establishing an accreditation relationship with a Canadian institution, but this still only provided a vestigial presence in the academy. It was part of Kent's genius that he not only forged a place as a distinguished New Testament scholar, but also invested himself in the structures of Higher Education (HE), striving to build faithful partnerships, working alongside colleagues in the University and HE sector, helping to shape a space for confessional colleges to thrive in a setting that was not adversarial but complementary and collaborative. Over those almost fifty years the landscape has changed: this paper attempts to assess the nature and implication of those changes.*

Theological education is in a time of transition. As Alice Hunt writes, "Almost everything about theological education has changed and faces continual change. The basic assumptions of theological education, including presuppositions about the business model, outcomes, and curriculum of theological education no longer function."[1] In Europe, according to the "Global Survey on Theological Education," the overall number of students involved in theological education is significantly decreasing—one of the only world areas where this is the case.[2] And theological education in the United Kingdom reflects these patterns: changes are taking place in models of delivery, in patterns of validation, in levels of engagement. Narrative

---

1. Hunt, "Waiting for a Divine Bailout," 61.
2. "Global Survey on Theological Education, 2011–2013," 4.

accounts describe some of these transitions,[3] but data to support the analysis is limited, particularly when examining changes beyond the University sector.

If theological education is, to use Cheesman's working definition, "the training of men and women to know and serve God," then where is such training currently taking place in the UK?[4] What are key features of the current landscape, and how is that landscape changing? A general analysis suggests three primary settings for theological education in the UK: theological education takes places *within universities*, typically in departments of Theology and Religious Studies (TRS), or in linked divinity colleges or private halls; it is also delivered within *validated Colleges*, either linked to denominations or non-denominational; and it is offered in *unvalidated settings*, often supported by and located within individual churches or mission organizations.

Statistics have, for many years, been systematically collected and published about the university sector by the Higher Education Statistics Agency (HESA), and so the trajectory of TRS within the university can be mapped and analyzed.[5] But for most of that period validated colleges (or "alternative providers," as they were designated) were not reported in that data. Validated Colleges now do have the option of registering with the Office for Students (OfS), so data on their enrolment is now also published by HESA. But some validated Colleges choose to avoid the regulatory demands of the OfS, and so are not reported in HESA data.[6] Unvalidated colleges and courses are also not centrally registered, and little data on them exists: it is difficult to comment on the scope of their provision with any degree of certainty.

The complexity of the sector is compounded by the fact that the three settings noted above have areas of overlap. Validated colleges and University private halls often deliver unvalidated provision alongside their degree offerings: this may be continued professional development; it may include short-term vocational courses; it may be sub-degree level lay-training.

---

3. See, for example, Cheesman, "Relationship of Evangelicals in the UK";"Hewlett, "Theological Education in England"; Higton, "Theological Education between the University and the Church."

4. Cheesman, "Theological Education," 1.

5. Data on full time undergraduate student applications and acceptances (by subject) are published by UCAS; data on full and part time student enrolment, both undergraduate and postgraduate, are published (by subject) by HESA.

6. OfS regulation, though it opens access to student finance and other resources, places a high regulatory demand on institutions, so some have avoided this, whilst others have de-registered, having found the regulatory burden too onerous.

Colleges without UK validation may, nonetheless, offer awards that are "accredited" by non-UK bodies (such as US-based Colleges, or by accrediting agencies such as the European Council for Theological Education), or offer awards that are outside the normal UK Qualifications and Credit Framework (QCF).[7]

This study will attempt two things:

- First, it reviews the state of Theology and Religious Studies in UK universities, drawing on the statistical data noted above, and offers a brief analysis of the implications of the data.
- Second, in the light of that review, the study considers validated theological institutions, and uses current HESA data, supplementing that with data from a small institutional survey, to describe and analyze the part of the sector not fully reported in the HESA data.[8]

THEOLOGY AND RELIGIOUS STUDIES IN UK UNIVERSITIES

Within the University sector, historically the home of much theological education in the UK, two significant patterns have emerged in recent years. One reflects a pattern of falling student enrolment; the second notes a general restructuring and contraction of TRS departments in the UK.

Student numbers enrolled in Theology and Religious Studies at British Universities have decreased significantly and steadily since 2005–6:[9] In 2005–6, there were 15,895 students taking theology and religious studies (6420 full time, 9470 part time; 4880 postgraduate, 11,010 undergraduate). By 2018–19, this had fallen to 7075 students (5065 full time, 2010 part time; 2650 postgraduate, 4420 undergraduate:[10] a 55-percent drop from the peak in 2005–6. The following year (2019–20) HESA changed its calculations

---

7. Tilsley College, for instance, offers a diploma validated by the ECTE; Capenwray is validated, outside the QCF, by NCFE; the now-closed Manchester International Christian College was not validated, but prepared students for University of London external examinations.

8. The unpublished survey, conducted by the author, collected student enrolment data in validated theological colleges, and explored student distribution across types of institution, types of awards (undergraduate; taught postgraduate; research), and types of delivery (full time; part time; distance/online learning).

9. HESA, "What do HE Students Study?"

10. This data is confirmed by a 2019 study from the British Academy, which notes that full time Undergraduate numbers fell 31 percent between 2012–2018, Foundation Degrees by 83 percent, and "other undergraduate programmes" by 69 percent.

to include data from registered validated providers in its statistics, but if the data are adjusted for this, numbers continue to decline: by 2020–21 the number of registered students (excluding validated providers) in University TRS had fallen a further 8 percent, to 6530—a total decline of 59 percent.

This decline is even more stark when set against a rise in HE enrolment generally. Between 2005–6 and 2018–19 (when data collection protocols changed),[11] overall student numbers in HE in the UK rose by 42 percent. In that same period student overall numbers in Theology and Religious studies fell by 55 percent. This reversed the pattern of the previous decade, which had seen a healthy increase in TRS student numbers: over 45 percent growth in Theology and Religious Studies between 1998 and 2006–7, somewhat ahead of the growth in overall numbers at UK universities, which was around 30 percent.[12] There has been a "performance gap" between TRS and the rest of the academy over the last fifteen years in terms of student recruitment.

The second significant pattern of note is that a number of Theology and Religious Studies departments have closed or been rationalized in the last decade. David Hewlett comments on "the [small] number of university departments of theology that are robust and have not morphed into departments of religion."[13] It is no longer controversial to observe that "the academic study of Christian theology in British universities and higher education colleges faces huge uncertainties; some might say a crisis."[14] Over recent years departments have closed or significantly contracted at Universities in Sheffield (biblical studies), Stirling (religious studies), Heythrop (undergraduate), Kings College London, and other university departments have seen staff reductions in TRS.

What has driven these changes within the Universities? One might point to the changing religious landscape of the UK, and the growing secularization of British society, leading to a decline in interest in religion and theology: the 2011 census reported a fall in those identifying as Christian, from 72 percent of the population (in 2001) to 59 percent; those who did identify as Christian had the oldest age profile of all religions, with 22 percent over the age of 65 (so the decline was greatest amongst those most commonly represented in HE).[15] Church membership and attendance showed

---

11. 2018–2019 was the final year in which data from "Alternative providers" was not included in the full data: comparisons become more complex beyond that period.
12. Universities UK, "Patterns," 2009.
13. Hewlett, "Theological Education," 567.
14. Pears, "Study of Christian Theology," 159.
15. Office for National Statistics, "Census 2011."

a similar decline.[16] Data from the 2021 census show a further decline, with only 46.2 percent identifying as Christian.[17]

Might it also be that TRS departments have not proven attractive to the "new demographic" within confessional settings? HESA data reveals that about 12 percent of UK-based TRS students (2014–15) were from non-white backgrounds, below the overall average (18 percent) for university admissions for all subjects, and well below the 25 percent reported to HESA from the small group of theological colleges who provided data in that year.[18] By 2020–21, though, the TRS percentage of non-white students had increased to 26 percent, just below the university average of 27 percent (and the 29 percent from HESA-reporting validated colleges). Since recent data suggests that it is growth from immigration, and growth from ethnic minorities, that is helping to arrest decline in many church traditions in the UK, this is an important increase.[19] It may also be that students from this new demographic are seeking theology with a vocational edge, or theology in a confessional context: most university TRS programmes are not designed to be vocational, so do not include field-based study or practice, and although many TRS faculty are themselves people of faith, it is unusual for such departments to practice faith in corporate settings.

Changing patterns of student finance might also be a factor: the decline in TRS numbers has coincided with the introduction of £9,000 student fees, in 2012, which also saw a sharp drop in part time and mature students. Whereas part time students composed 27 percent of the overall student cohort in 2012, they made up over 45 percent of students in Theology and Religious Studies, so the sector adjustment had a greater effect in TRS.

Changing government and university policies have a huge impact: increased government funding for STEM subjects has undoubtedly encouraged universities to invest in subject areas with a higher return, and focus their institutional strategies accordingly, choosing to disinvest in subject areas with a lower level of return.

---

16. UK Church Membership slipped from 17 percent to 11 percent between 2005 and 2010. Brierley, "Statistics," 47.

17. Office for National Statistics, "Census 2021."

18. In 2014–2015 not all QAA-reviewed colleges were required to provide HESA data (only those of a certain size), and so only six theological providers did so, and this data only covered undergraduate designated courses. HESA, "HE student enrolments."

19. Brierley, *Statistics*, 4.

BEYOND THE UNIVERSITY SECTOR: SURVEY OF VALIDATED THEOLOGICAL COLLEGES

Beyond University departments, the picture is far less easily summarized. On the one hand, the sector has seen the closure of many theological colleges over the past decades. A study in 1990, by Ian Bunting, surveyed 87 colleges and study course providers: of these, over a third have ceased to operate, or have merged with other bodies.[20] However, during the same period other providers have been established, and flourished, often using new methods of delivery: part-time, online, and distance learning options have multiplied, and church-based training schemes, often located in larger churches, are common. Narratives suggest that full time, residential models of theological education are declining, to be replaced by in-service training, e-learning, or modularized study.[21]

There has been, however, relatively little statistical information available about theological education beyond University departments, and, as a result, drawing accurate conclusions about the state of health or the direction of travel is difficult. There are several reasons for this absence of data: the most obvious is that central regulatory bodies have not, until recent years, required such information, and there is no single organization to which all theological institutions subscribe (in the USA, the Association of Theological Schools offers a relatively reliable compendium of such data).[22] Information on student numbers is also institutionally sensitive: reports of a decline in student numbers might be perceived to affect student recruitment. Limited statistics on UK Colleges and Bible Schools were collected for some 25 years by Peter Brierley's *Christian Research*, and published as part of the Christian Resources Handbook:[23] but this ceased publication in 2010, and even before then, although the handbook "provided a semblance of editorial unity . . . in practice, this involve[d] a significant degree of shoe-horning of data to fit the tabulations and of estimation (perhaps even guesswork on occasion)."[24]

The effect of this absence of information can be seen at multiple levels: for the validated provider, governance decisions are made more difficult when data on trends and patterns cannot be considered and examined,

20. Bunting, *Places to Train*.

21. Oxenham, "Theological Education in Western Europe."

22. Contrast this with the US, where accrediting bodies always collect data on student numbers and FTE. This may well change in the UK, at least for Colleges that fall under the remit of the OfS, as the submission of HESA data becomes a requirement.

23. *UK Christian Resources Handbook*.

24. Field, "Religious Statistics in Great Britain," 53–54.

and institutional strategy established in light of a broader analysis. For the researcher working in the discipline, analyzing the effect of sector change becomes problematic, and identifying future trends more difficult. And for the sector, speaking authoritatively to government or regulatory bodies becomes more complex when the scope and nature of the educational institutions which compose it are not known.

If we do not fully understand the landscape of theological education in our own time, and our own place, then anticipating the shape of things to come becomes a perilous exercise. Graham Cheesman wrote, in 1993, that "Theological Education today is complex, diverse and often unsure of itself."[25] This is still the case. David Hewlett wrote, in 2010, that "The last 20 years have seen a revolution in the way theological education is understood, organised and structured in England. This has in many ways been creative and liberating, enabling the learning and formation of the churches' ministers to be responsive to rapidly changing needs and opportunities. There are no signs that the changes are completed."[26]

Analysis of trends in the UK might also be instructive for a wider audience. Writing of the future of theological education in North America, Daniel Aleshire's predictions for 2032 sound remarkably like the current landscape of Theological Education in Europe. He anticipates that institutions will be "multiracial and multi-ethnic"; foresees a "changed community" of schools, with many closing or merging; expects increasing "educational diversity" in delivery and practice; predicts the "disciplinary shape" of college faculties will change to focus more on practical theology; sees the continued reduction of denominational subsidies for theological education; expects schools which survive to become more "deeply missional and entrepreneurial"; and looks to a heightened awareness of scholarship from the global south.[27] If, indeed, these patterns are already present within theological education in the UK, it may be that an analysis of the trends and patterns of the UK landscape might prove valuable reading internationally.

A small 2016 survey of validated colleges attempted to collect student enrolment data in theological colleges, to explore student distribution across types of institution, types of awards, and types of delivery; and second, to attempt to assemble comparable data for 2005/6, to try to establish how the sector was changing over time. It was sent to theological colleges that offered UK-recognized academic awards at FHEQ level four and above.

25. Cheesman, "Competing Paradigms," 484.
26. Hewlett, "Theological Education," 568.
27. Aleshire, "Future," 380–85.

The survey was sent to 42 institutions, all of which held UK validation. Of these, 27 (64 percent) completed the survey. Disappointingly, three of the larger colleges did not respond. Overall, the 27 institutions reported 5229 students, with an FTE of 3113 FTE.[28]

Some 18 of the 27 reporting colleges were able to provide comparative data for 2006. These 18 reported a 45 percent increase in enrolment, from 2179 to 3162. Undergraduate numbers were up by 30 percent; taught postgraduate numbers by 130 percent; and postgraduate research numbers were up by 85 percent. Campus-based numbers showed an increase of 33 percent; learning in "off-site hubs," reported as nil in 2006, made up 10 percent of enrollment by 2016; while online learning showed an increase of only 1 percent. This data seems to run counter to the narrative of scarcity and falling numbers that we instinctively "know" about the sector. So was the data wrong, or was the perception mistaken?

There certainly might be problems with the data: the data was incomplete, and the numbers self-reported and unverifiable. It may be that those whose numbers were less encouraging did not respond to the survey, and so it may be that there was greatest response from institutions who were keen to proclaim their success. It may be that the earlier data was unreliable or recorded in different ways. And, of course, the numbers did not allow for the fact that numbers of institutions in the sector have closed, or amalgamated, in the time period under scrutiny: the rationalization of institutions may simply have meant that, whilst the fewer remaining entities were larger, the overall number in theological education was still shrinking.

Notwithstanding the potential for inconsistencies, the survey presented some interesting trends in validated colleges: Numbers more than doubled at MA level (PGT) between 2006–2016, perhaps because programmes have been developed that offer professional development for those in ministry. PhD numbers also rose significantly, a general upward drift of qualifications at theological colleges, perhaps seeing an opportunity to develop markets at postgraduate level where undergraduate recruitment options were limited, or a growing appetite for academic engagement in constituencies that might previously have been hesitant to engage. The survey pre-dated the availability of MA loans for alternative providers (2017–18).

One of the most surprising statistics in 2016 was the absence of an apparent significant increase in online learning. Although colleges mentioned this in narrative responses as a factor that they thought would affect the structure of theological education, in 2016 there was no identifiable

---

28. Some of these Colleges were registered with the Quality Assurance Agency (QAA): limited data collected on the 27 QAA-registered colleges indicated a total of 5745 students, but no FTE was calculated.

increase in online delivery by any of the institutions who completed a survey. That will undoubtedly have changed significantly with the influence of the pandemic, but the HESA data does not allow detailed enquiry into delivery mode.

Overall, the survey provided data that told an incomplete story. It was unable to provide a comprehensive platform for 2016, and comparative data for a decade earlier, whilst of interest, was unreliable.

HESA DATA ON VALIDATED COLLEGES

The HESA data on theological colleges, though not comprehensive, makes interesting reading. In 2014–15, there were only seven validated theological colleges that submitted data to HESA. By 2015–16 that had risen to 19, and that figure has remained relatively stable. These are not newly founded institutions, but newly-reporting institutions. The level of reported enrolment, however, has remained relatively stable since peaking in 2017–18.

HESA Data	2014–15	2015–16	2016–17	2017–18	2018–19	2019–20	2020–21
Number of validated Theological Colleges reporting to HESA	7	19	19	19	21	22	21
College Enrolment	950	2465	2590	3660	3615	3325	3355
TRS Enrolment *excluding* validated provision	9305	8510	8115	7585	7075	6585	6530
Combined enrolment in TRS	10262	10994	10724	11264	10711	9910	9855
Validated provision as **percentage** of total HESA Enrolment in the subject area	9.4	22.4	24.1	32.5	33.7	33.5	34
Validated provision as **percentage** of total TRS Enrolment in the University sector	10.2	28.9	31.9	48.2	51.1	50.5	52.4

Table 1: HESA-reported enrolment at validated theological colleges, 2015–21[29]

It would seem that alternative providers were somewhat more resilient than TRS in Universities to enrolment slippage in the period covered by these statistics—though there has nevertheless been a plateauing in enrolment in these colleges, and they have suffered from enrolment slippage in the

29. Table 1—*HE student enrolments by HE provider, 2014-15 to 2020-21*, Table DT051, https://www.hesa.ac.uk/data-and-analysis/students/table-1.

pandemic years. But given that the HESA data only offers information on roughly half of the validated providers in the UK identified in the 2016 survey, it is likely that the number of students studying in these institutions is approaching parity with those studying in the university sector.[30]

REFLECTION AND IMPLICATIONS

But is this a cause for celebration or despair? It is surely to no-one's benefit to see theology decline as a serious subject of academic study in the university sector, or for it to be healthy only in confessional settings. Are there ways in which confessional colleges should be supporting colleagues in the University, or finding new models of collaboration across the sector? Those are subjects for further study.

This study reveals important dynamics in theological education: theological colleges, rarely considered a significant part of the formal higher education landscape prior to the late 1980's, now have an enrollment that is virtually equivalent to that in the university sector. Though this is particularly significant at undergraduate level, the growth of postgraduate courses, and research degrees, is a further trend that bears analysis. How has this affected the founding mission of these institutions; have they become less vocational through this academic upward drift, or any less committed to "the training of men and women to know and serve God"? How has it affected the qualification and profile of its staff?

And the landscape continues to change: falling church attendance in the UK is having an impact on all forms of theological education, and a post-pandemic decline in admissions is testing the resilience of many theological colleges. It is as yet unclear whether this is a temporary slump or a longer-term pattern. One UK theological college has attained full degree-awarding powers, and now has validating powers itself: perhaps a "significant moment . . . for the theological education sector."[31] But whether this embeds faith-based learning at the heart of UK HE, or offers a Christian alternative, remains to be seen. One thing is certain: changes within theological education continue, and institutions will have to adapt to survive.

---

30. HESA data also does not include off-shore students: those who are not resident in the UK for at least eight concurrent weeks in the year. This excludes postgraduate international students who are resident for shorter time periods, and students studying online but based overseas.

31. Spurgeon's College.

WORKS CITED

Aleshire, Daniel. "The Future of Theological Education: A Speculative Glimpse at 2032." *Dialog* 50 (2011) 380–85.
Brierley, Peter. *UK Church Statistics, 2005–2015*. Tonbridge, UK: ADBC Publishers, 2011.
The British Academy. "Theology and Religious Studies Provision in UK Higher Education." London: The British Academic, 2019. https://www.thebritishacademy.ac.uk/documents/288/theology-religious-studies.pdf.
Bunting, Ian. *Places to Train*. London: Marc Europe, 1990.
Cheesman, Graham. "Competing Paradigms in Theological Education Today." *Evangelical Review of Theology* 17 (1993) 484–499.
Cheesman, Graham. "The Relationship of Evangelicals in the UK to the Theology of the Academy in the 20th Century." https://theologicaleducationorg.files.wordpress.com/2010/09/academy.pdf.
———. "Theological Education: An Introduction to the Idea." https://theologicaleducationorg.wordpress.com/category/library-1-graham-cheesman/.
Field, Clive D. "Religious Statistics in Great Britain." In *British Religion in Numbers*, 53–54. Manchester: University of Manchester, 2010.
"Global Survey on Theological Education, 2011–2013." https://www.oikoumene.org/resources/documents/global-survey-on-theological-education.
HESA. "HE Student Enrolments by HE Provider 2014/15 to 2021/22." https://www.hesa.ac.uk/data-and-analysis/students/table-1.
———. "What do HE Students Study?" https://www.hesa.ac.uk/data-and-analysis/students/what-study.
Hewlett, David. "Theological Education in England since 1987." In *Handbook of Theological Education in World Christianity*, edited by Dietrich Werner et al., 563–68. Oxford: Regnum, 2010.
Higton, Mike. "Theological Education between the University and the Church." *Journal of Adult Theological Education* 10 (2013) 25–37.
Hunt, Alice. "Waiting for a Divine Bailout: Theological Education for Today and Tomorrow." *Theological Education* 46 (2011) 61–67.
Office for National Statistics. http://visual.ons.gov.uk/2011-census-religion/.
Oxenham, Marvin. "Theological Education in Western Europe." http://theologicaleducation.net/articles/view.htm?id=303.
Pears, Angie. "The Study of Christian Theology in the British Academy." *Journal of Adult Theological Education* 1 (2004) 159–174.
"Spurgeon's College Secures Full Degree Awarding Powers." https://www.spurgeons.ac.uk/spurgeons-college-secures-full-degree-awarding-powers/.
UK Christian Resources Handbook. Swindon, UK: Bible Society Resources, 2009.
Universities UK. *Patterns of Higher Education Institutions in the UK: 9th Report*. UUK. 2009.

African Communalism as a Paradigm for Theological Education

Samantha Chambo

INTRODUCTION

A key purpose of theological education is to prepare men and women to serve as ministers of the gospel of Jesus Christ in their respective contexts. However, the context in which theological graduates will work is changing significantly. Those called to serve in the twenty-first century are faced with increasing globalization, gender identification issues, justice concerns, displacement of people and wars, the ecological crisis, and racial and religious divisions. These are all just the tip of the iceberg. Theological education also faces the challenge of preparing ministers for an increasingly divided world that also yearns for unity and cooperation. One task of theological education is to prepare ministers to be relevant and effective, preparing people to connect with God within their circumstances. Traditional paradigms and methods might need to be revised to accomplish this mammoth task.

College-age students are part of generation Z. This generation cares deeply about the above-mentioned issues. There is also an increase in middle-aged or second-career people who profess a call to vocational ministry. The challenge with this group is the existing mindsets and parochialism, which may hinder their preparedness to serve in a context that demands creativity and flexibility. A re-orientation of theological education is thus needed. Peacock asserts, "Theology, in almost an essential sense, has perhaps more than any other discipline this emancipatory potential to transform not only the self but also the world."[1] How do we provide theological education that transforms students and prepares them to be agents of transformation?

1. Peacock, "Theological Education and Affirmative Alliances," 118.

A new theological education model should address or at least engage the existing challenges faced in this field. These include, but are not limited to the dichotomy between the goal of understanding and engaging in theology and the functional paradigm that focus on the specific skill clergy need to perform on the field.[2] Ideally, theological practitioners should be able theologians and vice versa. The second problem, as mentioned by Craig Dykstra, is the individualistic understanding of theological education. According to Dykstra, the overall picture that comes to mind is of an individual (the clergyperson) doing something to someone or a group of people.[3] For Dykstra, theological practice is inherently cooperative and, by nature, includes other people.[4] Third, the hegemony of the Western white male experience as the dominant voice in theological education has received increased criticism from the global community.[5]

This paper aims to address the following question: Can African communalism provide a new paradigm for theological education that can help address the above problems? This spiritual communalism goes by various names across the continent, but in Southern Africa, it is described as *Ubuntu*.[6] The hypothesis guiding this paper is that *Ubuntu* can translate into an alternative theological education paradigm with more potential for transformation.

1. AFRICAN COMMUNALISM

Africa is a vast continent characterized by various expressions of the African communal philosophy. However, various commonalities unite the continent.[7] According to Jacob Olupona, Africans believe in a three-tiered model of the cosmos that is made up of the realms of the gods, the realm of the ancestors,[8] and the realm of the living, which is sandwiched somewhere between the two realms.[9]

---

2. Wheeler and Farley, *Shifting Boundaries*, 15.
3. Dykstra, "Practice," 35.
4. Dykstra, "Practice," 42.
5. Wheeler, *Shifting Boundaries*, 14.
6. Khoza. *Attuned Leadership*, xxvii.
7. Khoza, *Attuned Leadership*, loc. 751.
8. Ancestors are family members who have passed away but still play a very active role in the lives of their kin.
9. Olupona, *African Religions*, 4.

It is a view held by most Africans who believe there is continuous interaction between inhabitants of the various realms.[10] The conviction that there is a connection between the realms of the living and the divine makes for a sacramental universe with very little differentiation between the physical and the spiritual.[11] This conviction is the framework for *Ubuntu* that assumes a continued connection between the spiritual world, amongst fellow humans, and with all of creation. According to Bediako, this spiritual communalism is the key to the African worldview.[12]

These transcendental relationships are what Vincent Mulago calls "vital participation."[13] Vital participation "is the vital link which unites vertically and horizontally the living and departed; it is the life-giving principle which is found in them all. It results from a communion or participation in the same reality, the same vital principle, which unites a number of beings with one another."[14] This communal worldview is not restricted to the people's religious life but finds expression in all aspects of African society. It is encompassed in the idea that a person is a person because of other people and is based on an ethic of mutual dependence.[15]

The African worldview is thus spiritual and communal in its very essence, and creation, family, friends, strangers, and even those existing in different realms form part of this kinship.[16] This communalism determines how people live. It is evident in the elaborate rituals and the moral and social codes that govern society.[17]

2. TOWARDS A UNIFIED PARADIGM FOR THEOLOGICAL EDUCATION

First, we will discuss if *Ubuntu* could address the issue of whether theological education is viewed as a theological problem or a matter of practical application and skills. Could *Ubuntu* aid in informing a more unified model for theological education?[18]

---

10. Olupona, *African Religions*, 4.
11. Bediako, *Christianity in Africa*, 96.
12. Bediako, *Christianity*, 196.
13. Bediako, *Christianity*, 103.
14. Mulago, "Vital Participation," 138.
15. Khoza, *Attuned Leadership*, loc. 751.
16. Kunene, *Communal Holiness*, loc. 26606.
17. Musopole, *Being Human in Africa*, 10.
18. Wheeler and Farley, *Shifting Boundaries*, 9.

Such a model would provide curricula related to life, and it would better prepare students for ministry. This preparation would address the need to learn skills to perform tasks but also embrace the centrality of the nature of the Christian community as redemptive, thus emphasizing engagement with the received traditions and the central convictions that govern the faith.[19] Instead of just focusing on the fourfold pattern of theological education (biblical, historical, systematic, and practical theology) separately, theological education should seek new methods that integrate all aspects for well-rounded clergy.[20]

According to Kwame Bediako, the central aspect of the African worldview is the conviction that humans live in a sacramental cosmos and that there is no dichotomy between the physical and the spiritual.[21] This conviction is exemplified in the elaborate rituals practiced by the various tribes and the insistence that every aspect of physical, daily life has its origin in the spiritual realm.[22] According to Gatumu, this conviction is theoretical because it refers to the beliefs in the supernatural but it is also practical, referring to the rituals, practices, and *mode de vie* of communities.[23]

The training of African traditional healers[24] might give some insights into such an integrated, holistic approach to training spiritual leaders because it is rooted in *Ubuntu*. Traditional healers must undertake formal or informal training, although this training differs according to the tribal beliefs and the preferences of the mentors.[25] According to D. Oyebola, who studied the training methods of traditional healers and midwives among the Yoruba of Nigeria, training may last between seven to ten years.[26] Trainees learn while serving as an apprentice to established practitioners.[27] This training includes memorizing traditional narratives and incantations, observing various procedures, and involvement in practical work. In addition, trainees learn the art of recognizing various herbal medications, diagnosing

---

19. Ferris, *Renewal in Theological Education*, 19.
20. Farley, *Theologia*, 127–28.
21. Bediako, *Christianity*, 96.
22. Gatumu, *Supernatural Powers*, 13.
23. Gatumu, *Supernatural Powers*, 14.
24. Traditional healers refer to people who are trained to provide holistic health care to the communities by using plants, animals, and help from spiritual powers. It should be differentiated from "witch doctors," a derogatory term for those who practice divination to harm human beings.
25. Mbiti, *African Religions and Philosophy*, 163.
26. Oyebola, "Method," 31.
27. Oyebola, "Method," 32.

and managing disease, and divination skills.[28] Graduation is usually an elaborate ceremony where the graduate demonstrates his or her spiritual sensitivity and capabilities by doing prayers and divinations while solving real-life scenarios created especially for this graduation.[29]

This example from the Yoruba tribe gives an overview of some aspects that may generally be present in the training of traditional healers. It demonstrates how *Ubuntu* results in a pedagogy that consistently weaves spiritual beliefs and practical applications together. Trainees learn practical skills through practice while absorbing the belief structure of their tribes and simultaneously interacting with the spiritual entities they believe in.

3. THE ROLE OF SPIRITUAL POWERS IN THE PEDAGOGICAL PROCESS

A Eurocentric knowledge system has dominated theological education, and focuses on science and rationality to the neglect of the spiritual realities that clergy will confront in their ministries.[30] Such an approach can help students conquer their subjects' content effectively, but it is lacking in transformative capacity. In contrast with western education, which holds that the main parts of education include the teacher, student, and subject, the African context adds a fourth part: the role of spiritual power in the learning process.

African traditional healers are trained as a scientist in that they are required to have a broad knowledge of plants and animals and the environment, and they have to know how to administer these medications to effect healing for the afflicted.[31] But they also operate under the paradigm that there is a connection between the physical and the spiritual and, therefore, always work in consultation with the spiritual realm, be it the ancestors, the creator, or other spiritual entities. Such spiritual learning outcomes include knowledge of myths undergirding the belief system of the tribe, performing rituals and divination to connect with the spiritual to diagnose diseases, creating charms and adornments to give to patients, and keeping or enforcing taboos.[32] The existing belief is that true healing is a gift from the ancestors, and therefore everything must be done in their presence.

A more holistic approach to education should consider the spiritual dimensions of human beings and embrace the spiritual as a method in

28. Oyebola, "Method," 31.
29. Oyebola, "Method," 31.
30. Matsika, "Education," 61.
31. Matsika, "Education," 74.
32. Matsika, "Education," 68–69.

pedagogy.[33] It acknowledges the fundamental Christian axiom that transformation is a function of the Holy Spirit, and humans prepare the way for the Holy Spirit to operate.[34] Such an approach would exceed regular chapel services and small group meetings on campuses but would embrace the spiritual as the framework and springboard for all aspects of theological education.

A spiritual approach to theological education can significantly impact individuals and communities by fostering personal growth, spiritual development, and a deeper understanding of faith. This approach can lead to a greater sense of connection to God, a more profound sense of purpose, and a more substantial commitment to living a life aligned with God's will. Additionally, a spiritual approach to theological education can help individuals develop the skills and knowledge necessary to serve as spiritual leaders and guides within their communities, promoting a deeper sense of connection and unity among members. Ultimately, a spiritual approach to theological education can lead to a greater sense of meaning and purpose in life and a deeper understanding of the relationship between faith and the world around us. This will produce leaders who are agents of transformation in their communities.

4. FROM INDIVIDUALISM TO COMMUNALISM

Next, we will address the individualism that marks Eurocentric models of theological education. Such a model sees the personal transformation of the student as a result of their piety and devotion and the possible transformation they could bring to their congregations due to their charisma and skills.

This is the opposite of the African philosophy, where personhood is achieved only within communal life, and communal transformation is always a result of community cooperation.[35] An example of this is the training of traditional healers in Zimbabwe. According to Matsika, the trainee is generally called by the ancestral spirits to serve as a healer, training takes place within the apprenticeship relationship with a seasoned practitioner, learning and practice takes place in the community where the trainee is allowed to practice incrementally, and they can only graduate after they have made a demonstration of their spiritual knowledge and healing capacity to the gathered community.[36] Training is thus communal from initiation to graduation.

33. Kang and Feldman, "Transformed by the Transfiguration," 365–75.
34. Kang and Feldman, "Transformed by the Transfiguration," 372.
35. Ifeanyi, "Person and Community," 72.
36. Matsika, "Education," 61–62.

Transformation in theological education must include the worshiping community.[37] This refers to students, teachers, the local churches, the communities where students are called to serve, and even those departed saints through the great wealth of wisdom they left behind in the form of Christian traditions.

A communal approach would prioritize apprenticeship and mentorship. According to Robert Ferris, who studied the strategies of institutions that successfully implemented renewal in their theological institutions, this factor was cardinal to their success. Ferris observed that faculty and staff made themselves vulnerable to students in their mentoring relationships while a conscious effort was made toward the spiritual direction and formation of students.[38] He also noted that care is given to the relationships with the constituent church and the needs of the communities. This necessitated open communication and linkages with all concerned parties.[39]

However, transforming practice is more than just a group of people doing things together. According to Dykstra, "Practice is participation in a co-operatively formed pattern of activity that emerges out of a complex tradition of interactions among many people, sustained over a long period of time."[40] Thus, for collaborative practice in education to be transformative, it needs to be complex, coherent and anchored in values and tradition. This will not only affirm existing axioms but also generate new and contextual ones.

5. INCLUSION OF DIVERSE VOICES IN THEOLOGICAL EDUCATION

Third, theological education must exchange the hegemony of Western, white, male experience as the dominant voices in theological education for a model that features the diversity of the global catholic church. This would allow for the inclusion of culture, heritage, and experiences as valid components in theological discourse.

An interesting aspect of traditional healing is that there is only one prerequisite to start training; that is evidence that the person has been selected or approved by the ancestors to serve as a traditional healer.[41] Thus, children as young as six years old to the aged, males or females, and even people not of African descent may train as traditional healers. This openness

---

37. Kang and Feldman, "Transformed," 373.
38. Ferris, *Renewal*, 129.
39. Ferris, *Renewal*, 131.
40. Dykstra, "Reconceiving Practice," 43.
41. Oyebola, "Method," 32.

is rooted in the belief that all humans have their origin in the creator god and are therefore considered kin.[42] This disposition contrasts with theological education, where homogeneity is valued, and programs are geared towards creating sameness and uniformity.[43]

Theological education needs to affirm and celebrate cultural and religious plurality and resist the various forms of political domination if it is to be transformative in the complexity where contemporary theologians must work.[44] Such an approach would value the historical character of theological education but will strive to address the present concerns and challenges of diverse cultural contexts.[45] It involves more than integrating diverse peoples into the current system but reorientating it to reflect and showcase the input from around the globe. It means going beyond counting the number of people from diverse backgrounds in our institutions and allowing the institutions to be shaped by the people it serves.

Using *Ubuntu* as a framework for theological education means encouraging students to explore different perspectives and engage in open dialogue about their beliefs rather than enforcing a specific viewpoint that might not translate culturally. This principle is exemplified in how tribal chiefs govern villages in South Africa. Ruel Khoza gives an example from a Shangaan village in South Africa of how *Ubuntu* values all voices present during an *Indaba*.[46]

> The chief does not so much rule as assess the opinions that are expressed in open forum by ordinary people, while the gray-heads who are the repositories of folk wisdom sit listening and occasionally offer comment. Decisions are not taken by majority vote but by consensus when there is sufficient unanimity for the chief to speak with the voice of the people.[47]

This approach allows all present to express their views, state their cases and request what they need. It is based on the foundational principle that all humans have inherent value and dignity and fosters a disposition of understanding and empathizing with others. For Africans, the prime evil is disregarding the community members. Thus, honoring all that participate in kinship and complying with social responsibilities and rituals is essential.

42. Kunene, *Communal Holiness*, loc. 2595.
43. Peacock, "Theological Education," 121.
44. Taylor, "Celebrating Difference," 259–94.
45. Taylor, "Celebrating Difference," 261.
46. An Indaba is a communal meeting held to resolve problems affecting South Africa's community. It usually is presided over by the chief or the community's elders.
47. Khoza, *Attuned Leadership*, loc. 181.

Prioritizing diversity in theological education results in a better understanding of different perspectives. When diverse voices are included in theological education, students are exposed to a broader range of experiences. This can help them understand the complexity of theological issues and the diversity of beliefs and practices within their faith tradition.

Including diverse voices also leads to increased empathy and compassion by hearing the perspectives of people with different backgrounds. This approach challenges biases and stereotypes by including voices from different races, genders, and other backgrounds. It may improve critical thinking skills because students are exposed to a wide range of perspectives and can better engage in critical thinking and analysis. This can help them develop the skills necessary to engage in theological reflection and dialogue in a nuanced and thoughtful way.

CONCLUSION

Using Ubuntu as a paradigm for theological education can have a significant impact on the way theology is studied and understood.

First, it can resolve the dichotomy between doing theology as a discipline and a functional paradigm that focuses on the specific skills clergy need to perform on the field. This is because the African worldview is holistic, where all of life is viewed as sacred, and practice is always rooted in the deep-rooted belief system, in communion with the spiritual. This also improves the possibility of transformation, as students, lecturers, and administrators depend on the Holy Spirit for transformation.

Second, it addresses the individualism characteristic of Eurocentric education models by focusing on communalism. A communal approach to transformation in theological education would include collaborative and collective efforts by all interested parties to bring about renewal and contextualization. It involves engaging all members of the theological network, including marginalized groups, in planning, implementing, and evaluating initiatives that address specific issues or challenges. This approach recognizes the value of local knowledge and resources to create relevant, contextual solutions. It also focuses on building solid relationships and partnerships among theological institutes, communities, and organizations to support the collective efforts toward transformation.

Third, the belief that all humanity forms part of a universal kinship allows for the inclusion of diverse voices in theological education that can lead to a more nuanced and inclusive understanding of theology and how it impacts the world.

WORKS CITED

Bediako, Kwame. *Christianity in Africa: The Renewal of a Non-Western Religion*. Edinburgh: Edinburgh University Press, 1995.

Dykstra, Craig. "Reconceiving Practice." In *Shifting Boundaries: Contextual Approaches to the Structure of Theological Education*, edited by Barbara G. Wheeler and Edward Farley, 35–43. Louisville, KY: Westminster/ John Knox, 1991.

Farley, Edward. *Theologia: The Fragmentation and Unity of Theological Education*. Eugene, OR: Wipf & Stock, 2001.

Ferris, Robert W. *Renewal in Theological Education: Strategies for Change*. Wheaton, IL: Billy Graham Center, 1990.

Gatumu, Kabir wa. *The Pauline Concept of Supernatural Powers: A reading from the African Worldview*. Eugene, OR: Wipf & Stock, 2008.

Kang, S. Steve, and Michael Feldman. "Transformed by the Transfiguration: Reflections on a Biblical understanding of Transformation and its Implications for Christian Education." *Christian Education Journal* 3 (2013) 365–75.

Khoza, Reuel J. *Attuned Leadership: African Humanism as Compass*. Johannesburg: Penguin, 2012.

Kunene, Musa. *Communal Holiness in the Gospel of John*. Carlisle: Langham, 2012.

Matsika, Chrispen. "The Education of Traditional Healers in Zimbabwe: A Pedagogy of Conflicting Paradigms." *Journal of Pan African Studies* 8 (2015) 60–74.

Mbiti, John S. *African Religions and Philosophy*. 2nd and rev. ed. Johannesburg: Heinemann, 1989.

Menkitti S., Ifeanyi. "Person and Community in African Traditional Thought." In *African Philosophy*, edited by Richard Wright, 171–82. 3rd ed. Lanham: University Press of America, 1984.

Mulago, Vincent. "Vital Participation." In *Biblical Revelation and African Beliefs*, edited by Kwesi Dickson and Paul Ellingworth, 137–58. New York: Orbis, 1969.

Musopole, Augustine C. *Being Human in Africa: Towards an African Christian Anthropology*. New York: Peter Lang, 1994.

Olupona, Jacob K. *Africa Religions: A Very Short Introduction*. Oxford: Oxford University Press, 2014.

Oyebola, D. D. O. "The Method of Training Traditional Healers and Midwives among the Yoruba of Nigeria." *Social Science and Medicine* 14A (1980) 31–37.

Peacock, Philip V. "Theological Education and Affirmative Alliances: Embracing otherness." *Bangalore Theological Forum* 50 (2018) 118–31.

Taylor, Mark K. "Celebrating Difference, Resisting Domination: The Need for Synchronic Strategies in Theological Education." In *Shifting Boundaries: Contextual Approaches to Structures of Theological Education*, 259–94. Louisville, KY: Westminster, 1991.

Wheeler, Barbara, and Edward Farley. *Shifting Boundaries: Contextual Approaches to the Structure of Theological Education*. Louisville, KY: Westminster/ John Knox, 1991.

www.ingramcontent.com/pod-product-compliance
Lightning Source LLC
Chambersburg PA
CBHW050348230426
43663CB00010B/2032